Interpreting Hong Kong's Basic Law

Interpreting Hong Kong's Basic Law: The Struggle for Coherence

Edited by Hualing Fu, Lison Harris,
and Simon N. M. Young

palgrave
macmillan

INTERPRETING HONG KONG'S BASIC LAW

First published in 2007 by
PALGRAVE MACMILLAN™
175 Fifth Avenue, New York, N.Y. 10010 and
Houndmills, Basingstoke, Hampshire, England RG21 6XS.
Companies and representatives throughout the world.

PALGRAVE MACMILLAN is the global academic imprint of the Palgrave Macmillan division of St. Martin's Press, LLC and of Palgrave Macmillan Ltd. Macmillan® is a registered trademark in the United States, United Kingdom and other countries. Palgrave is a registered trademark in the European Union and other countries.

ISBN-13: 978-0-230-60041-6
ISBN-10: 0-230-60041-7

Library of Congress Cataloging-in-Publication Data is available from the Library of Congress.

A catalogue record of the book is available from the British Library.

Design by Scribe Inc.

First edition: January 2008

10 9 8 7 6 5 4 3 2 1

Printed in the United States of America.

Contents

Foreword

After reunification on July 1, 1997, Hong Kong is a Special Administrative Region of the People's Republic of China under the principle of "one country, two systems," and is governed by the Basic Law. The principle of "one country, two systems" is a novel and imaginative concept. In the context of our new constitutional framework, interesting and challenging questions of constitutional interpretation have to be addressed.

In the last ten years, useful experience of the interpretation of the Basic Law has been gained. This book on constitutional interpretation is timely. It consists of a collection of papers written by distinguished scholars in and outside Hong Kong. With the benefit of the experience over the last ten years, these papers explore the subject of constitutional interpretation from a wide range of perspectives. The book makes an important contribution to the lively discussion and debate of many interesting questions. Readers will find the book useful and stimulating and will derive considerable benefit from it.

Andrew Li
Chief Justice
The Court of Final Appeal
Hong Kong Special Administrative Region
People's Republic of China
September 18, 2007

Acknowledgments

The chapters in this book arose from a Centre for Comparative and Public Law conference that was supported by the Faculty of Law, the University of Hong Kong, and the Constitutional Law Project, funded by the University of Hong Kong's Strategic Research Theme initiative. In addition, we would like to thank Cheng Yulin, Choy Dick Wan, and Xing Fei for their editorial assistance.

INTRODUCTION

Interpreting Hong Kong's Basic Law

The Struggle for Coherence

Hualing Fu, Lison Harris, and Simon N. M. Young

Introduction

The establishment of the autonomous Hong Kong Special Administrative Region (HKSAR) of the People's Republic of China (PRC) in 1997 formed a union of two very different legal, political, and social systems. Hong Kong's Basic Law, passed by the National People's Congress (NPC) of the PRC in April 1990, was designed to form the connection between the two systems and also to define their separation. The respective powers of the central and HKSAR governments are set out sometimes in great detail in the Basic Law but sometimes in broad—even obscure—terms. The power to interpret the Basic Law therefore defines and shapes the relationship between the HKSAR and the central authorities. The two institutions with jurisdiction to interpret the Basic Law are the courts of Hong Kong and the Standing Committee of the NPC (NPCSC). Although the distinct ideological settings of the NPCSC and the Court of Final Appeal (CFA)[1] mean that they will inevitably disagree over the interpretation of the Basic Law, the two systems must avoid becoming locked, or being seen to be locked, in a battle for "the soul of Hong Kong; instead the struggle must be towards coherence."[2]

The authors of this book examine the coherence of the law relating to the relationship between Hong Kong and Mainland China, and the extent to which the interpretation of the Basic Law is founded on a struggle for the soul of Hong Kong. They also assess the obstacles that they see to be hampering the development and protection of Hong Kong's autonomy, and how such obstacles may be overcome. Is the CFA, having positioned itself as a champion of the common law and international human rights norms, allowing for the creation of a unique jurisprudence that will promote a stable and coherent body of law relating to Hong Kong's autonomy? Is the NPCSC too steeped in its ideological setting to recognize creative solutions to the conflict between the two systems?

The international community has watched the relationship between Hong Kong and China with interest, as it is a measure of China's ability to interact with Western-style constitutional values. The "one country, two systems" (OCTS) formula, which is the foundation of Hong Kong's autonomy, was intended to serve as a model for Taiwan's reintegration into the Mainland. The formula also has broader implications: China's responses to constitutional debates in Hong Kong are increasingly viewed as indicative of China's plans for the constitutional structures and processes in the Mainland. Legal and constitutional reforms on the Mainland may even have been accelerated by the need to deal constructively with the issues arising from the contrasting legal systems.

For both Hong Kong and the Mainland, autonomy was the favored approach to the resumption of Chinese sovereignty, although each side had their own reasons. The Basic Law is both a wedge to separate the two systems and at the same time a bridge that connects the HKSAR and the PRC: the objective was to "maintain the metaphorical and institutional distance" between China and Hong Kong, and also to "assert sovereignty and achieve unity."[3]

Hong Kong residents feared an assault on their civil liberties and their relatively well-developed rule of law and particularly wanted to safeguard the region's capitalist-market policies from China's socialist planned economy. The PRC Constitution[4] has been amended several times to incorporate certain market economy principles and statements about the rule of law and the protection of property rights and respect for human rights. Nonetheless, the system of checks and balances based on the separation of powers that is familiar to common-law jurisdictions is absent in China. In addition, while China cannot realistically be called an authoritarian state, the Chinese Communist Party (CCP) remains the repository of ultimate political power.[5]

For its part, China sought to preserve national unity by minimizing political contamination and the risk of social instability that might ensue if Hong Kong was fully integrated with the Mainland. The CCP has been familiar with the concept of OCTS for more than sixty years. During the anti–Japanese War in the late 1930s and early 1940s, the tiny region that was under CCP control was the "other system" in a country controlled by the Nationalist Party. This first OCTS experiment failed several years after its implementation and China plunged into a prolonged civil war. Immediately following the victory of the CCP in 1949, the party applied OCTS to Tibet. Once again, the OCTS experiment as applied in Tibet terminated. Since then, an autonomy system based on ethnicity has been a key part of the Chinese political system. OCTS is in no way unprecedented in CCP history, and the CCP is well versed with the potentials and dynamics of this system.

A particularly ambiguous point during the drafting of the Basic Law, however, was the compatibility between the Basic Law and the PRC Constitution.[6] The Basic Law provides that the HKSAR is to have competence over all matters apart from foreign affairs and defense and guarantees the continuation of Hong Kong's legal system. Article 5 of the Basic Law states that: "the socialist system and policies shall not be practiced in the Hong Kong Special Administrative Region, and the previous capitalist system and way of life shall remain unchanged for 50 years." Although Article 31 of the PRC Constitution authorizes the state to set up a Special Administrative Region (SAR) when necessary, it is not clear to what extent any newly established SAR may deviate from the socialist system.[7] As Yash Ghai notes, the question is what limits may apply to the broad powers of the NPC to establish new political-economic systems in an SAR[8]—does the PRC Constitution authorize the NPC to create any system it deems fit? Given the constitution's express statements about the socialist system and the dominant role of the communist vanguard in Chinese society, and given the clear superiority of the PRC Constitution, the constitutionality of the Basic Law may come into question. That is, Article 31 is subject to the Preamble and Article 1, if they are read as prescribing fundamental limits on the governance and economic structures that are permitted in the PRC.

But the political-legal system created by the Basic Law is fundamentally antagonistic to the political-legal system created by the PRC Constitution. Although political expediency, especially since 1997, may have lessened the textual and substantive antagonism between these two systems, current modes of legal interaction between the Basic Law and the PRC Constitution clearly lack doctrinal support within the PRC Constitution. The PRC Constitution has been forced to produce a deviant political system, which is so different that it has to be kept at a distance. To ensure that the constitutionality of the Basic Law would not be challenged, the NPC adopted a formal decision on the same day it passed the Basic Law, declaring that the Basic Law is consistent with the PRC Constitution.[9] The Basic Law forms the only valid constitutional connection between HKSAR laws and the PRC Constitution. There is no other official means by which PRC laws (including the PRC Constitution) may be applied in Hong Kong.

The Basic Law does not, however, establish a complete constitutional "firewall" around the HKSAR. Several "points of intersection"[10] allow the Mainland to influence Hong Kong's legislation and legal system. For example, Annex III sets out which national laws are to apply to Hong Kong;[11] the Hong Kong courts lack jurisdiction over "acts of state such as defence and foreign affairs";[12] and the NPCSC had power on handover to declare laws previously in force to be in contravention of the Basic Law.[13] The NPCSC also has the power to appoint—and therefore presumably to refuse to appoint—the elected chief executive.[14] Furthermore, the structure and electoral processes of the legislature and the relationship between the executive and the legislature are such that the central government may influence government policy.[15]

The inevitable processes of intermingling between the two systems will not necessarily threaten Hong Kong's autonomy as long as there exists an institution committed to protecting it: an independent judiciary who will "speak for" Hong Kong's constitution.[16] Article 158 of the Basic Law has become the most controversial link between the two legal systems, as it places the power to interpret the Basic Law with the NPCSC. Article 158 authorizes the Hong Kong courts to interpret provisions of the Basic Law that "are within the limits of the autonomy of the Region." If the courts need to interpret provisions that are "the responsibility of the Central People's Government, or concerning the relationship between the Central Authorities and the Region," they must seek an interpretation from the NPCSC, which, if issued, the courts are obliged to follow.[17]

The Court of Final Appeal has not yet asked the NPCSC for such an interpretation, but the NPCSC has issued three interpretations of provisions of the Basic Law. One was in response to a CFA ruling, on the request of the government of the HKSAR; the second was issued without any court proceedings' having been instituted but in the midst of public debate about the pace of democratization in the region; and the third was made in anticipation of the commencement of legal proceedings on the issue of the term of office of a new chief executive. Clearly, the NPCSC's exercise of its interpretative powers raised questions about the independence and jurisdiction of the courts in Hong Kong and about the true extent of the region's autonomy.

OCTS as practiced in Hong Kong has fared better than previous autonomous regions in China largely because of Hong Kong's unique political and economic position. In contrast to other autonomous regions in China, Hong Kong is the first "minority" region in the Middle Kingdom to be regarded as having more developed political and economic systems than the center. The central authorities have therefore largely taken a hands-off approach in dealing with Hong Kong–related matters. However, Beijing's restraint is tested by the pragmatic concerns raised by Hong Kong's reintegration and more importantly by the fundamental inconsistencies between the two systems.

Sources of Basic Law Interpretation

The first part of this book examines the sources of interpretative materials and the practice of constitutional interpretation in Hong Kong. One interpretative source is history. Legislative history, or the original intent of the framers of a constitution, is in many jurisdictions treated respectfully as a useful tool in constitutional interpretation. But the legislative intent of the Basic Law has been treated with great suspicion because of the undemocratic nature of the legislature that passed the law, political manipulation and control of the drafting process, and the secrecy of the legislative process. Yet Simon Young argues convincingly for a restricted form of original intent analysis in appropriate cases based on the legislative history of the Basic Law, as a means of achieving consistent and similar outcomes despite the different approaches to interpretation in the two legal systems. The first necessary step is to establish a comprehensive public archive that contains all the important documents pertaining to the drafting of the Basic Law.

A second guide to legal interpretation is international law and common law as practiced in other common-law jurisdictions. Hong Kong law needs to tap into the rich jurisprudence in other jurisdictions for survival. Fortunately, as Carole Petersen observes, the Basic Law encourages the use of international legal norms in Hong Kong, and judges in Hong Kong are increasingly referring to foreign judgments to guide their decisions. In particular, Petersen argues, the entrenchment of the International Covenant on Civil and Political Rights in Hong Kong is "a link to international standards, thus keeping Hong Kong firmly attached to the universalist approach to human rights" (p. 37). These common-law ties with other jurisdictions help to ensure Hong Kong's rule of law and the respect for an international standard of human rights. Nonetheless, Petersen points out, the courts' enthusiastic support for civil and political rights is not matched by an embrace of the social and economic rights contained in the International Covenant on Economic, Social and Cultural Rights.

The common law may not be a necessary or sufficient condition for democratic reform or for the development of a coherent legal system, however. Michael Dowdle asserts that the entrenchment of the common-law system by Article 8 of the Basic Law could well be detrimental to Hong Kong's constitutional progress. He argues that Dicey's common-law constitutionalism, which he sees as espoused by the Basic Law, suppressed rather than promoted constitutionalism in England and now limits the available responses to Hong Kong's unique constitutional situation. Hong Kong thus needs to look beyond a narrow view of the common law for its constitutional aspirations.

Another interpretative source, as Michael Davis describes it, is the dynamic interaction of local politics, Beijing's interests, and foreign interests. Hong Kong's constitutionalism is a result of this process of contention and compromise. Davis sees the NPCSC's use of its interpretation power to intervene in the discussion about democratic reform in Hong Kong as a grave challenge to the OCTS principle, which may undermine the rule of law in Hong Kong.

What Davis regards as abnormal becomes normal for Robert Morris, who writes that such interpretative angst is founded on misunderstandings about the nature and role of the Basic Law. The Basic Law was passed by the NPC and is therefore subject to interpretation according to whatever interpretative rules exist in Chinese law. For Morris, Article 158 is unambiguous: the NPCSC has a plenary power to interpret the Basic Law, limited only by the Hong Kong courts' exceptional power to interpret the Basic Law in certain defined circumstances. Common-law commentators fail to appreciate the significance of Marxist dialectical and historical materialism to Deng's formulation of the OCTS principle and therefore unduly restrict their responses to the NPCSC's exercise of its powers.

Basic Law Interpretation and the Dialogue between Hong Kong Courts and the NPCSC

Federalism and autonomy systems fail when: (a) there is no common legal framework to accommodate differences; and (b) no independent institutions exist to settle disputes between the center and the region. The Basic Law provides for neither of these mechanisms. The Basic Law recognizes and preserves Hong Kong's internal political, economic, and social differences. But it lacks a detailed framework and institutional structure to generate positive consensus between Beijing and Hong Kong. In particular, it lacks institutions with the ability to restrain the Mainland authorities from possible interference in the political and legal systems of Hong Kong. In this context, the authors in the second part analyze the circumstances and implications of the interpretations of the Hong Kong Basic Law issued by the NPCSC, discussing the limits and potential of NPCSC interpretations as a mechanism of constitutional interaction and for dialogue between Hong Kong courts and the NPCSC.

To understand fully the NPCSC's interpretative power, it is necessary to situate it in a proper historical and comparative context. This is the aim of Yash Ghai's chapter's "Political Economy of Interpretation." Ghai traces the origins of three different interpretative approaches. Judicial interpretation, which he traces to the United States Constitution and the famous judgment of *Marbury v. Madison*,[18] is the approach familiar to common-law countries that regards the courts as the exclusive interpreter of the constitution. Ghai traces the second approach, which he describes as legislative interpretation, to the French Revolution and the strong leftist forces who wanted to ensure that the general will of the people embodied in the legislature remained sovereign over legal proceedings and interpretation. The third approach, which Ghai describes as the Marxist approach, is similar to the second one in that it involves interpretation by the legislature but is fundamentally different, given its grounding in Leninist concepts of law and state power and its rejection of the separation of powers doctrine. Ghai argues that the NPCSC power of interpretation should be understood as coming within the third and not the second approach. Ghai notes the increasing convergence between the U.S. and French approaches, especially with the establishment of the French constitutional court in 1958, but he is far less optimistic about possible convergence of these two approaches with the NPCSC approach.

If convergence is not possible, then what about dialogue? The political and legal differences between Hong Kong and the Mainland may render any meaningful dialogue impossible. Lin Feng and P. Y. Lo discuss why a different result ensued when lawyers from Hong Kong and the Mainland interpreted the same provision of the Basic Law, using the example of the NPCSC's third interpretation relating to the length of the term of a chief executive who replaces a chief executive who has resigned without serving out his or her whole term. The interpretation highlights, they say, the difference in approach between those people trained in Chinese law and those from a common-law background. As the methods of interpretation are similar, the authors conclude that the difference must be the constitutional context of interpretation—the Mainland interpreters based their decision on their experience of the people's congress system and other government organs, while Hong Kong commentators looked to their common-law context. Nonetheless, the Mainland interpretative context should not be a relevant consideration for Hong Kong decision makers: The Court of Final Appeal has confirmed that the Basic Law is to be interpreted according to common-law principles, not Chinese constitutional conventions.

Nonetheless, as P. Y. Lo argues in the following chapter, courts in Hong Kong do react strategically—and, he argues, controversially—to NPCSC interpretations. Lo examines the mechanism of "judicial reference," the requirement that the CFA refer certain provisions of the Basic Law to the NPCSC for interpretation, under Article 158(3) of the Basic Law. He compares the reference requirement with its prototype, the preliminary reference mechanism under the legal system of the European Union. He concludes that the CFA's reluctance to refer matters to the NPCSC has immobilized the process and contrasts this with the success of the European model.

Although Hong Kong courts have, in one way or another, responded strategically to the NPCSC's interpretations of the Basic Law, the NPCSC should take China's commitment to Hong Kong's high degree of autonomy as its priority in Basic Law interpretation. Yu Xingzhong assesses Hong Kong's constitutional development as exhibiting a tendency toward constitutional formalism based on the pedigree thesis of legal positivism. The consequence is that constitutional development depends on ad hoc activism and reactive policy making. Furthermore, this tendency could justify an acceptance that the rule of recognition for Hong Kong is in Chinese law, or in China's Constitution, rather than in the Basic Law. This conclusion would erode Hong Kong's constitutional autonomy. The solution, according to Yu, is to encourage constitutional commitments by both parties.

Legislative Interpretations in the Chinese Context

The NPCSC will no doubt continue to interpret the Basic Law, especially those provisions related to the democratic process in Hong Kong and those with a potential impact on the Party and State in China. As Hong Kong's political future depends on past and future NPCSC interpretations, it is prudent to understand the nature, functions, and process of legislative interpretation as it is practiced in the Mainland.

Many scholars and officials, mainly those based in the Mainland, argue that legislative interpretation is congruent with the civil-law tradition in which the legislature rather than the courts interpret the constitution and laws. As mentioned already, Ghai in his chapter vehemently disputes this claim. Moreover, specific examples are difficult to find of any civil-law country relying on legislative interpretation by the body that made the law.

The process for legislative interpretation in China was as much based on Stalinist concepts imported from the former Soviet Union as it was on civil-law traditions. Following on Ghai's thesis, Sophia Woodman examines the Stalinist roots of the PRC Constitution and the way in which Soviet thinking influenced and continues to influence key elements of the Chinese legal system, particularly in relation to the role of law in a socialist state. In the Soviet Union, legislation was designed to provide general rules, while interpretation through edicts by the presidium ensured the "correct" application of those rules. She concludes that the NPCSC's power to interpret law is most usefully categorized as part of a general power to make decisions, rather than an usurpation of Hong Kong's independent judicial power.

Hong Kong does not have to content itself with waiting passively for a revolution to take place in Beijing but rather can influence the interpretative process in the NPCSC. Two bridging institutions within the framework of the Basic Law theoretically have the potential to generate positive consensus between the Mainland and the HKSAR so as to manage and accommodate regional differences: the Basic Law Committee (BLC)[19] and, to a lesser degree, the NPC deputies from Hong Kong. Hualing Fu and D. W. Choy examine the limits and potential for Hong Kong deputies to the NPC in facilitating dialogue and generating consensus. All powers within China's socialist state, according to the PRC Constitution, are vested in the NPC. Given the legal importance of the NPC, the Hong Kong delegation to the NPC might be expected to represent the voice of Hong Kong in the organ of supreme state power and also to serve as a bridging institution between Beijing and the HKSAR. The HKSAR NPC deputies are selected through a small-circle election process, however, and do not genuinely represent Hong Kong. The existing electoral rules effectively limit HKSAR NPC membership to the "pro-China" faction within Hong Kong. The HKSAR NPC deputies also do not enjoy any legal authority in either the Mainland or Hong Kong in terms of supervising the Hong Kong government. For the most part, the deputies lack sufficient political and social standing in the community, and therefore, despite efforts to make their role more meaningful, they act essentially in a symbolic capacity. Notwithstanding the limits, Fu and Choy argue, Hong Kong deputies as an institution are likely to play a more significant role in the cross-border constitutional relations. Given the growing importance of the NPC in lawmaking and legal interpretation, Hong Kong may have a vested interest in being more widely and better represented in the "highest organ of state power."

The growing importance of the NPC is only part of the larger effort by the postauthoritarian state to entrench its power through developing the rule of law, upholding the authority of the constitution, and the general improvement of human rights in China. Lison Harris examines the role of the PRC Constitution in the Chinese political and legal system. She notes that constitutionalism in China has rejected liberal democratic values and argues that one must therefore ascertain the context in which the CCP intends the constitution to be interpreted and applied. In this way, the development of constitutionalism—even an independent judiciary—may not contradict some form of one-party rule, as any political party policies and judicial decision making would take place within a constitutionalized CCP ideology.

A coherent legal framework for Hong Kong's autonomy may only be achieved through compromise. However, the contributors to this book do not all agree on the extent to which compromise would threaten the freedoms and legal certainties that are the foundation of Hong Kong's way of life. The CFA is playing a vital role in entrenching these elements, but by doing so, it may be sacrificing its ability to develop an innovative jurisprudence that will be preserved after 2047. The court cannot and should not apply the PRC Constitution and Mainland laws directly to the adjudication of cases in Hong Kong, but it could make more effective use of the judicial reference system and the Basic Law drafting materials to encourage the development of a more stable and predictable relationship with the Mainland legal system. For this process to function smoothly, the NPCSC must respond by issuing principled, persuasive, and focused interpretations. Only in the most urgent cases should it intervene directly and then only for the sake of coherence. Prudence, then, must guide the progress of Hong Kong's constitutional development.

Notes

1. Yash Ghai warns that "this duality is not merely that of legal techniques, but is also rooted in fundamentally opposed notions of authority and governance." See Ghai, *Hong Kong's New Constitutional Order: The Resumption of Chinese Sovereignty and the Basic Law*, 2nd ed. (Hong Kong: Hong Kong University Press, 1999), 211.
2. Ghai, *Hong Kong's New Constitutional Order*, 212.
3. Peter Wesley-Smith, "Law in Hong Kong and China: The Meshing of Systems," *Annals of the American Academy of Political and Social Sciences*, September 1996, 106.
4. Constitution of the People's Republic of China (1982); hereinafter "the PRC Constitution."
5. Preamble, the PRC Constitution.
6. Hungdah Chiu, ed., *The Draft Basic Law of Hong Kong: Analysis and Documents*, Occasional Papers/Reprints Series in Contemporary Asian Studies No. 5, 1988, School of Law, University of Maryland.
7. Article 31 of the PRC Constitution states that, "the state may establish special administrative regions when necessary. The systems to be instituted in special administrative regions shall be prescribed by law enacted by the National People's Congress in the light of specific conditions." Article 62(13) further provides that the NPC has the power "to decide on the establishment of special administrative regions and the systems to be instituted there."
8. Ghai, *Hong Kong's New Constitutional Order*, 89.
9. Decision of the National People's Congress on the Basic Law of the Hong Kong Special Administrative Region of the People's Republic of China (Adopted at the Third Session of the Seventh National People's Congress on April 4, 1990).
10. Wesley-Smith, "Law in Hong Kong and China: The Meshing of Systems," 111.
11. These include matters such as the national flag and emblem, the national day, territorial seas, the Nationality Law, and regulations on diplomatic immunity.
12. Article 19 requires courts to obtain a binding certificate from the chief executive on questions of fact concerning acts of state. The chief executive is required to obtain a certifying document from the Central People's Government. Wesley-Smith suggested that this

provision "if abused, could almost wholly destroy the jurisdiction of the courts in any case involving the interests of the central authorities"; see Wesley-Smith, "Law in Hong Kong and China," 112-13.

13. Article 160. The NPCSC issued a decision on disallowing only a handful of ordinances and sections of ordinances, although its choices clearly showed its disapproval of the liberalization policy applied by the last colonial governor.
14. See Wesley-Smith, "Law in Hong Kong and China," 113.
15. See Albert H. Y. Chen, "'Executive-Led Government,' Strong and Weak Governments and Consensus Democracy," in *Hong Kong's Constitutional Debates, ed.* Johannes Chan and Lison Harris (Hong Kong: Hong Kong University Press, 2005), 9; and Christine Loh and Civic Exchange, eds., *Functional Constituencies: A Unique Feature of the Hong Kong Legislative Council* (Hong Kong: Hong Kong University Press, 2006).
16. Wesley-Smith, "Law in Hong Kong and China," 117: "The Basic Law provides the means to give autonomy and separateness genuine prospects: by ensuring an independent judiciary" who will "speak for" the constitution.
17. Basic Law, Article 158.
18. *Marbury v. Madison*, 5 US 137 (1803).
19. The BLC is an advisory committee of the Standing Committee of the NPC (NPCSC). The BLC was established by an NPC Decision adopted on April 4, 1990, the same day on which the NPC passed the Basic Law. The BLC is composed of twelve members, six each from the Mainland and Hong Kong. They are appointed by the NPCSC for a term of five years. The BLC is limited to giving opinions to the NPCSC on matters relating to Articles 17, 18, 158, and 159 of the Basic Law. The NPCSC should, under the relevant Basic Law provisions, consult the BLC before it finds any HKSAR law inconsistent with Basic Law (Article 17); adds to, or deletes from, the list of national laws in Annex III of the Basic Law applicable to HKSAR (Article 18); interprets the Basic Law (Article 158); or amends the Basic Law (Article 159). Given the qualifications of the members in the BLC, however, the advice it gives will be more political than legal.

PART I

Interpreting Hong Kong's Basic Law

CHAPTER 1

Legislative History, Original Intent, and the Interpretation of the Basic Law

Simon N. M. Young[*]

Introduction

In this chapter, I examine the admissibility and use of legislative history in the interpretation of the Basic Law. I discuss the different approaches of the Standing Committee of the National People's Congress (NPCSC) and the Court of Final Appeal (CFA) to the use of legislative materials in their interpretations. I consider the issues of alignment and harmonization of the different approaches and discuss the possibility of the CFA applying "original intent" analysis to constitutional interpretation. I argue that by adapting established common-law doctrines, it is possible for the CFA to adopt a restricted form of original intent analysis in appropriate cases. After explaining the parameters of this approach, this chapter concludes with a discussion of possible challenges that could be made against the argument.

The Two Approaches to Interpretation

The NPCSC and the CFA each apply a different approach to interpreting the Basic Law. However their approaches might be characterized or distinguished, they are evidently different in terms of how legislative materials are admitted

* I acknowledge assistance from the Constitutional Law Project funded by the University of Hong Kong's URC Strategic Research Theme initiative. I wish to thank Lison Harris, Lin Feng, and Hualing Fu for their comments on an earlier draft of this chapter

and used in the interpretive process. I define *legislative materials* broadly to include all official documents concerning the drafting and enactment of the Basic Law (1985–90), the establishment of the HKSAR (1990–97), and the legislative interpretation of the Basic Law (1997–). I have deliberately left out the 1984 Sino-British Joint Declaration (JD) and the materials surrounding the JD from this definition because the JD, as the international agreement behind the Basic Law, presents other issues when considering its legitimacy as an interpretive source.

The NPCSC treats legislative materials as a primary source for interpretation. Such materials are intrinsic to an interpretive approach based on the original intent of those responsible for drafting and enacting the Basic Law. While the intention sought is an original one (i.e., one that existed at the time of drafting and enactment), the approach does not preclude postenactment (post-1990) materials from being used as evidence of the original intention. This could even include *ex post facto* statements, such as those contained in the published memoir of a drafter, that shed light on the intended meaning of words used in the Basic Law.

Reliance on legislative materials was clearly seen in the first and third NPCSC Interpretations of the Basic Law. In the first interpretation of June 26, 1999, it was stated that "the interpretation of the Court of Final Appeal [was] not consistent with the legislative intent," and that the "legislative intent" of the relevant Basic Law provisions was reflected in a written opinion "adopted at the Fourth Plenary Meeting of the Preparatory Committee for the Hong Kong Special Administrative Region of the National People's Congress on 10 August 1996."[1] This item of legislative material created after 1990 but before the establishment of the HKSAR was the only cited source in the text of the interpretation. Although no legislative materials were cited in the third Interpretation of April 27, 2005,[2] the explanation of the draft Interpretation given by Mr. Li Fei, deputy director of the Legislative Affairs Committee of the NPCSC on April 24, 2005, made it clear that the Interpretation was giving effect to the "original legislative intent" of Article 53 of the Basic Law.[3]

For the CFA, legislative materials are only an extrinsic aid to interpretation. In *Director of Immigration v. Chong Fung Yuen*, the chief justice discussed the role of extrinsic materials in the interpretation of the Basic Law:

> To assist in the task of interpretation of the provision in question, the courts consider what is within the Basic Law, including provisions in the Basic Law other than the provision in question and the Preamble. These are internal aids to interpretation.

> Extrinsic materials which throw light on the context or purpose of the Basic Law or its particular provisions may generally be used as an aid to the interpretation of the Basic Law. Extrinsic materials which can be considered include the Joint Declaration and the Explanations on the Basic Law (draft) given at the NPC on 28 March 1990 shortly before its adoption on 4 April 1990. The state of domestic legislation at that time and the time of the Joint Declaration will often also serve as an aid to the interpretation of the Basic Law. Because the context and purpose of the Basic Law were established at the time of its enactment in 1990, the extrinsic materials relevant to its interpretation are, generally speaking, pre-enactment materials, that is, materials brought into existence prior to or contemporaneous with the enactment of the Basic Law, although it only came into effect on 1 July 1997. [4]

The CFA adopts an interpretive approach that gives primary attention to the text of the Basic Law when read in the light of its context and purpose, that is, the textual-purposive approach.[5] The starting point for interpretation is the words of the Basic Law rather than its history or the intentions of its drafters. Legislative materials are only of secondary importance to the extent that they are relevant to the context and purpose that informs the language used in the Basic Law. This is different from using the statements and reports made by the drafters as direct evidence of the meaning of the words in the Basic Law.

Aligning the CFA with the NPCSC?

One might debate whether the coexistence of these two different interpretive approaches in one country is sustainable. Given that the NPCSC has plenary authority to interpret and the CFA has only a limited derivative authority,[6] one might suppose that the CFA (at least in the long run) should try to bring its method of interpretation in line with that of the NPCSC, which after all is the body that authorizes the CFA to interpret the Basic Law.[7] The greatest pressure to align will probably be felt by lower courts if and when asked to interpret an excluded provision, that is, one in which the CFA is duty-bound to refer to the NPCSC for an interpretation.[8] Lower courts may feel that, because the excluded provision will ultimately be interpreted by the NPCSC (without substantive consideration by the CFA), they should strive to reach the same interpretation as the NPCSC would to avoid inconsistency, conflict, or any possible legal instability caused by a NPCSC overruling. Some lower courts might try to stay the proceeding until the reference issue has been decided by the CFA, and, if necessary, the NPCSC has made its interpretation.

However, such practice seems contrary to the intention behind Article 158, which appears to contemplate that lower courts will attempt the interpretation first and only where necessary before final adjudication would the issue be referred to the NPCSC.

However much debate this question of alignment generates, it seems, for the time being, that its answer lies in the Basic Law. Under the principle of "one country, two systems," the high degree of autonomy given to Hong Kong contemplates that Hong Kong will continue to have its own separate legal system and the two different legal systems can and will coexist. This not only means the coexistence of different laws, legal practices, and legal culture, it also extends to the application of different interpretive methods to the same law, whether or not such methods lead to different interpretations.

Harmonization of the Two Approaches

Even if the coexistence of separate systems is permitted, one might still ask whether there should be greater harmonization in interpretive approaches on the theory that if the two bodies are applying the same or almost the same interpretive approach it is more likely that they will arrive at the same or a similar interpretation. On this theory, harmonization can help to further legal certainty, stability in the legal system, and the avoidance of constitutional confrontations. Accordingly, it will also reduce the need to seek interpretations from the NPCSC.

Greater harmonization can occur in one of two ways. First, the NPCSC may come to adopt more common-law-like principles and approaches to its interpretations of the Basic Law. This is not a far-fetched idea. With the presence of the six Hong Kong members, there is a common-law influence in the Basic Law Committee, which the NPCSC must consult before making an interpretation. There is also the influence of the Hong Kong government, who will have a greater tendency to draw on familiar common-law ideas in their request for an interpretation. Finally, there are the increasing exchanges between Hong Kong and mainland academics that can potentially lead to a greater cross-pollination of ideas. Indeed, one might detect a semblance of common-law reasoning in the third Interpretation, which appeared to apply contextual analysis by citing and drawing inferences from other parts of the Basic Law.[9]

The second path to harmonization sees the CFA construing the Basic Law according to the original intention of its drafters. This idea is not unreal and would not necessarily involve a surrender of judicial autonomy.[10] The CFA has not expressly ruled out all forms of original intent analysis, although it has called for caution and prudence, recognizing that "under a common law system which includes a separation of powers, the interpretation of laws once enacted is a matter for the courts."[11] Nevertheless, originalism is accepted as a legitimate theory of interpretation by some common-law judges, particularly in the United States.[12] Within English common law, the original intent of ordinary statutes can be given effect to by courts but only in accordance with the strict conditions set down in *Pepper v. Hart*.[13]

Adapting *Pepper v. Hart* for the Basic Law

Status of Pepper v. Hart

In *Pepper v. Hart*, the House of Lords relaxed the old exclusionary rule prohibiting reference to parliamentary materials to construe legislation. Six of the seven Law Lords set down three prerequisite conditions that had to be satisfied before such reference was possible:

> (a) [the] legislation is ambiguous or obscure, or leads to an absurdity;
> (b) the material relied upon consists of one or more statements by a Minister or other promoter of the Bill together if necessary with such other Parliamentary material as is necessary to understand such statements and their effect; and
> (c) the statements relied upon are clear.[14]

Once these three conditions are satisfied, the court is entitled to refer to the minister's statement and to use it directly to reach a conclusive interpretation of the provision in question. In this sense, the legislative history is evidence of an original legislative intent and does not merely form part of the context and purpose of the text. Lord Browne-Wilkinson justified this relaxation on the basis that the court in the situation described by the three conditions would be giving effect to Parliament's true intention rather than thwarting it.[15] His lordship preferred this approach over one in which the court ignorant of the relevant parliamentary history was "forced to adopt one of the . . . possible meanings using highly technical rules of construction."[16] Lord Mackay opposed the change in the law not on principle but because of the practical problems it would cause in researching the Hansard and increasing the cost of litigation.[17] The other Law Lords acknowledged the practical problems but did not think them so great to "outweigh the basic need for the courts to give effect to the words enacted by Parliament in the sense that they were intended by Parliament to bear."[18]

The facts of *Pepper* illustrate the significance of the change in the law. *Pepper* concerned schoolmasters who paid only concessionary fees to have their children educated at the school where they were employed. The legal issue was how this benefit enjoyed by the schoolmasters would be taxed. The legislation provided that the benefit would be assessed according to the "cost of the benefit," which was the "amount of any expense incurred in or in connection with its provision." At the relevant time, the school was not full to capacity and the concessionary fees were more than enough to cover the additional cost of educating the taxpayers' children. Accordingly, the taxpayers argued that cost of the benefit was nil. On the other side, the revenue argued that the cost of the benefit was the proportionate cost of educating a student based on the total cost to the school.

A majority of the Law Lords in both the first and second hearing would have decided the case in favor of the revenue had no reference been made to the parliamentary materials. After the second hearing, however, the reference to Hansard was of such significance that all the Law Lords now accepted the taxpayers' position.[19] The parliamentary history showed that when the Finance Bill 1976 was initially proposed, there was a clause in the bill that would have taxed these so-called in-house benefits on the basis of the price that the public paid for the facility or service. After the second reading and while the clause was being considered in standing committee, the financial secretary to the Treasury stated that having discussed the matter with the public the clause was to be withdrawn because of the possible injustice it could cause where there was a large difference between the cost of the benefit to the employer and the assessed value of the benefit.[20] Later, the financial secretary made several more statements (particularly in response to questions from members wanting to confirm the legal effect of withdrawing the clause) to the effect that the benefits would be taxed on the same basis as before and the amount of the charge would be small or nil.[21] From this history, Lord Browne-Wilkinson found that "these repeated assurances are quite inconsistent with the Minister having had, or communicated, any intention other than that the words 'the expense incurred in or in connection with' the provision of the benefit would produce a charge to tax on the additional or marginal cost only, not a charge on the average cost of the benefit."[22]

Although it is clear that *Pepper* is still good law in England, there has been a great debate about the scope of its *ratio decidendi*. Essentially, the debate sees the contest between the broad holding, which would relax the exclusionary rule in all cases, and the narrow holding, which would relax the rule only in cases where the government in litigation was taking a different position from the one taken during the legislative process. The generally accepted reading of *Pepper* is that Lord Browne-Wilkinson and the others who joined with him were contemplating the broad holding in their decision to relax the rule. However, the narrow holding has gained footing in recent times particularly because of an influential article written by Lord Steyn, published in 2001.[23]

Lord Steyn argued that the true ratio in *Pepper* was that reference to parliamentary materials would only be permitted insofar as it formed the basis of an estoppel argument to prevent the government in litigation from resiling from an interpretive position it took at the time it was promoting the passage of the law.[24] To take *Pepper* any further, according to Lord Steyn, would violate the constitutional principle that reserves legislative power to Parliament and not the executive.[25] Put simply, if the ministerial statements were treated as a "source of law" it would enable "the executive to make law," which would be "constitutionally unacceptable."[26]

As one might expect, the extrajudicial views of Lord Steyn have led some courts and judges to question the ratio in *Pepper*.[27] Despite this apparent retreat from *Pepper*, some have come to its defense. In particular, Professor Stefan Vogenauer has responded to the constitutional objection and highlighted problems with the estoppel argument.[28] Vogenauer argues that it is necessary to distinguish between admissibility and weight in respect of the use of parliamentary materials. *Pepper* laid down a rule of admissibility of such materials as an aid to interpretation. The weight to be given to the interpretive criteria is a matter for the court to decide in the circumstances of the case, and there is no rule that categorically accords greater weight to ministerial statements. It follows, according to Vogenauer, that Lord Steyn's characterization of treating such statements as a "source of law" was going too far.[29] As for the estoppel argument, Vogenauer argues that it could lead to the undesirable consequence of having "a different meaning assigned to one and the same statutory provision, depending purely on the private or public law nature of one of the litigants."[30]

It is unclear whether the House of Lords will ever adopt the narrower holding of *Pepper*. The most recent indication in a 2006 decision is that the House of Lords is still prepared to uphold the broad holding. *Harding v. Wealands* concerned a motor vehicle accident that occurred in New South Wales, Australia.[31] The claimant passenger who became severely disabled from the accident sued the defendant driver in England. Liability was admitted; the only issue was the assessment of damages and particularly whether the assessment would be governed by English law or New South Wales law. If it was the latter, the claimant stood to recover 30 percent less than he would under English law.[32]

The issue turned on whether the assessment of damages was a "question of procedure," and if it was then under the English legislation, the issue would be decided according to English law. The parliamentary history showed that this very issue was addressed at the Report stage in the House of Lords. In response to a proposed amendment by Lord Howie, the Lord Chancellor

(Lord Mackay of Clashfern) stated that the amendment would be unnecessary because "issues relating to the quantum or measure of damages are at present and will continue under Part III to be governed by the law of the forum; in other words, by the law of one of the three jurisdictions in the United Kingdom. Issues of this kind are regarded as procedural."[33] Lord Howie withdrew his proposed amendment. As Lord Hoffmann wrote in his judgment (in respect of the second and third conditions of the *Pepper* test), this was "as clear a case within the principle stated in *Pepper v. Hart* [1993] AC 593 as anyone could hope to find."[34]

Although all five Law Lords ultimately found in favor of the claimant, their treatment of the parliamentary materials is of some interest. Most significantly, none of the Law Lords held that *Pepper* was inapplicable on the basis of the narrow holding, even though the opportunity clearly presented itself, as this was a case involving only private parties. No doubt, the Law Lords would have all been aware of the trenchant critique by Lord Steyn. Four of the five Law Lords did not find the relevant provision to be ambiguous, and thus for them it was unnecessary to resort to Hansard. Yet, the majority (as expressed in the opinions of Lord Woolf and Lord Hoffmann) went on to review the Hansard evidence and say that had the first condition of ambiguity been met they would have applied *Pepper*. Lord Rodger (who came within the majority given his "full agreement" with Lord Hoffmann's opinion) cited and relied on the Hansard materials to confirm the construction he had already reached without any mention of the *Pepper* test.[35] Lord Carswell, who was the sole member to embrace *Pepper* fully, found the three conditions of the *Pepper* test to be satisfied and came to *Pepper*'s defense generally with the following words:

> *Pepper v Hart* has been out of judicial favour in recent years (no doubt largely because there were some instances of its over-use, though there have been some trenchant and irreconcilable critics), and courts have constantly striven to avoid resorting to it. I do consider, however, that the principle has a place in statutory interpretation. As Lord Nicholls of Birkenhead remarked in *R (Jackson) v Attorney General* [2005] UKHL 56; [2006] 1 AC 262, 291–292 at para 65, it would be unfortunate if *Pepper v Hart* were now to be sidelined, as there are occasions when ministerial statements are useful in practice as an interpretative aid, perhaps especially as a confirmatory aid. I would simply remark myself that it would be wilful blindness for courts to deprive themselves of its assistance in proper cases.[36]

Whether this sentiment of Lord Carswell will spark a change in judicial attitude remains to be seen, but it is at least fair to say that *Harding* confirms the vitality of the broad holding in *Pepper*.

Pepper v. Hart and Hong Kong

Before 1997, courts in Hong Kong had accepted and applied *Pepper* in a handful of cases.[37] In early 1997, the Law Reform Commission of Hong Kong published a report on the use of extrinsic materials for statutory interpretation in which it recommended codifying and extending the *Pepper* position.[38] The recommendations have yet to be adopted. Since July 1, 1997, *Pepper* has been cited in quite a number of judgments, but the CFA has yet to hold definitively the extent to which the approach in *Pepper* constitutes the law in Hong Kong post-1997.[39]

In *PCCW-HKT Telephone Ltd v Telecommunications Authority*, Justice Bokhary (with whom all the other justices agreed) had no difficulty with a limited relaxation of the rule excluding reference to legislative materials but felt that "more adventurous use of ministerial statements about the meaning and effect of proposed legislation would give rise to practical, conceptual and constitutional problems."[40] These sentiments of caution, however, are a contrast to the more favorable treatment of legislative materials by Sir Anthony Mason NPJ in an earlier judgment.[41] Although the CFA was aware of the ongoing intellectual controversy over *Pepper*, it appears to be waiting for the issue to be reconsidered by the House of Lords before engaging in the debate. It is hoped that *Harding* will assure the court to see the continued legitimacy of the broad holding.

Pepper has yet to be applied in the context of the Basic Law. The main constitutional objection of Lord Steyn must be reconsidered in this unique context. Lord Steyn's objection was that to treat ministerial statements as "canonical" would undermine the separation of powers between the executive and the legislature.[42] Although this argument may have force in the context of lawmaking in a political system that adheres to the principle of separation of powers, the genesis, drafting, and promulgation of the Basic Law did not occur within such a context. Hong Kong's future after 1997 was decided by the executive authorities of the United Kingdom and China in 1984 when the Joint Declaration was signed between the two sovereigns. From 1985 to 1990, a process undertaken by China with some Hong Kong participation took place during which the Basic Law was discussed and drafted in two official bodies, which have long since been disbanded, with some public consultation and ultimately promulgated by the president of China. The process did not involve a distinct executive and legislative body and thus to speak of the separation between the executive and legislative powers would be inapposite.[43]

I believe *Pepper* when properly adapted points the way to the introduction of original intent analysis to the interpretation of the Basic Law. Where the words of the Basic Law read contextually and purposively are "reasonably capable of sustaining competing alternative interpretations," then adopting the interpretation that gives effect to the clear intention of the drafters (assuming such can be found) can be justified for reasons of harmonization and respect for the participatory process behind the drafting of the Basic Law.[44] The main objection to applying *Pepper* will probably be the argument that it unjustifiably freezes the meaning of words in some historical era. Although I address this argument later, I do not believe that it outweighs the two considerations of harmonization and respect for the participatory process.

Adapting Pepper v. Hart

Applying *Pepper* to the legislative materials of the Basic Law requires an adaptation of condition (b) obviously because the Basic Law was not enacted within a parliamentary and ministerial system. Condition (b) is mainly concerned with capturing authoritative statements of the collective intentions and understandings of the legislative body however much a fiction this involves.[45] *Pepper* purposely confined the scope of relevant statements to only those of the minister or person promoting the bill because of concerns that otherwise an excessive amount of time would have to be spent reading the debates in *Hansard*.

By all standards, the drafting process of the Basic Law was unique. Although it was not a democratic process, it could be described as a participatory process in which members of the public in Hong Kong and China were given the opportunity to provide input through formal and informal channels. Unlike the parliamentary process where bills are prepared and introduced by government and sent through an established set of procedures for debating, amending, and enacting the bill, the drafting of the Basic Law was more ad hoc, spanning the course of almost five years.[46]

The task of drafting was given to the Basic Law Drafting Committee (BLDC), a body consisting of fifty-nine Mainland and Hong Kong members established by the NPCSC. The BLDC established the Basic Law Consultative Committee (BLCC), a local body made up exclusively of 180 Hong Kong members drawn from various sectors and strata in Hong Kong. The BLDC began its work by agreeing on an architectural skeleton of the Basic

Law. It formed five main subgroups that were responsible for drafting various parts of the Basic Law. Each subgroup had two co-convenors, one from the Mainland and the other from Hong Kong. During the course of its work, the members of the BLDC engaged the members of the BLCC for purposes of informing the public of its work and soliciting feedback on proposals. The BLCC set up eight special groups for this purpose. Many of the Hong Kong BLDC members played a leading role in the BLCC. After publishing and soliciting public feedback on two draft versions of the Basic Law, the final draft came before the National People's Congress (NPC) in the spring of 1990. It was passed by the NPC and promulgated by President Yang Shangkun on April 4, 1990.

If *Pepper* was applied literally to the enactment of the Basic Law, it would mean that only the short "Explanations" speech by Ji Pengfei, chairman of the BLDC, addressed to the National People's Congress on March 28, 1990, could be included within condition (b). Such an approach is clearly unsatisfactory, given the extensive involvement of the BLDC subgroups in the drafting process, the amount of consultations with the public and members of the BLCC, and the numerous amendments made to the two versions of the Basic Law draft. A more flexible approach is needed to enable a fair ascertainment of the legislative intent behind all 160 articles in the Basic Law. This flexible approach should admit clear statements of legislative intent found in the official reports of the BLDC and its subgroups, particularly where such statements disclose the reasons for pertinent changes in earlier drafts of the Basic Law. This approach is akin to the approach of domestic and international tribunals using the *travaux préparatoires* to interpret ambiguous provisions in international treaties.[47]

Although a flexible approach is recommended, it is doubtful that a common-law court, keeping within the spirit of *Pepper*, will extend the approach to include postenactment documents, for example, opinions of the Preparatory Committee or statements made in subsequent NPCSC interpretations.[48] While these documents may be relevant to showing an original intent, they will have a marginally decreased probative value, given faded memories with the passage of time. Such *ex post facto* documents have an inherent risk of attributing an intention to the drafters that was not held at the time. Postenactment materials are distinguishable from preenactment contemporaneous statements, which, as direct evidence of original intent, have stronger probative value and less risk of containing error arising from either an innocent or deliberate misconstruction of past events.

Even if condition (b) is adapted and made more flexible, a major hurdle to referring to the Basic Law legislative history lies in condition (c). This condition requires that the intention be clear. Essentially, it requires that the drafters had turned their minds to the same issue before the court and had expressed a clear view on the matter. It is insufficient to point simply to pertinent changes in the text and then to leave it to the court to infer what must have been in the minds of the drafters when they made the changes. There needs to be evidence as to the reasons for the changes.[49] If an inference were to be drawn, it would certainly have to be a compelling one. Lord Hope, in discussing the analogous situation of using a treaty's *travaux préparatoires* as an aid to treaty interpretation, called for caution, "as the delegates may not have shared a common view. An expression by one of them as to his own view is likely to be of little value if it was met simply by silence on the part of the other delegates. It will only be helpful if, after proper analysis, the *travaux* clearly and indisputably point to a definite intention on the part of the delegates as to how the point at issue should be resolved."[50]

In the same case, Lord Hobhouse highlighted the need for an objective interpretation: "It may well be that different delegates may have had different beliefs. The views of one delegate, however distinguished, articulate and well-published, may not represent the views of others. The examination must be an objective one."[51] Given the extensive coverage of different subject matters within the Basic Law, many of the interpretive issues that are now arising were never at all in the contemplation of those who drafted the Basic Law. In these cases, the legislative history will be of little use to the court.

Issue of Accessibility

In addition to the three *Pepper* conditions, a common-law court would be minded to add a fourth condition in light of the unique circumstances surrounding the legislative history of the Basic Law. It is that the legislative material relied on must be and have been publicly accessible at the time the court makes the interpretation. This is the same precondition that the House of Lords has imposed in the context of using the *travaux préparatoires* of an international treaty.[52] In *Fothergill v. Monarch Airlines Ltd.*, Lord Wilberforce stated that the *travaux* could profitably be used where "two conditions are fulfilled, first, that the material involved is public and accessible, and secondly, that the *travaux préparatoires* clearly and indisputably point to a definite legislative intention."[53]

The rationale for this precondition is a concern for fairness and transparency. The legislative material must be a public record for all to access, to research, and to verify. It would be unfair to allow one party, such as the government, who might have greater accessibility to such materials to admit what would appear to the other party a secret document that might have a decisive effect in the case. The other party and the general public might question the authenticity of the document and wonder whether there existed other "secret" documents that could indicate a different intention.

This fourth precondition presents serious challenges for using the legislative history of the Basic Law, given its current state of public accessibility. It is well known that the secretariats of both the BLDC and BLCC kept detailed records (although not verbatim records) of all the proceedings surrounding the drafting and consultation processes. These records have always been treated as classified, and a full set has never been made a public record. Although the Hong Kong government in conjunction with the Basic Law Institute established a Basic Law Library in December 2004, its collection of the legislative history is far from complete.[54] A more or less complete collection of the BLCC proceedings can be pieced together from the various public libraries in Hong Kong.[55] However, the same cannot be said for the BLDC records, particularly those of the subgroups. In respect of the chief executive's remaining term issue, the effect of this fourth precondition would have precluded the Hong Kong government from relying on some of the legislative material, which led it to change its position, as those materials were not publicly available.[56]

One might argue that given the current state of public accessibility categorically there should be no reference to the legislative history (even to those parts which are publicly accessible) because one is unable to know if there might be inaccessible material that could undermine or qualify an otherwise clear intention. The difficulty with this argument is that it can be made on pure speculation. A better approach is to consider the problem under condition (c) in terms of whether there is sufficient clarity in the intention. If there is evidence to suggest that a document, which is not publicly accessible, contains a material contradictory intention then this might be enough to tip the balance in favor of disallowing the available material on grounds that the legislative intent is insufficiently clear. In other words, one might argue that the clarity of the intention as drawn from the legislative materials must be beyond reasonable doubt before original intent analysis can be employed for the interpretation of the Basic Law.

Possible Arguments against Adopting Original Intent Analysis

Three challenges might be made against the adoption of original intent analysis by Hong Kong courts. First, it could be argued that it undermines the "living tree" approach to constitutional interpretation. The original intent approach confines the meaning of the constitution to its time of creation and inhibits the possibility of future development in light of changing societal conditions. This challenge is answered by the existing purposive approach applied by the court together with *Pepper*'s condition (a). I am not arguing that the court should abandon its existing textual-purposive approach to interpretation. The limited original intent approach only becomes applicable where, after applying the textual-purposive approach, there is still ambiguity in the provision.

There are two sides to the living tree metaphor. Although the tree should have the capacity to grow and develop, it is still a tree rooted in the ground. The textual-purposive approach allows for growth and change, but when this approach fails to provide a clear answer, the original intent approach, as the trunk and roots of the living instrument, is a natural alternative.

Following from this, the second challenge questions whether *Pepper*'s condition (a) would ever be satisfied since the textual-purposive approach is capable of providing a definite interpretation in all cases. Although this position has some theoretical appeal, the reality is that the courts will find ambiguity when it wants to find ambiguity. There is often much room for judges to debate whether certain words are reasonably capable of sustaining competing alternative interpretations. Judges may also disagree on how to apply the textual-purposive approach, particularly regarding what purposes to give effect to, and what logical inferences should be drawn from the contextual evidence. In these circumstances when traditional canons of interpretation prove to be unsatisfactory, then courts should be allowed to give effect to a clear legislative intent found in the legislative history.

Finally, there is the challenge that by allowing our courts to apply original intent analysis the door is opened for Chinese legal doctrines and views to enter our separate legal system in a way that was not contemplated in the Basic Law. It would be misleading and unfair to characterize all the final views expressed by the Basic Law drafters as representing Chinese legal doctrines and views. Even though it is true that the Hong Kong BLDC members were in the minority, the synergistic dialogue between the Hong Kong and Mainland BLDC members and the exchanges with people in Hong Kong resulted in something that was truly *sui generis*. Many of the ideas incorporated in the Basic Law were inspired by practices in other countries or were simply unique in order to give effect to the "one country, two systems" concept.

Conclusion

The proposal in this chapter for original intent analysis in judicial interpretations of the Basic Law is a modest one. As the proposal excludes postenactment materials from its ambit, it is an approach that is more limited than the approach evidently applied by the NPCSC. Nevertheless, the adoption of such a proposal has a tendency to bring the two interpretive bodies in greater harmony with each other and to eschew constitutional conflicts over interpretations.

Whether the proposal is adopted, public debate on the propriety of original intent analysis is positive if only to bring attention to the deficient public character of the Basic Law legislative history. Those who hold the keys to the records should make it a priority to release them for research and review by the public. Increasing the public accessibility of the legislative history, according to the argument in this chapter, will contribute to judicial acceptability of original intent analysis. It will also allow the public to gain a deeper understanding of the historical thinking behind the Basic Law and the limits of those original intentions.

Notes

1. The Interpretation by the Standing Committee of the National People's Congress of Articles 22(4) and 24(2)(3) of the Basic Law of the Hong Kong Special Administrative Region of the People's Republic of China (adopted by the Standing Committee of the Ninth National People's Congress at its Tenth Session on June 26, 1999), L.N. 167 of 1999, Legal Supp. No. 2 to the Hong Kong Gazette Extraordinary No. 10/1999; hereinafter "first Interpretation." For analysis of the first Interpretation, see J. M. M. Chan, H. L. Fu, and Y. Ghai, eds., *Hong Kong's Constitutional Debate: Conflict Over Interpretation* (Hong Kong: Hong Kong University Press, 2000).
2. Interpretation of Paragraph 2, Article 53 of the Basic Law of the Hong Kong Special Administrative Region of the People's Republic of China by the Standing Committee of the National People's Congress (adopted at the Fifteenth Session of the Standing Committee of the Tenth National People's Congress on April 27, 2005), L.N. 61 of 2005, Legal Supp. No. 2 to Hong Kong Gazette No. 17/2005; hereinafter "third Interpretation."
3. Li Fei, "Explanations on the Draft Interpretation of Paragraph 2, Article 53 of the Basic Law of the Hong Kong Special Administrative Region of the People's Republic of China by the Standing Committee of the National People's Congress," delivered at the Fifteenth Session of the Standing Committee of the Tenth National People's Congress on April 24, 2005, which can be found at http://www.info.gov.hk/basic_law/fulltext/article2.pdf. See also the analysis of the third Interpretation by Lin and Lo in Chapter 7 of this volume.
4. See *Director of Immigration v. Chong Fung Yuen* (2001) 4 HKCFAR 211, 224.
5. Ibid. See also *Ng Ka Ling & Others v. Director of Immigration* (1999) 2 HKCFAR 4, 28–29.
6. The CFA acknowledged this in *Lau Kong Yung & Others v. Director of Immigration* (1999) 2 HKCFAR 300, 322–24. See also Article 158 of the Basic Law.
7. On the interpretive power of the NPCSC, see Chapters 5 (Morris), 7 (Lin and Lo), 8 (Lo), and 11 (Woodman) in this volume.
8. Article 158 of the Basic Law provides *inter alia* that if Hong Kong courts "in adjudicating cases, need to interpret the provisions of [the Basic Law] concerning affairs which

are the responsibility of the Central People's Government, or concerning the relationship between the Central Authorities and the Region, and if such interpretation will affect the judgments on the cases, the courts of the Region shall, before making their final judgments which are not appealable, seek an interpretation of the relevant provisions" from the NPCSC. See also Lo, Chapter 8 in this volume.

9. See the discussion in Lin and Lo, Chapter 7, in this volume. Compare the common-law interpretation attempted by Robert Morris in R. J. Morris, "The 'Replacement' Chief Executive's Two-Year Term: A Pure and Unambiguous Common Law Analysis," 35 *Hong Kong Law Journal* (2005): 17–27.
10. Professor Albert Chen has argued that originalism, when applied in a particular manner, is an appropriate approach to constitutional interpretation that could be adopted by Hong Kong courts; see A. Chen, "The Interpretation of the Basic Law—Common Law and Mainland Chinese Perspectives," *Hong Kong Law Journal* 30, no. 380 (2000): 421–22.
11. *Director of Immigration v. Chong Fung Yuen*, 225. The court left open the question of whether a greater reliance on extrinsic materials could be made where the provision was ambiguous.
12. Most notably, Justices Antonin Scalia and Clarence Thomas of the U. S. Supreme Court. See, e.g., A. Scalia, "Originalism: The Lesser Evil," *University of Cincinnati Law Review* 57 (1989): 849 and his judgment in *Crawford v Washington*, 541 US 36 (2004). However both judges subscribe to the "original meaning" family of originalism, which looks to the objective meaning of the words of the law at the time it was enacted rather than to the actual intentions of the drafters.
13. *Pepper v. Hart* [1993] AC 593 (HL).
14. Ibid., 640.
15. Ibid., 634–35, 646.
16. Ibid., 634.
17. Ibid., 614–16.
18. Ibid., 637, per Lord Browne-Wilkinson.
19. Lord Mackay, however, accepted the taxpayers' position without the aid of parliamentary materials. See ibid.
20. Ibid., 627.
21. Ibid., 641.
22. Ibid.
23. J. Steyn, "*Pepper v Hart*: A Re-examination," *Oxford Journal of Legal Studies* 21 (2001): 59.
24. Ibid., 67.
25. Ibid., 68.
26. Ibid.
27. See the cases discussed in S. Vogenauer, "A Retreat from *Pepper v. Hart*? A Reply to Lord Steyn," *Oxford Journal of Legal Studies* 25 (2005): 629, 638–48.
28. Ibid. See also P. Sales, "*Pepper v. Hart*: A Footnote to Professor Vogenauer's Reply to Lord Steyn," *Oxford Journal of Legal Studies* 26 (2006): 585.
29. Ibid., 657–61.
30. Ibid., 669.
31. *Harding v. Wealands* [2006] UKHL 32, 3 WLR 83.
32. Ibid., para. 18.
33. Ibid., para. 37.
34. Ibid.
35. Ibid., paras. 70 and 78.

36. Ibid., para. 81.
37. See *Matheson PFC Ltd v. Jansen* [1994] 2 HKC 250 (CA), per Penlington JA; *Canon Kabushiki Kaisha v. Green Cartridge Co. (Hong Kong) Ltd. & Another* [1995] 1 HKC 729 (HC); *Attorney General v. Pham Si Dung* [1993] HKCFI 135 (HC). The Privy Council did not have the opportunity to consider the application of *Pepper* in any cases from Hong Kong.
38. See The Law Reform Commission of Hong Kong, *Report on Extrinsic Materials as an Aid to Statutory Interpretation* (Hong Kong: Law Reform Commission of Hong Kong, March 1997).
39. The court expressly left the question open in the following two cases: *PCCW-HKT Telephone Ltd v. Telecommunications Authority* (2005) 8 HKCFAR 337, 354; *Lam Pak Chiu & Another v. Tsang Mei Ying & Another* (2001) 4 HKCFAR 34, 44.
40. *PCCW-HKT Telephone Ltd v. Telecommunications Authority*, ibid.
41. See *Commissioner of Ratings & Valuation v. Agrila Ltd & Others* (2001) 4 HKCFAR 83, 102–4, where his lordship relied on legislative history to confirm the interpretation that he had reached by other means. All the other judges agreed with this judgment.
42. See Steyn, "*Pepper v. Hart*: A Re-examination," 68.
43. It is also worth noting the lack of adherence to the separation of powers doctrine in the Chinese system. Professor Albert Chen writes, "under the Constitution of the PRC (1982), although there is a functional division of powers among legislative, executive, judicial and procuratorial organs, all such organs are subject to the principle of the leadership of the Communist Party," and later, "The orthodox view expressed in most textbooks is that the doctrine of the separation of three powers is not applicable to China"; see A. H. Y. Chen, *An Introduction to the Legal System of the People's Republic of China*, 3rd ed. (Hong Kong: LexisNexis, 2004), 40, 51.
44. This is the definition of *ambiguity* given in *Director of Immigration v. Chong Fung Yuen*, 224.
45. See Lord Steyn's criticisms in "*Pepper v Hart*: A Re-examination," 64–66.
46. For an official report of the drafting history, see Secretariat of the Consultative Committee for the Basic Law, *The Draft Basic Law of the Hong Kong Special Administrative Region of the People's Republic of China (For Solicitation of Opinions) (with Introduction and Summary)* (Hong Kong: Drafting Committee for the Basic Law, April 1988), 1–4. Criticisms of the drafting history can be found in S. H. Lo, "The Politics of Cooptation in Hong Kong: A Study of the Basic Law Drafting Process," *Asian Journal of Public Administration* 14 (1992): 3–24; EWH Lau, "The Early History of the Drafting Process," in *The Basic Law and Hong Kong's Future, ed.* A. H. Y. Chen and P. Wesley-Smith (Hong Kong: Butterworths, 1988), 90.
47. Article 32 of the Vienna Convention on the Law of Treaties provides that recourse may be had to the preparatory work of the treaty and the circumstances of its conclusion as a supplementary means of interpretation to either confirm the meaning resulting from the application of Article 31 or to determine the meaning when the interpretation according to Article 31: (a) leaves the meaning ambiguous or obscure; or (b) leads to a result which is manifestly absurd or unreasonable. See also n. 52.
48. The Preparatory Committee was an official Chinese body that was in existence in the year leading up July 1, 1997, to facilitate the actual transfer of sovereignty.
49. See the similar sentiments expressed by Lord Lloyd in *Adan v. Home Secretary for the Home Department* [1999] 1 AC 293, 305 (HL).
50. *King v. Bristow Helicopters Ltd.* [2002] 2 AC 628, para. 79 (HL).
51. Ibid., para. 148.

52. See Lord Wilberforce's judgment in *Fothergill v. Monarch Airlines Ltd.* [1981] AC 251, 278 (HL). See also *In re Deep Vein Thrombosis and Air Travel Group Litigation* [2006] 1 AC 495, para. 54 (HL); *King v. Bristow Helicopters Ltd.*, ibid.; *Effort Shipping Co. Ltd. v. Linden Management S.A. and Another* [1998] AC 605 (HL).
53. Ibid., 278.
54. Alan Hoo SC, chairman of the Basic Law Institute and the person who co-opted the Hong Kong government to establish the Basic Law Library, is still awaiting the declassification of a set of basic materials given to him by Wu Jianfan (a well-known drafter who passed away in 2004) before he can make them public; see K. Lee, "Speed Release of Papers on Basic Law, Urges Chairman," *South China Morning Post*, February 26, 2007, p. A3.
55. Online access to these materials is available via Basic Law Drafting History Online (http://sunzi1.lib.hku.hk/bldho/), a project of the Centre for Comparative and Public Law and HKU Libraries.
56. In a reply to the Bar Association, the government stated that it had relied on nine background documents and conceded that at least five were public documents available in the Basic Law Library; see Department of Justice, "The Chief Executive's Term of Office: Response of the Department of Justice to The Hong Kong Bar Association's Statement of 17 March 2005," April 1, 2005, which can be found at http://www.doj.gov.hk.

CHAPTER 2

Embracing Universal Standards?

The Role of International Human Rights Treaties in Hong Kong's Constitutional Jurisprudence

Carole J. Petersen

Introduction

In this chapter, I analyze the extent to which international human rights treaties, and interpretative materials that inform and update our understanding of those treaties, are considered and relied on by the Hong Kong judiciary. I adopt a fairly broad definition of "interpretative materials" to include not only international and foreign judgments but also commentary by international treaty monitoring bodies, periodic reports submitted by the Hong Kong government regarding its implementation of the treaties, and other nonjudicial commentary.

The chapter is organized by treaty, beginning with the treaty that has done the most to bring international materials and developments into Hong Kong's constitutional discourse—the International Covenant on Civil and Political Rights (the ICCPR). The ICCPR was incorporated into Hong Kong's domestic law in 1991[1] and further entrenched in July 1997, through Article 39 of the Basic Law of the Hong Kong Special Administrative Region (the Basic Law). I argue, however, that the impact of the ICCPR also owes much to the approach taken to the treaty by Hong Kong judges, lawyers, and government officials. As discussed in the next section of this chapter, the ICCPR is treated as a sort of human rights "gold standard", against which Hong Kong laws and policies are regularly assessed. In some situations this heavy reliance upon the ICCPR may permit restrictions on rights that need not have been upheld.[2] In general, however, the ICCPR plays a positive role in Hong Kong's constitutional jurisprudence, largely because the courts regularly look to international judgments and other international sources for guidance in interpreting the treaty. While judges are sometimes selective in deciding which sources to mention they consistently treat the ICCPR as a link between the Basic Law and international standards and often embrace recent developments. Thus, the incorporation of the ICCPR in Article 39 (which can be traced back to the language of the Joint Declaration[3]) has arguably become the single most powerful element in the Basic Law's framework for the protection of human rights, firmly connecting Hong Kong to some of the most advanced jurisdictions in the field, even though the Basic Law contains many other provisions protecting human rights, which are far more detailed than Article 39. Although the Standing Committee of the National People's Congress has the power to issue a contrary interpretation of Article 39 (one that would make the ICCPR less enforceable in our local courts), the political costs to China of issuing such an interpretation would be extremely high, not only in Hong Kong but in the international community.

The impact of other human rights treaties in Hong Kong's constitutional jurisprudence is less clear. The third and fourth sections of this chapter analyze two cases in which Hong Kong judges have made good use of two specialist human rights treaties—the Convention Against Torture and Other Cruel, Inhuman, or Degrading Treatment or Punishment (CAT) and the Convention on the Elimination of All Forms of Discrimination Against Women (CEDAW). In each case, the court's decision regarding the government's obligations was significantly informed by the treaties. However, as demonstrated in the fifth section of the chapter, the International Covenant on Economic, Social and Cultural Rights (ICESCR) plays a surprisingly limited role, although it is referred to in Article 39 of the Basic Law in precisely the same language as the ICCPR. The limited Hong Kong case law on this treaty reflects an outdated view of the treaty and little awareness of recent commentary on the nature of the obligations that it imposes. The chapter concludes by considering the implications of this pattern for law and policy making in Hong Kong.

The International Covenant on Civil and Political Rights

The process by which the ICCPR became Hong Kong's gold standard started before Article 39 of the Basic Law came into force in 1997. The treaty was first incorporated into Hong Kong's domestic law in 1991 (through the enactment of the Bill of Rights Ordinance and the amendment to the Letters Patent). The courts thus began to exercise the power of judicial review well before the handover, using the standards set by the ICCPR and seeking guidance from international judgments and other materials. In one of the first important decisions interpreting the Bill of Rights, *R. v. Sin Yau-ming*, the Court of Appeal stated that guidance could be derived from "decisions taken in common-law jurisdictions which contain a constitutionally entrenched Bill of Rights," as well as from decisions of the European Court of Human Rights, the European Human Rights Commission, and the decisions and comments of the United Nations Human Rights Committee.[4] The Privy Council later sounded a note of caution with respect to the use of comparative materials, in *A.G. v. Lee Kwong-kut*,[5] and some commentators have argued that this was the start of a more narrow and technical approach to the Bill of Rights. Yet, the general principles stated in *Sin Yau-ming* still stand, and Hong Kong judges regularly cite foreign and international judgments for guidance on the meaning of the ICCPR. They also refer to a wide range of additional materials, such as the periodic reports by the Hong Kong government to the Human Rights Committee, the general comments of the Human Rights Committee, and the Siracusa Principles on the Limitation and Derogation of Provisions in the ICCPR.[6]

The prominence of the ICCPR has been facilitated by the Hong Kong government's approach to constitutional litigation. Government lawyers have frequently acknowledged that local laws must be declared invalid if they cannot be interpreted in a way that is consistent with the ICCPR. For example, in *HKSAR v. Ng Kung Siu*, the government accepted in court that Article 19 of the ICCPR is incorporated into the Basic Law by its Article 39 and that "by virtue of Article 39(2) of the Basic Law, a restriction on freedom of expression cannot contravene the provisions of the ICCPR."[7] This was a significant concession, particularly because one of the two ordinances challenged in the case was the National Flag Ordinance, which was enacted to fulfill the local legislature's obligation to implement a national law placed on Annex III to the Basic Law. The government apparently did not take the position that an ordinance enacted to implement a law on Annex III could trump the ICCPR. Rather, the government based its case on the argument that a prohibition on flag desecration does not violate the ICCPR, relying heavily on the fact that at least some democratic nations that embrace the ICCPR and international standards of human rights also have laws prohibiting flag desecration. The Court of Final Appeal (CFA) also cited these examples and emphasized the fact that a prohibition on flag desecration is a narrow restriction on the form, as opposed to the content, of expression. It also relied on several international sources (including the Siracusa Principles and an Advisory Opinion of the Inter-American Court of Human Rights) to bolster its conclusion that the concept of *ordre public* was wide enough to include societal interests in protecting the national and regional flags. Although the court also indirectly referred to Hong Kong's constitutional duty to implement national laws in Annex III (which may have provided the more compelling reason to find that the National Flag Ordinance was necessary for *ordre public*), the court's stated reason for upholding the two flag ordinances was that it accepted the government's position—a prohibition on flag desecration could be reconciled with the ICCPR. Although some of us may disagree with the judgment (particularly the analysis of "necessary"), the case does not stand for the proposition that the ICCPR is not enforceable in Hong Kong. Indeed, it is regularly cited for the opposite principle—that the ICCPR is incorporated into the Basic Law.

Another example of the prominence of the ICCPR in Hong Kong's constitutional framework is the 2003 debate on the National Security (Legislative Provisions) Bill 2003. During that debate the government did its best to persuade legislators, lawyers, and the general community that the legislative proposals could be reconciled with the ICCPR and frequently pointed to comparable laws in liberal democracies. The government's addition of the "Pannick clauses," while considered superfluous by many local lawyers, further illustrates the ICCPR's privileged status in Hong Kong's human rights discourse. The government retained David Pannick, a British Queen's Counsel, to give an opinion on the content of the legislative proposals. He stated that the proposals would be consistent with international human rights standards, as long as they were interpreted consistently with Article 39 of the Basic Law, which provides for the continued application of the ICCPR.[8] The government later added specific clauses to the bill stating that the legislation should be so interpreted. The government believed that it could gain support by linking these proposals explicitly to the ICCPR and an international expert in the field. Government officials also regularly assured the public that vague clauses in the National Security Bill would be interpreted by the courts to be consistent with the ICCPR and that provisions that could not be so interpreted would be declared invalid by the courts under Article 39.[9] I have argued elsewhere that this was an inappropriate approach, not only because the government should be more precise when drafting legislation to implement Article 23 but because vague laws could put the Hong Kong courts on a collision course with the Standing Committee of the National People's Congress.[10] Still, it is noteworthy that the government was so ready to concede that even legislation implementing Article 23 must be struck down if it cannot be interpreted so as to comply with the ICCPR.

The actual impact of the ICCPR depends, of course, on the way that the local courts apply it. In general, Hong Kong judges rely on comparative materials and treat the ICCPR as a link to international standards, thus keeping

Hong Kong firmly attached to the universalist approach to human rights. For example, in *Leung Kwok Hung v. Hong Kong SAR*,[11] the CFA held that one of the powers that the Public Order Ordinance gave to the police—the power to restrict or prohibit a demonstration on the ground of *ordre public*—was unconstitutionally vague and failed to meet the requirement in the ICCPR that any such restriction be "prescribed by law." In some ways, the judgment is fairly conservative in that it upheld the prior notification requirement and did not condemn the harsh criminal penalties that can be imposed for merely failing to notify the police of a procession, even if the demonstration remains peaceful. The dissenting judgment of Justice Bokhary went further and decided that the overall scheme of prior restraint was unconstitutional, including the criminal penalties. Nonetheless, the majority judgment makes a valuable contribution that arguably extends beyond the remedy granted at the conclusion of the case, which was to sever the words *ordre public* from the Public Order Ordinance. For example, the CFA emphasized that freedom of assembly is a fundamental right and that the commissioner of police must exercise his powers in such a manner that any restriction imposed upon demonstrators is no more than necessary to accomplish the relevant statutory legitimate purpose. The CFA also stressed that the police must give reasons for any restrictions and that these reasons must not be simply a "bald assertion of a conclusion" but rather must be specific enough to "show that he has properly applied the proportionality test in making his decision."[12] The CFA's use of interpretive materials was particularly interesting in this case. It relied in part upon the Hong Kong government's *Second Periodic Report* to the United Nations Human Rights Committee as support for the proposition that the right of assembly imposes a positive duty on the government to enable lawful assemblies to take place.[13] It also cited the Siracusa Principles, Nowak's commentary on the ICCPR, and numerous judgments from outside Hong Kong (the European Court of Human Rights, as well as courts in Canada, the United Kingdom, and South Africa). The dissenting judgment of Justice Bokhary also referred to the 1999 Concluding Observations of the United Nations Human Rights Committee, in which the committee expressed its concerns regarding the Public Order Ordinance.[14]

The CFA's judgment in *Yeung May-wan v. HKSAR*[15] is another example of the influence of comparative jurisprudence in Hong Kong. To the general public, this case is best known for having reaffirmed that members of the Falun Gong (which is banned in Mainland China) have the same right to public assembly as others in Hong Kong.[16] However, the case plays a broader role in that it allowed the CFA to review foreign authorities on the law of obstruction and reasonable use of the highway and to bring Hong Kong jurisprudence up to date on the question of what constitutes a reasonable suspicion for the purposes of determining whether an arrest is lawful. The CFA reviewed several cases from the United Kingdom and the European Court of Human Rights before reaching the conclusion that the Hong Kong police were not acting in the due execution of their duties when they arrested the defendants. These cases formed an important part of the CFA's analysis, leading to the fairly dramatic conclusion that the defendants had every right to use a certain amount of force to resist their unlawful arrests. The CFA implicitly acknowledged the role that comparative case law had played in its analysis when it emphasized that "no criticism" of the police was intended by the judgment because the police had been presented "with a difficult situation in relation to an area of the law which has been developing."[17] The case also confirms that protesters have a right to demonstrate where relevant officials will see them and need not comply with arbitrary orders given by the police.

Hong Kong courts other than the CFA have also made good use of comparative sources and generally resist arguments that would tend to distance Hong Kong from emerging international trends. For example, in *HKSAR v. Hung Chan Wa*,[18] the government argued that Hong Kong should not follow the decision of the House of Lords in *R. v. Lambert*[19] because Hong Kong had developed a more "robust and flexible" approach than England to the right to be presumed innocent. The Court of Appeal rejected this argument in strong language, stating that "attempts to cajole the courts of this jurisdiction to adopt a 'robust' approach to the balancing exercise" must be resisted when that approach runs the risk of undermining a fundamental right.[20] The Court thus made it clear that it views the ICCPR not as a means of freezing Hong Kong jurisprudence in its pre-1997 state but rather as a link to the most recent foreign and international cases in the field, including jurisprudence in the UK arising from the Human Rights Act 1998. The CFA affirmed the judgment[21] and similarly embraced the approach taken by the majority of the House of Lords in *Lambert*.

A particularly compelling example is the case of *Leung T. C. William Roy v. Secretary for Justice*,[22] which held that criminal provisions setting an unequal age of consent for anal and vaginal intercourse were unconstitutional because they discriminated on the ground of sexual orientation. The judgment by the Court of First Instance relied heavily on comparative jurisprudence and on recent medical research on homosexuality. For example, the court cited the 1994 British Medical Association's report, which found that sexual orientation is well established before the age of puberty and undermines the argument that men between sixteen and twenty-one require special protection from homosexual conduct. Justice Hartman noted that the discriminatory age of consent was enacted before the Bill of Rights or the Basic Law came into force. This is correct, but the need to comply with the ICCPR was certainly on the government's mind when it introduced the law. It was part of a package of legislation that partially decriminalized homosexual conduct, which the government persuaded the Legislative Council to adopt on the ground that it was necessary in order to comply with the ICCPR.[23] Perhaps the government recognized the possible conflict with the ICCPR but viewed the discriminatory age of consent as a compromise, necessary to gain the legislature's support for decriminalization. Alternatively, perhaps the government honestly believed, in 1991, that an older age of consent for homosexual intercourse could be justified as an acceptable departure from the general principle of equal treatment. Implicit in Justice Hartman's decision is a recognition that the standards imposed by the ICCPR have progressed since 1991, due to recent medical research on homosexuality and a broader conception of the rights to equality and privacy. The judge used the ICCPR as a vehicle to bring these updated standards into Hong Kong's jurisprudence. In rejecting the government's appeal, the Court of Appeal endorsed Justice Hartman's approach and made similar use of comparative materials. The case may have implications that go well beyond the age of consent, as the Court of Appeal expressly held that the ICCPR prohibits discrimination on the ground of sexual orientation (it falls within "other status" in Articles 2 and 26 of the ICCPR[24]) and stated that "where there is an apparent breach of rights based upon race, sex or sexual orientation, the court will scrutinize with intensity 'the reasons said to constitute justification.'"[25] Unsubstantiated theories will not be accepted by the courts as justifications for unequal treatment.

The cases discussed here are just a few examples of the many cases in which Hong Kong courts have used international materials, including quite recent developments, to inform their interpretation and application of the ICCPR. Although this approach has often put the government on the losing side of litigation, the government has arguably facilitated this process through its own treatment of, and reliance on, the ICCPR.

The Convention Against Torture

Given that it is a specialist human rights treaty, it is not surprising that the Convention Against Torture and Other Cruel, Inhuman or Degrading Treatment or Punishment (CAT) is cited far less often than the ICCPR. Nonetheless, CAT has had an important impact in Hong Kong, in part because of the willingness of the judiciary to scrutinize the government's compliance.[26]

The obligation to prohibit torture in Hong Kong is implemented through several local ordinances, including Article 28 of the Basic Law, Article 3 of the Bill of Rights Ordinance (which is based on Article 7 of the ICCPR); and the Crimes (Torture) Ordinance, which was enacted for the express purpose of complying with CAT.[27] However, the treaty imposes obligations that go beyond simply preventing torture within the territory. Article 3 of CAT provides that "no State Party shall return a person to another State where there are substantial grounds for believing that he would be in danger of being subjected to torture." This is significant because Hong Kong is not a party to the Convention on the Status of Refugees. Special legislation was enacted to address the Vietnamese "boat people" issue pre-1997, but the government has always opposed general legislation on political refugees, arguing that Hong Kong's relative prosperity would attract many people and that it is too small to accept a large number of refugees. The Hong Kong government does, however, permit the UNHCR to screen people in Hong Kong who claim refugee status, on the understanding that anyone who is determined to be a refugee will then be resettled in another country.

There is no provision in the Crimes (Torture) Ordinance that is expressly based on Article 3 of CAT (and it is therefore arguably an incomplete effort to incorporate CAT into domestic law). However, the obligation may also exist under the Bill of Rights Ordinance and the Hong Kong government has, in any event, assured the United Nations Committee Against Torture that a claim of torture by a potential deportee will be carefully assessed and the person will not be deported if the claim is well founded.[28] This statement was put to the test in the case of *Secretary for Security v. Sakthevel Prabakar*.[29] In this case, the secretary for security had issued a deportation order against a Sri Lankan man who alleged that he had been a victim of torture and would be subjected to torture again if returned to Sri Lanka. Mr. Prabakar had not intended to enter Hong Kong. He had fled Sri Lanka and was on his way to Canada but had to change planes in Hong Kong. Immigration officials questioned Mr. Prabakar in the transit lounge of the Hong Kong airport, discovered a forged Canadian passport, and charged him with possession of a forged travel document. While he was in prison, Mr. Prabakar sent a letter to the UNHCR and the Immigration Department describing the treatment that he had received in Sri Lanka. Nonetheless, the secretary for security signed a deportation order without investigating Mr. Prabakar's allegations of torture. The government apparently relied on the fact that the UNHCR initially decided not to recognize him as a refugee.[30]

The UNHCR eventually changed its decision and recognized Mr. Prabakar as a refugee under the mandate of the UNHCR. At this point, Mr. Prabakar was released by the Immigration Department on recognisance and the secretary for security made a representation that he would not be deported, pending identification of a resettlement country. Nonetheless, the deportation order was not rescinded and thus Mr. Prabakar's attorneys applied for an order to quash it. The application was dismissed in the Court of First Instance, but Mr. Prabakar successfully appealed to the Court of Appeal.[31] The Court of Appeal cited the obligation under CAT and the Hong Kong government's 1999 report on the implementation of CAT, in which it had assured the committee that any claim of torture by a potential deportee would be carefully assessed and that no person with a well-founded claim of torture would be returned against his will. The government's report had also stated that its assessment would take into account the human rights situation in the home country, as required by CAT.[32] The Court of Appeal emphasised that this responsibility to properly investigate a claim of torture could not be delegated to the UNHCR, in part because the criteria for determining refugee status could differ but also because the Hong Kong government had no way of knowing what investigative steps are taken by the UNHRC and the UNHCR gives no reasons for its decisions.[33] Thus the Court of Appeal used CAT, together with the government's own statements in its periodic reports to the treaty monitoring body, to define a duty that can be enforced against the government in a domestic court.

The government appealed to the Court of Final Appeal. By this time, the case was arguably moot because Mr. Prabakar had reached Canada and had been accepted there as a refugee. Nonetheless, the CFA agreed to hear the appeal and identified, as one of the questions, "whether the 1984 United Nations Convention Against Torture imposes duties on the Secretary for Security under our domestic law."[34] This is an interesting question, but the CFA never answered it, apparently deciding that it did not have to be resolved after all.[35] Instead, the CFA decided the appeal on the basis of the standard of fairness that must be observed by the secretary for security in determining the validity of a person's claim of torture, in accordance with the government's stated policy of not deporting a person who has a genuine fear of torture. The CFA decided that the standard of fairness required could not possibly have been met by merely following the UNHCR's unexplained rejection of refugee status. More importantly, for future cases, the CFA stated that the standard of fairness in such cases is very high, given the severe consequences of a mistaken conclusion that the person's fear of torture is not well founded. It also elaborated, in some detail, on the nature of the investigation that will be required before the government can lawfully deport a person who alleges that she will be tortured.[36]

What was not decided by the CFA is whether the government is free to change its stated policy of not deporting a person who is at risk of being tortured. The CFA did, however, cite numerous international materials, including the government's periodic report to the Committee Against Torture (in which the government stated that it will not order deportation of people who make well-founded claims that they will be subjected to torture) and the General Comment No. 1 by the Committee Against Torture (the CFA suggested that this document could serve as a "useful reference" for the secretary for security about the matters to be considered when properly assessing claims of torture).[37] The citation of these materials indicates that the CFA will treat any government statements to the committee as evidence of its policy and then hold the secretary for security to a high standard of fairness in implementing it. Since the Hong Kong government will not want to announce to the Committee Against Torture that it is no longer complying with Article 3, the CFA's decision—combined with its willingness to review government reports to the committee—has the same practical effect as a holding that the government has a legal obligation in domestic law to comply with Article 3 of CAT. The impact can be seen in Hong Kong's most recent periodic report, in which the government assured the Committee Against Torture that it had developed new procedures for assessing torture claims to meet the "high standards of fairness laid down by the CFA."[38] In March 2005, the Hong Kong government had fifty-eight Article 3 claims under investigation, involving seventy-four persons.[39]

The Convention on the Elimination of All Forms of Discrimination Against Women (CEDAW)

The Convention on the Elimination of All Forms of Discrimination Against Women (CEDAW) has applied to Hong Kong since 1996, the same year that the Sex Discrimination Ordinance (SDO) was brought into force.[40] The SDO does not contain a provision expressly stating that it incorporates CEDAW or that it must be interpreted to comply with the treaty because the government successfully opposed amendments proposed by legislators that would have added such language to the SDO. Although there was some concern that this legislative history might inhibit efforts to rely on CEDAW in the courts, it is a general rule of statutory construction that the legislature is presumed to intend to conform to public international law. Moreover, when the Hong Kong government announced that it would propose a Sex Discrimination Bill, it expressly informed the legislature that it was doing so to comply with CEDAW (which the government had by that time conceded would soon be extended to Hong Kong).[41]

In some jurisdictions, including the United Kingdom, judges seem reluctant to cite CEDAW as a guide to interpreting domestic sex discrimination law.[42] However, in Hong Kong CEDAW was relied on in one of first important cases under the SDO, *EOC v. Director of Education*.[43] The case arose from an application for judicial review by the Equal Opportunities Commission (EOC) and led to a declaration that the Education Department's system of allocating students to secondary schools was unlawful. Hong Kong operates an ability-segregated system of secondary schools. Students are assessed in the last two years of primary school and then divided into bands, with "band 1" ranking the highest. The elite schools have become known as "band 1 schools" (reflecting the banding of the majority of students who are admitted). A student who is admitted to one of these elite schools can expect a bright future, while the lower band schools are considered to be dead ends.

Prior to 1999 it was widely believed that students applying to secondary school were "banded" entirely on the basis of academic assessments. However, in 1999 an EOC formal investigation determined that the system violated the SDO. Female students completing primary school generally performed better than male students on the relevant assessments but the Education Department was scaling the results on the basis of gender. It also "banded" male and female students separately and applied gender quotas to the elite co-educational schools. The purpose of these adjustments was to prevent girls from obtaining a majority of the places in the elite schools.[44] As a result, fewer girls than boys were being allocated to their first choice of school, despite the girls' better examination results.

The government initially indicated that it would comply with the EOC's recommendations and change the system. However, in early 2000, the government announced that it had obtained new legal advice and could now justify the unequal treatment. It argued that boys developed later than girls and required "special measures," permitted under Section 48 of the SDO (which provides an exemption for voluntary affirmative action in certain circumstances). The EOC eventually applied for judicial review and the Court of First Instance issued a declaration that all three elements of the government's allocation system were unlawful.

In rejecting the government's defenses the Court of First Instance cited several foreign judgments and held that the SDO should be interpreted so as to carry out Hong Kong's obligations under CEDAW, including the obligation (in Article 10) to eliminate stereotyped concepts of men and women. The court found that the government's assumption that all boys develop later than all girls reinforced stereotypes and ignored the fact that some girls may also be late developers. The court also held that any special measures must comply with Article 4 of CEDAW, essentially incorporating the requirements of Article 4 into Section 48 of the SDO: "The article contemplates that state parties may wish, for the purpose of accelerating de facto equality, to take special measures to bring about such equality. The measures, however, are to be temporary. But the essential qualification is that such measures shall in no way entail as a consequence the maintenance of unequal standards; in short, as I read it, any special measures that are taken must not be allowed to undermine the purpose of the Convention itself; namely the abolition of sex discrimination."[45]

The court then rejected the government's defenses, noting that the Department of Education had no plans to phase out the system (which had been in place since the mid-1980s). The judge also commented on the fact that the government's mechanisms made no effort to ascertain or address the reasons why boys performed at a lower standard than girls. The system simply boosted the boys' scores, entrenching a pattern of unequal standards and sex discrimination.

The court's conclusion—that special measures must be temporary—would be disputed by some feminists. However, in Hong Kong, this may be of little consequence because the government is unlikely to introduce special measures to benefit women. What is beneficial in the judgment is the general holding that the SDO must be interpreted, where reasonably capable of bearing such a meaning to carry out Hong Kong's obligations under CEDAW. This could have significant ramifications for future cases. For example, Section 11 of the SDO prohibits discrimination in the "terms and conditions" of employment. This requires equal pay for equal work but doubts have been expressed about whether it requires equal pay for work of equal value. It should be interpreted so as to require equal pay for work of equal value because this is provided for in CEDAW and Section 11 of the SDO is certainly broad enough to bear this meaning. Thus, if nurses (who have argued claims based on equal pay for work of equal value in other jurisdictions) were to bring a claim against the hospital authority it would be difficult for their employer to argue that Section 11 does not require equal pay for work of equal value.[46] Indeed, the government has essentially admitted this in published statements, including statements to the CEDAW committee.[47] If a public-sector employer tried to deny that it was obligated to abide by the principle of equal pay for work of equal value under the SDO, one would expect the Hong Kong courts to look to these government statements—in much the same manner that the courts examined the government's reports to the Committee Against Torture in *Secretary for Security v. Sakthevel Prabakar.*

The International Covenant on Economic, Social and Cultural Rights

In theory, the ICESCR is entrenched by Article 39 of the Basic Law, which provides that the treaty "shall remain in force and shall be implemented through the laws" of Hong Kong. This is the same language used to refer to the ICCPR in Article 39. The Hong Kong government has also assured the United Nations Committee on Economic, Social and Cultural Rights that the ICESCR is fully incorporated into Hong Kong's domestic law through the Basic Law (particularly Articles 27, 36, 37, 137, 144, and 149) and more than fifty local ordinances.[48]

Unfortunately, there is a widespread perception that the ICESCR does not contain justiciable rights. This is partly because Article 2 of the ICESCR provides that state parties undertake to achieve "progressively the full realisation of the rights recognised" in the treaty and expressly permits developing countries to determine the extent to which they will guarantee the economic rights. Many of the rights stated in the ICESCR discuss economic entitlements, the allocation of which is difficult (but not necessarily impossible) for a court to review. However, the ICESCR contains some rights that could be more easily enforced against the government and recent literature argues for the justiciability of economic, social, and cultural rights.[49] The United Nations Committee on Economic, Social and Cultural Rights has also been working hard to counter the perception that the ICESCR is not justiciable and to promote the notion that the covenant places enforceable obligations on state parties. For example, the committee's Third General Comment, entitled "The Nature of States Parties' Obligations," interprets Article 2(1) in a manner that includes a duty to implement immediately some of the treaty's obligations.[50] The campaign for an optional complaints mechanism for the ICESCR is also intended to enhance the enforceability of the treaty.[51]

Unlike the ICCPR (which is largely copied into the Bill of Rights Ordinance), the provisions of the ICESCR have not been copied into a single domestic ordinance. The Committee on Economic, Social and Cultural Rights has urged the Hong Kong government to enact such a law, expressing its concern that the ICESCR continues to have a different status than the ICCPR in Hong Kong's domestic legal order.[52] This is consistent with the committee's General Comment Nine, "The Domestic Application of the Covenant," which requires state parties to incorporate the covenant as binding law in the domestic legal order. However, the Hong Kong government has declined to enact a "Bill of Rights equivalent" for the ICESCR, insisting that the provisions of the covenant are *already incorporated* into Hong Kong's domestic law "through several Articles of the Basic Law (for example Articles 27, 36, 37, 137, 144, and 149) and through over 50 ordinances."[53] The government maintains that "specific measures of this kind more effectively protect Covenant rights than would the mere re-iteration in domestic law of the Covenant Provisions themselves."[54]

Given the government's position, one would expect that the ICESCR could be used as a guide to interpreting some of the many ordinances that the government claims incorporate the treaty into Hong Kong's domestic law. There are, however, very few citations to the ICESCR in decided cases. Most of the limited jurisprudence has arisen in the area of immigration, which is perhaps not the best area in which to attempt to develop the justiciability of the treaty. For example, in *Chan Mei Yee v. Director of Immigration*[55] one of the applicants sought judicial review of a removal order and asked for permission to remain in Hong Kong so that she could care for her young daughter, who had permanent resident status and suffered from epilepsy. In addition to the ICCPR and the Convention on the Rights of the Child (CRC), the applicant cited Article 10 of the ICESCR, which provides that the "widest possible protection and assistance should be accorded to the family, which is the natural and fundamental group unit of society . . . particularly while it is responsible for the care and education of dependent children."

Unlike the ICCPR and the CRC, there is no reservation for immigration matters regarding the application of the ICESCR to Hong Kong. Article 10 of the treaty arguably provides a strong claim for the applicant in *Chan Mei Yee*, especially given the reference to the ICESCR in Article 39 of the Hong Kong Basic Law. Yet the attempt to rely upon the ICESCR failed, largely because the judge decided that the treaty is only promotional or aspirational in nature. The court cited commentary by international experts, which discussed the reasoning behind Article 2 of the ICESCR – the notion that the fulfilment of many of the obligations in the treaty are necessarily limited by the resources available to the State. Interestingly, the judge did not discuss whether the right asserted in this particular case required any public resources (the applicant was simply asking the government to refrain from deporting her). Rather, the judge appears to have lumped all the rights stated in ICESCR together and to have treated the entire treaty as a "promotional" document. According to the judge, the most that the ICESCR could provide was a "framework in which government decisions or discretions are to be considered."[56]

In a later case, *Chan to Foon v. Director of Immigration*,[57] Justice Hartman also held that the ICESCR is merely promotional in nature and rejected the notion that it might be used even as basis for legitimate expectation. Justice Hartman did give some consideration, it seems, to the question of whether the right to family reunion requires government resources, noting the opinion of the director of immigration that unchecked immigration could "threaten the Territory's social fabric." [58] Justice Hartman apparently concluded that the *reason* that no reservation to the ICESCR was entered for immigration matters was that the British government viewed the treaty as aspirational and therefore assumed that no reservation was necessary. Immigration matters are a sensitive area and may not be the best place to test the enforceability of the ICESCR. What is worrying, however, is that the courts do not seem to recognize the possibility that the ICESCR might provide a source of an enforceable right in other contexts or that it might offer useful guidance when interpreting local ordinances.

Although the Committee on Economic, Social and Cultural Rights recognizes that the Hong Kong courts are independent of the government, it nonetheless issued sharp criticism to the government following these judgments in the Court of First Instance. The committee urged the government "not to argue in court proceedings that the covenant is only 'promotional' or 'aspirational' in nature."[59] Interestingly, the Hong Kong government responded (in its next periodic report) by stating that: "We note the Committee's observation that the Covenant is not merely 'promotional' or 'aspirational' in nature and accept that it creates binding obligations at the international level."[60] Thus, it would appear that the government has implicitly accepted the fact that the treaty is not simply promotional. However, the words "at the international level" may indicate that the government does not consider the ICESCR to be enforceable as part of Hong Kong's domestic law, despite the reference to it in Article 39 of the Basic Law.

The judgment of the Court of Final Appeal in *Ho Choi Wan v. Hong Kong Housing Authority*[61] presented an opportunity to adopt a more progressive interpretation of the obligations imposed by the ICESCR. Unfortunately, the treaty is only mentioned in the dissenting judgment of Justice Bokhary. Justice Bokhary stated that the treaty is relevant to the case and acknowledged that Article 39 speaks of the ICESCR "in the same breath" as it does of the ICCPR. He also recognized that the right to adequate housing is of "central importance for the enjoyment of all economic, social and cultural rights."[62] He thus concluded that the ICESCR can be a powerful aid in construing the Housing Ordinance as imposing a duty to provide affordable housing. Yet even this judgment never expressly criticised the theory that the treaty is only promotional, although that view is increasingly rejected as outdated.[63] Nor did he refer to any of the recent commentary by the Committee on Economic, Social and Cultural Rights arguing that the treaty contains justiciable obligations. Justice Bokhary's view of the treaty is perhaps best reflected by the statement: "I am not saying that economic, social and cultural rights enjoy precisely the same status as civil and political rights under our constitutional arrangement."[64]

Justice Bokhary noted that there is no equivalent to the Bill of Rights Ordinance for the ICESCR, and this apparently influenced his view that the ICESCR does not enjoy the same status in Hong Kong as the ICCPR. There is a certain irony in this point. The Hong Kong government has assured the Committee on Economic, Social and Cultural Rights that there is no need for a special ordinance to incorporate the ICESCR because it is already "fully incorporated" into domestic law. Yet the government can rest assured that the judiciary will draw a distinction between the ICESCR and the ICCPR, in part because of the lack of such an ordinance.

There is also a striking contrast between the lack of judicial references to the comments made by the Committee on Economic, Social, and Cultural Rights and the judiciary's willingness to consider the exchanges between the Hong Kong government and the enforcement bodies for other treaties. For example, in his dissenting opinion in *Leung Kwok Hung*, Justice Bokhary cited the Human Rights Committee's criticism of the Public Order Ordinance. The CFA has also cited the government's reports to treaty monitoring bodies, such as the report under the ICCPR (in *Leung Kwok Hung*) and the report under CAT (in *Sakthevel Prabakar v. Secretary for Security*). This prevents the government from taking a different position in court than it takes before the relevant international committee. The judiciary does not seem as interested in the dialogue between the government and the Committee on Economic, Social and Cultural Rights.

The lack of judicial references to the ICESCR and materials relating to it is unfortunate because the treaty contains certain rights that are not otherwise provided for in the Basic Law. For example, the ICESCR contains (at Articles 6–8) numerous provisions on workers' rights.[65] Interestingly, the Committee on Economic, Social and Cultural Rights has frequently criticized the Hong Kong government for the lack of protection for workers.[66] The committee has also condemned the controversial "two-week rule," an immigration policy that discriminates against foreign domestic workers and makes them vulnerable to abuse by employers and employment agencies.[67] Changing the two-week rule would not require an expenditure of public money and therefore the "resource constraint" argument is not an excuse for failing to implement the committee's recommendation. Nonetheless, in the current legal and political environment, it would be almost impossible to use the ICESCR as a tool for legally challenging the two-week rule or any other policies that interfere with the realization of the rights stated in the ICESCR.

Conclusion

If the trends discussed here continue, then fulfillment of economic, social, and cultural rights will remain largely a matter of executive policy in Hong Kong, with relatively little influence from emerging trends in international human rights law. There will be a discourse on these rights, but it will not be a constitutional discourse, despite the language of Article 39. The debate will focus almost entirely on what is appropriate for Hong Kong's "unique context" rather than on what is necessary to comply with universal standards or the government's obligations under international law. The debate on economic, social, and cultural rights will also continue to be dominated by the business classes, as long as they occupy a privileged position in Hong Kong's undemocratic political system.

In contrast, the ICCPR will enjoy an elevated status in Hong Kong's judicial discourse, even though Article 39 of the Basic Law refers to the ICCPR in the "same breath" as the ICESCR. Because Hong Kong judges actively embrace universal standards of civil liberties, the discourse on these rights will be regularly refreshed by international and comparative materials, not only by foreign and international judgments but also by the broad range of interpretative materials arising from the international monitoring process for the ICCPR. Certain specialist treaties (such as CEDAW and CAT) will also have an effect on judicial interpretation of the domestic laws that have been enacted to comply with these treaties. The judiciary clearly has an interest in these specialist treaties and a willingness to look to comparative materials regarding them. This interest may arise in part from the fact that CEDAW and CAT build upon rights that were initially recognized in Hong Kong's gold standard, the ICCPR.

Notes

1. See Hong Kong Bill of Rights Ordinance (Cap 383). For a discussion of the enactment of the Bill of Rights in 1991 and the simultaneous amendment to the Letters Patent, see Yash Ghai, *Hong Kong's New Constitutional Order*, 2nd ed. (Hong Kong: Hong Kong University Press, 1999), 419–22; Andrew Byrnes, and Johannes Chan, eds., *Public Law and Human Rights: A Hong Kong Sourcebook* (Hong Kong: Butterworths, 1993), 215–29.
2. See Simon N. M. Young, "Restricting Basic Law Rights in Hong Kong," *Hong Kong Law Journal* 34 (2004): 130.
3. See Ghai, *Hong Kong's New Constitutional Order*, especially 48–51 and 415–19.
4. (1991) 1 HKPLR 88 (CA) (holding that certain provisions in the Dangerous Drugs Ordinance violated the presumption of innocence).
5. (1992) 3 HKPLR 72 (PC).
6. UN Doc E/CN.4/1984/4 (1984). The Siracusa Principles were adopted by a group of international human rights experts convened by the International Commission of Jurists,

the International Association of Penal Law, the American Association for the International Commission of Jurists, the Urban Morgan Institute for Human rights, and the International Institute of Higher Studies in Criminal Sciences in Siracusa, Italy, to consider the limitation and restriction provisions of the ICCPR.

7. (1999) 2 HKCFAR 442, CFA (at paras. 39–40).
8. For further discussion of the Pannick clauses and the debate on the Article 23 legislation, which was ultimately withdrawn by the government in response to public protests, see Carole J. Petersen, "Hong Kong's Spring of Discontent: The Rise and Fall of the National Security Bill in 2003," in *National Security and Fundamental Freedoms: Hong Kong's Article 23 Under Scrutiny*, ed. Hualing Fu, Carole J. Petersen, and Simon N. M. Young, chap. 1 (Hong Kong: Hong Kong University Press, 2005).
9. See, for example, the letter to the editor by James O'Neil, deputy solicitor general at the time, *South China Morning Post*, November 2, 2002.
10. Petersen, "Hong Kong's Spring of Discontent," 42–43.
11. [2005] 3 HKLRD 164, CFA.
12. Ibid., para. 59.
13. Ibid., para. 23 (citing para 221 of the *Second Periodic Report on the Hong Kong Special Administrative Region of the People's Republic of China in the Light of the International Covenant on Civil and Political Rights*).
14. Ibid., para. 106.
15. [2005] 2 HKLRD 212, CFA.
16. In this case, a group of Falun Gong practitioners successfully appealed their convictions for obstructing a public place and obstructing police while in the due execution of their duty. The group had been protesting outside the Hong Kong offices of the Liaison Office of the Central People's Government and were initially arrested because they refused to obey a police order to move to another location (which had apparently been given by the police at the urging of the Liaison Office). The Court of Appeal struck down the convictions for obstruction of a public place and the Court of Final Appeal went further, striking down the remaining convictions arising from the group's efforts to resist arrest. For further discussion of the significance of this case, see Carole J. Petersen, "From British Colony to Special Administrative Region of China," in *Human Rights in Asia: A Comparative Legal Study of Twelve Asian Jurisdictions and the USA*, ed. Randall Peerenboom, Carole J. Petersen, and Albert H. Y. Chen (London and New York: Routledge, 2006), especially pp. 241–42.
17. *Yeung May-wan* [2005] 2 HKLRD 212, CFA, para. 115.
18. [2005] 3 HKLRD 291, CA, aff'd [2006] 3 HKLRD 841, CFA.
19. [2002] 2 AC 545 (holding that the imposition of a persuasive burden of proof on the defendant to prove absence of knowledge to a charge of being in possession of cocaine with intent to supply was a derogation from the presumption of innocence protected under the European Convention on Human Rights and Fundamental Freedoms).
20. *Hung Chan Wa*, [2005] 3 HKLRD 291, CA.
21. *Hung Chan Wa*, aff'd [2006] 3 HKLRD 841, CFA.
22. [2005] 3 HKLRD 657, CFI, aff'd [2006] 4 HKLRD 211, CA.
23. For a discussion of the legislative debate and the legal and political developments that led to decriminalization, see Carole J. Petersen, "Values in Transition: The Development of the Gay and Lesbian Rights Movement in Hong Kong," *Loyola of Los Angeles International and Comparative Law Review* 19 (1997): 337.
24. The Court of Appeal noted that the government also accepted that homosexuality is a "status" for the purposes of Articles 1 and 22 of the Bill of Rights, which are copied from

Articles 2 and 26 of the ICCPR. See *William Roy*, aff'd [2006] 4 HKLRD 211, CA, para. 46.

25. *William Roy*, aff'd [2006] 4 HKLRD 211, CA, para. 53 (citing *Ghaidan v. Goldin-Mendoza* [2004] 2 AC 557, 568).
26. CAT was ratified by the United Kingdom in 1988 but not extended to Hong Kong until December 1992, in part because the local government needed to introduce local legislation to comply with it. See Byrnes and Chan, *Public Law and Human Rights*, 316.
27. Crimes (Torture) Ordinance, Cap 427.
28. See Hong Kong Government, *Report on the Hong Kong Special Administrative Region under the Convention Against Torture and Other Cruel, Inhuman or Degrading Treatment or Punishment* (1999), para. 2.
29. [2005] 1 HKLRD 289, CFA.
30. Ibid., para. 32.
31. *Sakthevel Prabakar v. Secretary for Security*, CACV000211/2002 (CA 27 November 2002).
32. Ibid., para. 19.
33. Ibid., paras. 21–24.
34. Decision on Application for Leave to Appeal [2004], 1 HKLRD 568, CFA, para. 8.
35. *Prabakar*, [2005] 1 HKLRD 289, CFA, para. 4.
36. Ibid., paras. 44–60.
37. Ibid., paras. 10 and 52.
38. *Second Periodic Report on the Hong Kong Special Administrative Region under the Convention Against Torture and Other Cruel, Inhuman or Degrading Treatment or Punishment* (submitted in June 2006 as part of the *Fourth and Fifth Reports of the People's Republic of China Under the Convention Against Torture and Other Cruel, Inhuman or Degrading Treatment or Punishment*), para. 66.
39. Ibid.
40. CEDAW was not applied to Hong Kong until a full decade after the United Kingdom's ratification, largely because the Hong Kong government objected to it. See Carole Petersen and Harriet Samuels, "The International Convention on the Elimination of All Forms of Discrimination Against Women: A Comparison of Its Implementation and the Role of Non-Governmental Organizations in the United Kingdom and Hong Kong," *Hastings International and Comparative Law Review* 26 (2002): 1.
41. In 1994, the government informed the Legislative Council that "we will need to introduce some form of legislation prohibiting discrimination, which would include equal pay legislation, before CEDAW is formally extended to Hong Kong." See Home Affairs Branch, "Legislative Council Brief: Equal Opportunities for Women and Men," June 1994, para. 10 (reprinted as Document No. 298, 336, in *Hong Kong Equal Opportunity Law—Legislative History Archive 1993–1997* [Centre for Comparative and Public Law, University of Hong Kong 1999]). Similarly, a government press release of June 3, 1994, stated that the "institution of sex discrimination legislation is a means to implement the provisions of CEDAW," ibid., Document No. 26, 333–35.
42. See Petersen and Samuels, "The International Convention on the Elimination of All Forms of Discrimination Against Women."
43. [2001] 1 HKLRD 690 (CFI). For a more detailed discussion of this case and the allocation system, see Carole J. Petersen, "The Right to Equality in the Public Sector: An Assessment of Post-Colonial Hong Kong," *Hong Kong Law Journal 32* (2002): 103–34.
44. See Equal Opportunities Commission, *Formal Investigation Report: Secondary School Places Allocation (SSPA) System*, at Executive Summary, 1999, iv and chap. 4; 24, para. 29.

45. *EOC v. Director of Education*, [2001] 1 HKLRD 690 (CFI), para. 110. The court also held (at paras. 112–36) that the government's system failed to satisfy the requirements of rationality and proportionality.
46. For further discussion, see Carole J. Petersen, "Implementing Equal Pay for Work of Equal Value: A Feminist Perspective," in *Proceedings: Equal Pay for Work of Equal Value* (Hong Kong: EOC, 2000).
47. For examples of these admissions, see ibid.
48. See *Second Report on the Hong Kong Special Administrative Region of the People's Republic of China in the Light of the International Covenant on Economic, Social and Cultural Rights*, 2003; hereinafter "Second Periodic Report by Hong Kong under ICESR," para. 2.9.
49. See Kitty Arambulo, *Strengthening the Supervision of the International Covenant on Economic, Social and Cultural Rights: the Theoretical and Procedural Aspects* (Antwerpen: Intersentia, 1999); Beth Lyon, "A Post-Colonial 'Agenda' for the United Nations Committee on Economic, Social and Cultural Rights," *American University Journal of Gender, Social Policy and the Law* 10 (2002): 535.
50. UN Committee on Economic, Social and Cultural Rights, *General Comment 3*, available at http://www.unhchr.ch/tbs/doc.nsf/(Symbol)/94bdbaf59b43a424c12563ed0052b664?Opendocument, accessed February 20, 2007).
51. See Draft Optional Protocol to the International Convention on Economic, Social and Cultural Rights, available at http://www.ohchr.org/english/bodies/cescr/comments.htm, accessed February 20, 2007).
52. *Concluding Observations of the Committee on Economic, Social and Cultural Rights on the Initial Report of the Hong Kong Special Administrative Region*, May 11, 2001, E/C.12/1/Add.58, para. 15.
53. Interestingly, the government did not list Article 39 of the Basic Law as one of the articles that incorporates the ICESCR into Hong Kong's domestic law, although it is the only article that expressly refers to the ICESCR. This may indicate that the government wants to reserve the right to argue in court that the reference to the ICESCR in Article 39 has a different meaning than it does with respect to the ICCPR.
54. Second Periodic Report by Hong Kong under ICESCR, para. 2.9.
55. HCAL 77/1999 (CFI, July 13, 2000).
56. Ibid., para. 46.
57. HCAL 58/1998 (CFI, April 11, 2001).
58. Ibid., para. 72.
59. *Concluding Observations of the Committee on Economic, Social and Cultural Rights on the Initial Report of the Hong Kong Special Administrative Region*, paras. 16 and 27.
60. *Second Periodic Report by Hong Kong under ICESCR*, Article 2, para. 1.12.
61. [2005] 4 HKLRD 706, CFA.
62. Ibid., paras 65–68.
63. *Lyon*, "A Post-Colonial 'Agenda,'" maintains that "only the United States continues consistently to advance nonjusticiability as a serious proposition in the international human rights political arena." For a discussion of the arguments against justiciability and the drafting of the optional complaints mechanism for the ICESCR, see Michael J. Dennis and David P. Stewart (both attorneys in the U.S. Department of State), "Justiciability of Economic, Social and Cultural Rights: Should There Be an International Complaints Mechanism to Adjudicate the Rights to Food, Water, Housing, and Health?" *American Journal of International Law* 98 (2004): 462.
64. *Ho Choi Wan*, para. 65–68.

65. Although outside the scope of this chapter, it should be noted that Article 39 also refers to ILO conventions, which should help to bolster a claim asserting labor rights.
66. Legislation that would have expanded collective bargaining powers and protected against summary dismissal (enacted shortly before the handover) was repealed by the Provisional Legislative Council. See Wilson Chow and Anne Carver, "Employment and Trade Union Law: Ideology and the Politics of Hong Kong," in *The New Legal Order in Hong Kong*, ed. Ray Wacks (Hong Kong: Hong Kong University Press, 1999). Efforts to introduce similar bills since the handover have been frustrated by the limitations on private members bills in Article 74 of the Basic Law.
67. See Peggy Lee, and Carole Petersen, *Forced Labour and Dept Bondage in Hong Kong: A Study of Indonesian and Filipina Migrant Domestic Workers*, Centre for Comparative and Public Law Occasional Paper No. 16, June 2006, available at http://www.hku.hk/ccpl/.

CHAPTER 3

Constitutionalism in the Shadow of the Common Law

The Dysfunctional Interpretive Politics of Article 8 of the Hong Kong Basic Law

*Michael W. Dowdle**

Introduction

Article 8 of the Basic Law of the Hong Kong SAR commands that "the laws previously in force in Hong Kong, that is, the common law, rules of equity, ordinances, subordinate legislation and customary law shall be maintained." This introduces a unique element into Hong Kong's constitutional interpretation—its "interpretative politics": Hong Kong may be the only jurisdiction in the modern world to elevate a particular legal system to the status of a constitutional right.

The academics, lawyers, and commentators that make up the constitutional interpretive community in Hong Kong tend to regard this as a good thing. However, history suggests otherwise. The only other time the common-law system has been elevated to the status of a foundational constitutional norm was in the 1880s, when Albert Venn Dicey enshrined his particular vision of common-law constitutionalism in his famous notion of "rule of law." The result was exactly opposite that which most Hong Kong constitutional interpreters desire for Hong Kong. Dicey's common-law constitutionalism suppressed rather than promoted democracy. It weakened

* The author gratefully acknowledges the germinal contributions of Iris Lau, Joyce Chung-man Chan, Penny Leung Pui Yan, and Bryon Wong. If only I were as good a teacher as they.

and stunted rather than strengthened and reinforced the role that constitutional law played in British political society.

Article 8 basically imposes on Hong Kong a distinctly Diceyian vision of common-law constitutionalism. And in similar manner its constitutional sanctification of "the common law" has debilitating ramifications for Hong Kong's constitutional and democratic development. It reinforces the pronounced character of Hong Kong's legal system, a character at odds with the more open needs of constitutional discourse. It demands that in addressing Hong Kong's unprecedented constitutional issues and problems, Hong Kong constitutionalism must limit its responses to those that have already been sanctified by the historicist tropes of English attitudes and experience, and thus impedes Hong Kong's ability to develop original responses to its original constitutional circumstances. In addition, it may work to alienate a significant element of the Hong Kong polity—namely, that the large, working-class majority of the Hong Kong citizenry who do not speak English well enough to participate in an essentially English common-law discourse.

Dicey and the English Constitution

To see how Article 8 activates a distinctly Diceyian vision of constitutionalism, and what that means, we first need to understand what is so distinctive about Dicey's vision of common-law constitutionalism. I am not seeking to condemn the common law per se as an obstacle to popular government. There are different visions of the common-law construct, and it is the particular vision advanced by Dicey in his work on English constitutionalism that concerns us. As we shall see, Dicey's particular vision of a constitutionalized common law represented an ingenious, conservative reigning-in of an earlier, more democratically inclusive stage of English constitutional development associated with the rise of the working-class during the early nineteenth century. But this conservative twist prevented English constitutional thought from responding to the development of modern English democracy, which as we shall see subsequently in this chaper makes it particularly relevant to constitutional "interpretative politics" in present-day Hong Kong.

What Came Before: The Radical Constitutional Flowering in England ca. 1760–1820

Beginning around 1760, England underwent a constitutional flowering every bit as dramatic and revolutionary as that which was occurring across the Atlantic—a flowering that transformed the nature of constitutional legitimacy and authority in England just as the American Revolution had done in the former English colonies of North America. Before this transformation, one's authority to pronounce on constitutional issues in England derived from one's class. In a hagiography written in the 1760s to England's traditional constitution, William Blackstone in his germinal *Commentaries on the Laws of England* pronounced:

> We have taken occasion to admire at every turn the noble monuments of ancient simplicity, and the more curious refinements of modern art. Nor have its faults been concealed from view . . . defects chiefly arising from the decays of time, or the rage of unskillful improvements in later ages. To sustain, to repair, to beautify this noble pile, is a charge intrusted [sic] principally to the nobility, and such gentlemen of the kingdom as are delegated by the country to parliament. The protection of THE LIBERTY OF BRITAIN is a duty which they owe to themselves, who enjoy it; to their ancestors, who transmitted it down; and to their posterity, who will claim at their hands this, the best birthright, and the noblest inheritance of mankind.[1]

By the 1820s, however, this class-based vision of English constitutionalism had been superseded by an alternative understanding that located constitutional intelligence in a much more inclusive vision of the citizenry—a vision that included the landless and the working classes. Thus, in the celebrated impeachment proceedings brought in 1820 by the House of Lords against Princess Caroline, the consort to the Prince Regent (later George IV), the princess's advocate, Henry Brougham, was able to wield the constitutional authority of popular opinion so as to convince the Lords to reject the contrary constitutional arguments of the Prince Regent himself. At the end of his defense of the princess, he questioned, "What would be said by the people of England—what would be said by the world at large—if, upon this species of proof, acting, as you do, as judges and legislatures, you were to pass a bill, which must for ever debase and degrade an injured, an innocent women?" To this, he continued:

> My lords,—I pray your lordships to pause, standing as you do on the brink of a precipice, before you form your judgment—a judgment which, if pronounced in favour of the bill now under your lordships' consideration, will fail in its object, and will return upon those who give it. . . . Save yourselves from the consequences of an event by which you would risk the situation you hold in that country of which you are the ornament, but in which you would cease to flourish if no longer served by the people. . . . [Y]our lordships willed—the King willed that the Queen of these realms should be left without the solemn service of the church. In the absence of this solemnity, she sustained no loss, for she still enjoyed the heartfelt prayers of the people. Her Majesty

> wants not my prayers—but I now ardently and sincerely supplicate the Throne of Grace, that mercy may be poured down on the people in a larger proportion than their rulers deserve, and that your hearts may be turned towards justice.[2]

The ease with which this argument prevailed confirmed that by the 1820s the constitutional authority of working-class public opinion had become a *fait accompli*.[3]

The trial of the future Queen Caroline was part of a larger constitutional movement characterized by an unprecedented scope and inclusiveness of constitutional discourse in England. Never before had England's constitutional system been subjected to such an intensely popular scrutiny. It was a discourse that included critical contributions, not simply from the gentry but also from the working classes and from women.[4] It was this discourse that drove the expansion of the franchise and that exposed English governance to a newly public accountability.[5] It was a discourse that would ultimately usher England from a premodern aristocracy to a modern constitutional democracy.

Dicey and the "Counterreformation" of English Constitutionalism (ca. 1880–1920)

But many in Britain resisted this popularization of constitutionalism or at least the democratizing impulses it engendered. One such person was Albert Venn Dicey, who would later come to be regarded as the intellectual founder of what we might call "modern" British constitutionalism. Like many other intellectual and aristocratic elites of his day, Dicey was skeptical about the capacities of what we might call "lower classes"—"lower" in the sense that Dicey expressly uses the term *middle* class to identify the lower limits of constitutional intelligence—to understand the true sources of England's constitutional strengths. Not only did such classes lack the property interests necessary to align them with the interests of "the state" per se, but the combination of their lack of education and their understandable, constant need to concern themselves with their own private economic hardship made such classes particularly predisposed to advance "collectivist" legislation that would upset the security of property that gave the middle and superior classes their constitutional enlightenment.[6]

Most opponents of England's growing constitutional openness sought to contest democratic liberalization by contesting the spread of the franchise. Dicey's genius—and his constitutional import—came from his articulation of a fundamentally conservative, aristocratic vision of constitutionalism that nevertheless accommodated expanded suffrage. Unlike his fellow constitutional conservatives, Dicey recognized that as of the third quarter of the nineteenth century, universal male suffrage was largely a *fait accompli*. But he also saw that one could nevertheless contain the corrupting influences of these newly enfranchised lower classes and preserve the essentially aristocratic intelligence that gave the English constitutionalism its strength, by taking the constitutional discourse that had been popularized earlier in the nineteenth century and assigning it to the more aristocratic realm of the common-law judge and barrister.

This he did through his celebrated idea of "rule of law."[7] Like the constitutionalism of Blackstone, Dicey attributed the ultimate success of England's constitutionalism to certain foundational principles of its unique common-law system. Dicey's vision of rule-of-law referred to the ability of ordinary common-law courts—by which he meant common-law judges—to impose the demands of the common law even on the government itself. Locating the font of English constitutional wisdom in the person of the judge effectively insulated English constitutionalism from England's expanding political democracy. Judges were not elected, they were not beholding to persons that were elected, and they generally drew from the aristocratic remnants of English society. They would therefore ensure that English constitutionalism would continue to be driven primarily by the distinctively public-minded political understandings this class allegedly brought to the constitutional table.

From Dicey to Irrelevance: The Fate of Constitutionalism in Twentieth-Century England

Ultimately, Dicey's restorative conceptualization was to become the defining vision of English constitutionalism in the early twentieth century. But if his success represents a triumph over more earlier, more radical visions of "popular constitutionalism," it was very much a pyrrhic victory.[8] At the end of the day, Dicey's vision of an aristocratic, judge-led constitutionalism could not erase the effects of Britain's inexorable march to ever more economically-inclusive (and gender-inclusive) forms of economic and governmental decision making. Instead, what it did was render England's self-described "constitutional law" increasingly irrelevant to its actual constitutional system.

This was largely due to innately historicist nature of the common-law system. The common law sees legal authority as deriving primarily from history. However, society and constitutionalism often find themselves in historically uncharted territory. In such situations, their responses to new problems frequently have to operate outside of the historicist comprehension of the common law. Critical developments in the late-nineteenth-century constitutional state—developments such as the regulatory state, administrative litigation, and emerging practices of "social citizenship"—simply were not acknowledged by England's now Diceyian constitutional jurisprudence. In linking English constitutionalism with a historicist vision of the "common law," Dicey rendered that jurisprudence epistemically immune to the kind of innovation that was needed to bring constitutionalism in line with England's continually evolving social and economic arrangements. After Dicey, England's real constitutional innovations, including its ongoing democratization, would paradoxically occur outside the realm of its "constitutional law."[9]

Article 8 and the Dysfunctionality of Hong Kong's Interpretive Politics

Like many who follow Hong Kong's constitutional politics, I am of open mind about the ultimate success of Hong Kong's constitutional experiment. But unlike most if not all of my fellow observers, I do not derive my skepticism primarily from past National People's Congress (NPC) interventions in Basic Law interpretation, or from Beijing's resistance to direct election of the Chief Executive. I do not find the principal obstacle to Hong Kong's constitutional fulfillment to be sitting in the shadow of the Great Wall. In fact, I find it in what I suspect most of Hong Kong constitutional commentators regard to be a foundational bulwark of whatever effective constitutionalism Hong Kong does enjoy—the Basic Law's express preservation of Hong Kong's "common law" form of legal system, Article 8.

Article 8 commands that "the laws previously in force in Hong Kong, that is, the common law, rules of equity, ordinances, subordinate legislation and customary law shall be maintained." As previously noted, this effectively elevates the historicist "common law" to the status of a constitutional right. In this way, Article 8 establishes a distinctly Diceyian vision of common-law constitutionalism. And here is where I see the greatest threat to Hong Kong's constitutional vitality.

Of course, in England, as discussed previously, Dicey's constitutional vision was more irrelevant than corruptive. This is because the common law in England did not operate along Diceyian lines. But the common law of Hong Kong, in contrast, does indeed sport a pronounced Diceyian exclusionary and historicist character. For this reason, in Hong Kong, a Diceyian vision of common-law constitutionalism is much more likely to be dysfunctional rather than simply irrelevant.

Dicey's Vision of the Common Law

Dicey had hoped that the common law, as he envisioned it, would restrict lower-class input into constitutional politics in two ways. First, he believed that the insular and technocratic nature of common-law discourse would make it difficult for uneducated, lower-class citizens to inject their private interests into constitutional decision making. And because this language was distinctly historicist in character, he also believed that this historicism would innately preserve the long-standing aristocratic character that he argued gave English constitutionalism its particular strength.[10]

In fact, the technocratic language of judge and scholar is not nearly as exclusory or essentialist or historicist as Dicey (and many present-day post-modernists) assumed. In England, the technocratic language of the common law has always been fairly easy to learn. Since the thirteenth century, legal practice has historically been one of England's major avenues for social mobility.[11] By the early eighteenth century, even England's "inferior classes" had shown themselves to be more than adapt at picking up the language of the common law and turning it against their noble and aristocratic, juridical guardians.[12] Some of the foundational liberties underlying England's constitution were first articulated by ordinary citizens with no significant legal training. The constitutional prohibition against general warrants was first articulated by radical parliamentarian John Wilkes, as was the constitutional right to publicly report on parliamentary activity. The unconstitutionality of jury packing was first advanced publicly by the radical publisher, T. J. Wooler, in defending himself from charges of seditious libel. The inclusion of political satire under the constitutional protection of freedom of the press was identified by another radical publisher, William Hone. None of these men had any significant legal training before representing themselves at trial.

Nor is the common law as bound and determined by essentialist aspects of common-law history as Dicey's constitutionalism suggests. The common law has always been subject to legislative modification. The twentieth century in particular saw an explosion in legislative reworking of traditional common-law doctrines. Dicey's idea of rule of law was intended as to prevent this, by insulating the constitutional core of common law from legislative, that is, democratic, interference. However, it was not successful—the common law continued to evolve (albeit it did so, as we saw, largely outside of England's constitutional consciousness). Today, it is legislation, not historical judge-made doctrine, that is the principal foundation of legal order throughout the common-law world.

Even within its judge-made doctrine, the common law was never as essentialist as Dicey portrayed. It is not above borrowing from outside itself when new problems arise, even constitutional problems. For example, the foundational constitutional freedom against self-incrimination came from Catholic canon law. The constitutional transformation of early industrial England was critically informed by legal-constitutional concepts, like those of the "citizen" and "equality," imported from revolutionary France. More recently, England's system of judicial review has imported the important doctrine of proportionality from French administrative law.[13]

The Diceyian Dysfunctionality of Hong Kong's Common-Law Constitutionalism

In other words, Dicey's vision of a social exclusive, essentialist, and historicist common law was more illusory than real by the time the twentieth century rolled around. For this reason, his counterdemocratic constitution offered little real resistance to England's ongoing pursuit of a modern, constitutional democracy. However, as we shall see, in Hong Kong, the "common law" does indeed enjoy much more of the aristocratic exclusivity and historicist authority that Dicey attributed to it. Therefore, there is good reason to suspect that Article 8 may indeed have introduced or enshrined significant Diceyian obstacles to the realization of a true constitutional democracy in Hong Kong.

Linguistic and Social Alienation

Dicey assumed that the common law would be exclusive in part because he assumed that the technocratic language of the common law was exclusive. As we saw previously, that is not necessarily the case—the ordinary citizenry is significantly more able to understand and deploy the technocratic language of the common law than is often appreciated. But this is not as true in Hong Kong. In Hong Kong, the language of the common law is not simply technocratic, it is for the most part alien. In Hong Kong, the language of the common law is English—and not just English, but the English of English-educated social elites. Because the ordinary Hong Kong citizen has virtually no chance of developing such levels of English proficiency, the marrying of Hong Kong constitutionalism to the common law insulates Hong Kong constitutionalism from middle- and lower-class participation in the way that Dicey had intended for late-nineteenth-century England.

The nature of common law's social-linguistic exclusion in Hong Kong is multivariate. It is reflected, for example, in the profession's requiring that all Hong Kong lawyers be able to speak an advanced level of English; while simultaneously dismissing any ability to speak the language of the majority of the population, Cantonese, as professionally meaningless. Few appellate-level judges speak Cantonese, and only one of the five justices on the Court of Final Appeals (CFA) speaks Cantonese. Many important constitutional decisions, such as those affecting central/local relations, are not translated into Cantonese.[14] As of 2005, neither of the two seminal texts cited by the CFA on Hong Kong Constitutional Law, Yash Ghai's *Hong Kong's New Constitutional Order* and Peter Wesley-Smith's *Constitutional and Administrative Law in Hong Kong*, yet appeared in Chinese, despite being first published in 1997 and 1987, respectively.[15] Academic publications in Cantonese are not always as valued by Hong Kong law schools in hiring, rehiring, and promotion decisions as publications that appear in English.[16] As of 2005, only one of Hong Kong's three law school deans speaks or reads Cantonese or Mandarin. Only one has ever attended a Hong Kong university.

All this can be seen as suggesting that the only portion of the Hong Kong population that is truly capable of meaningful legal knowledge is its English-speaking population. Because Article 8 made legal knowledge a critical part of constitutional knowledge, this suggests that the particular experiences and concerns of Hong Kong's lower, middle, and working class populations—basically those who could not afford to attend Hong Kong's more expense, English-language schools—are of little constitutional significance.

One might respond that such a requirement is necessary to ensure that Hong Kong lawyers can read the English-language cases that inform Hong Kong's legal system. Whether this is as necessary as the Hong Kong legal community contends is an open question. But the profession's English-language requirements go far beyond simply demanding reading comprehension. They demand a level that is characteristic of Hong Kong's elite and distinctly Anglicized social classes.[17]

In fact, there is no real justification for making English per se a prerequisite for entry into the profession. One could simply require all prospective entrants into the profession to take a qualifying exam, administered in either English or Cantonese, depending on the entrant's preference, which tests the entrant's knowledge of the positive law. If English is indeed *essential* to legal comprehension, then there is no need to test or measure the applicants' English-language ability *independent* of her legal abilities. A test that measures one's English proficiency outside of one's demonstrated understanding of the law seems intended primarily to ensuring that the legal profession will be able to serve Hong Kong's elite, primarily English-speaking, social and economic classes.

And if Hong Kong legal system makes the particular ideas and concerns of the 80 percent of the population that tends to live their lives more or less exclusively in Cantonese irrelevant to the law, it also makes the law irrelevant to this population—and so too any constitution that claims that law as a critical component of its identity.

In fact, there is good reason to suspect that issues of socio-linguistic exclusion are far more important to Hong Kong's Cantonese-speaking middle and lower classes than is realized by most participants in Hong Kong's constitutional discourse. Socio-linguistic issues have been lightning rods for student mobilization in Hong Kong universities. When the City University of Hong Kong failed to renew the contracts of most of its Cantonese-speaking law faculty in fall of 2001, it triggered a wave of student protest. The issue also attracted considerable attention from the Cantonese-language press. Similarly, when the Chinese University of Hong Kong sought to promote English as its official language of instruction in 2005, students again mobilized in opposition (Chinese University's decision to promote English as the official language of instruction is particularly ironic given that, as evinced by its name, it actually was founded to provide the local population with a Cantonese-language university). Clearly, the problems of linguistic exclusion are problems to which the ordinary Cantonese-speaking population is especially sensitive.

The student protests described previously are particularly significant because they contradict the frequently heard canard about Hong Kong Cantonese being politically apathetic. These two instances demonstrate quite obviously that Hong Kong's Cantonese students, and the larger Hong Kong Cantonese population, are indeed willing and able to mobilize themselves politically. They simply do not mobilize in response to the kinds of constitutional issues that concern constitutional scholars and activists. Why is that? One possible reason is suggested by looking at the one Hong Kong institution in which Cantonese-speaking students do frequently mobilize in support of constitutional issues—Hong Kong University. Hong Kong University is distinguished from other academic institutions in Hong Kong by three related factors. First, Hong Kong University tends to draw from the elite social population, at least much more so than the other institutions. Relatedly, its students have a much higher level of English-language proficiency. And finally, Hong Kong University's law school is also distinguished by the attention it receives (vis-à-vis other Hong Kong law schools) from the elites of Hong Kong's common-law community.

Could it be that the ordinary Cantonese citizens' seeming lack of political concern for constitution issues is a product, not of some innate cultural apathy, but simply of feelings of socio-linguistic exclusion from constitutional debate—a feeling caused by the close association between constitutionalism and Hong Kong's exclusive common-law community? This is an issue that deserves much more study then it has heretofore received. In informal interviews, a number of Cantonese-speaking students in Chinese University's graduate programs report that "the law" is often regarded within Hong Kong's Cantonese-speaking middle class as something that the progeny of the elite, those whose families are wealthy and Anglicized enough to allow them to receive significant English-language education, do for the elite themselves. They see the law's principal concern as lying with the needs of multinational business, the needs that feature most prominently in discussions of Hong Kong's English-language needs. They suggest that when middle-class Hong Kongers seek redress for public grievances, they bring their complaint to the Legislative Council rather than to the legal system. They report that the idea of using the law (rather than politics) to effectuate social justice is alien to them because the law and the profession seem alien to them, uninterested in their more ordinary problems and concerns.

I suspect that this is a controversial claim. Clearly, the Cantonese-language press does sport frequent Cantonese articles and editorials on constitutional issues. However, the presence of such articles alone does not demonstrate necessarily popular engagement. They could simply demonstrate being preached to. As constitutional advocates for greater democracy in Hong Kong frequently point out, reading about a discussion is not the same as participating in that discussion.

I am merely trying to show that this issue of linguistic exclusion is one that needs more investigation. I am not claiming it to be an established fact. However, in suggesting it as a possibility, I am also suggesting that it is a possibility that Hong Kong constitutionalism continues to ignore at its peril. Constitutional activists and scholars seem largely insensitive to the feeling of alienation that Hong Kong's English-language common-law system can engender. This insensitivity was tellingly demonstrated in summer of 2002, when a Hong Kong High Court held that a Cantonese-speaking defendant in a criminal trial had no constitutional right to a trial in Cantonese even in cases in which he could not speak English,[18] even though Hong Kong is officially a bilingual jurisdiction. My own experience is that most foreign constitutional and legal scholars find this disturbing when informed of it. However, to my knowledge, no constitutional activist or scholar in Hong Kong has paid any significant attention to this issue or the serious implications it has for the political and constitutional exclusion of much of Hong Kong's population.

Instead, when these activists and scholars focus on threats of political exclusion, they focus exclusively on the issue of electoral democracy. However, of these two concerns, elections versus linguistic inclusion, there is good reason to suspect that the latter is actually more relevant to Hong Kong's constitutional progress. History is replete with polities that enjoy universal suffrage but are still constitutionally stunted and stagnate.[19] Recall that Dicey's own vision of constitutionalism in particular was founded on a desire to prevent the *fait accompli* of universal suffrage from "corrupting" the aristocratic nature of England's predemocratic constitution. By contrast, I believe that history provides no precedent for effective, modern, democratic constitutionalism that functioned in a legal language not spoken by at least a plurality of the citizenry.[20] It was popular discourse, not formalized elections, that drove the flowering of constitutionalism in England's early industrial era and in the Americas in the 1770s and 1780s.[21] It was popular discourse, and not formal elections, that established the constitutional identities of the formerly socialist countries of Eastern Europe.[22] However, such popular participation is difficult if not impossible if the language of constitutional discourse is alien to a supermajority of the citizenry.

Isolation and Hegemony

The distinctly Diceyian character of Hong Kong's constitutional discourse is further augmented by the pronounced, hierarchical, and hegemonic character of the legal community that drives that discourse. To a large extent, this hierarchical and hegemonic character is a structural correlate to the Hong Kong bar's worshipful reference for the English language. Hong Kong society does not produce a significant number of Anglicized English speakers. The smallness of this population allows a very closed collection of interpenetrated legal institutions—a professional-academic *Keiretzu* as it were—to direct the terms of legal-constitutional discourse. It is, to be sure, a very impressive *Keiretzu*, populated by many of the best legal minds the common law has to offer. But diversity is often more crucial to constitutionalization than quality.

This is because critical aspects of emerging constitutional knowledge frequently come from unforeseeable sources. England's constitutional reformation of the early nineteenth century initially emerged from outside its preordained fonts of constitutional-legal intelligence. In the United States, many foundational constitutional innovations, such as the delegitimation of slavery, the replacing of laissez-faire constitutionalism with the welfare state, and the delegitimation of racial exclusion, also emerged outside of formally identified repositories of national, constitutional-legal talent. In some cases, they emerged in spite of, rather than because of, the well-meaning efforts of the elite bar and legal academia to promote and preserve the quality of constitutional-legal discourse.[23]

For this reason, Hong Kong's constitutionalism desperately needs both a legal academia and a legal profession that allows for people to train in law from as many paths as is possible, and in pursuit of as wide a diversity of professional, social, and constitutional goals as possible, including that of bringing the dynamics and discourse of the law and the constitution to the large and presently excluded elements of Hong Kong's Cantonese-speaking populations. It probably needs more than three law schools. But in any event, *it certainly needs Cantonese as well as English language law schools.* What it needs, in other words, is a multiplicity of academic institutions, operating through a diversity of educational, scholarly, and linguistic approaches.

It also needs discourses and interactions among its law schools and legal scholars and professionals. The insularity that attends Hong Kong's institutions of higher legal education and its constitutional-legal civil societies in general is striking compared with, for example, those in Australia, New York, or London. It is still extraordinarily rare, virtually unheard of, to see the law or politics faculties of City University, Chinese University of Hong Kong, or Hong Kong University invite compatriots from sister faculties to give seminars or presentations. Tragically, it was depressingly common for me to hear academic and administrative figures from more self-consciously "elite" institutions, such as my own Chinese University, discredit the possible contributions of very competent compatriots at other institutions simply because they regard these institution less prestigious than their own.

Hong Kong's constitutional development also desperately needs legal professional organizations that are willing to afford equal respect to the full diversity of schools, approaches, and backgrounds that constitutionalism requires. It needs professional organizations that would not discriminate or privilege one school or its graduates over another in extending opportunities for entry into the profession. Insofar as Hong Kong legal academy is concerned, these professional organizations should simply and solely determine the minimal qualifications necessary to practice. They should not demand more idealized qualifications, and they should not set entry quotas—and they should most certainly not set entry quotas specific to each law school. Outside of perhaps requiring a degree from a recognized law school (wherein the standards for recognition are objective and focus exclusively on institutional resources), they should not dictate *how* these minimal professional qualifications are to be instilled or achieved.

They should not dictate the law school curricula. At present, Hong Kong appears to have no law school faculty who specializes in comparative law, legal history, or regulatory theory. Of course, such topics have proved to be absolutely invaluable in the development of common-law constitutional thought in the United States and the United Kingdom, and so their complete absence from Hong Kong legal education is troublesome. Some attribute this to Hong Kong students only being interested in practical courses that will help them make money. However, comparative law and regulatory theory courses offered by the Department of Government and Public Administration at Chinese University have no problem attracting Hong Kong students. A better explanation is that law school intake and the law school curriculum are so utterly constrained by the corporatist interests and power of the profession as to filter out or otherwise extinguish opportunity to or interest in exploring these more academic, but still very constitutionally-relevant topics.

Historicism

Hong Kong's constitutionalism also evinces a much more pronounced, Diceyian concern with preserving the historicist essentialisms of the common law than is found in the rest of the common-law world. We can get some idea of the comparative prominence of historicist essentialism in Hong Kong constitutional discourse by comparing that discourse with the constitutional discourse of contemporary Great Britain. The comparison is particularly apt because like that of Hong Kong, the common-law constitutional system of Great Britain has also recently become embedded into a larger constitutional framework that is alien to the common law. In the case of Hong Kong, that larger, alien constitutional system is obviously the socialist-civilian system of China. In the case of Great Britain, that larger, alien constitutional system is the corporatist-civilian system of the European Union.

Arguments about the historicist-essentialist nature of the England's distinctly common-law tradition has been much less prominent in the case of Great Britain's constitutional integration with the European Union than they have been in the case of Hong Kong's ongoing constitutional integration with the People's Republic of China (PRC). Constitutional textbooks in the United Kingdom, like Bradley and Ewing's *Constitutional and Administrative Law*, generally portray the United Kingdom's European integration as simply a next step in its constitutional evolution.[24] By contrast, the principal textbook on the Hong Kong Basic Law, Yash Ghai's *Hong Kong's New Constitutional Order*, portrays the conflicts between the civilian and socialist essences of China's constitutional legal system on the one hand, and the common-law essences of Hong Kong's legal system on the other as an almost Huntingtonian, intercivilizational contradiction.[25]

Of course, maybe it is. Hong Kongers by-and-large find the authoritarian-socialist regime of the PRC much more threatening than the British find the democratic-capitalist regime of the European Union. It is no doubt for this reason that Hong Kong's Basic-Law "mini-constitution" committed itself to maintaining in Hong Kong the "common-law system." And because the common law is a historicist construct, a commitment to maintain that system in the face of competition from another, threatening legal system would naturally seem to require a deference to the distinguishing, historicist essences that give the common-law its protecting essence.

Indeed, it was precisely this same type of threat that caused Dicey to adopt his own historicist-essentialist perspective. In Dicey's case, the threat was from the legal system of radical-collectivist France, which had significantly influenced the radical vision of "popular constitutionalism" that Dicey was seeking to remove from English constitutional discourse. Dicey identified the essentialist components of England common-law history (i.e., rule of law) primarily through their contrast with what was found in the French public-law system.[26]

Nevertheless, Hong Kong's common-law constitutionalism would do well to avoid obsessing over its seemingly "common-law" essences. The success of Hong Kong's constitutional arrangement is likely to depend primarily on Hong Kong interpretative ability to generate new understandings in response to new situations. These new understandings are not likely to be found simply by recycling traditional "common-law" solutions developed in the context of a now-gone past.

Indeed, insofar as constitutionalism is concerned, the idea of a "common-law" essence is virtually nonsensical. The interpretive diversity that exists among common-law constitutional systems is at least as great as that which exists between common-law and civil-law systems. There is probably no better example of this than the question of the NPC's power to "interpret" the Basic Law. The virtually universal trope that one hears from Hong Kong constitutional scholars is that such interpretative practice is contrary to the common-law system. China's practice of parliamentary interpretation is routinely ascribed to its civil-law or socialist-law heritage. But, we are told, in the common-law system, it is the judiciary, not the legislature, that interprets constitutional law.

In fact, this is categorically incorrect. Leaving aside for the moment the obvious but perhaps special counterexample of the English House of Lords, both the U.S. Congress and the Australian Parliament also frequently issue binding interpretations of law, including constitutional law, that that work to overrule some prior and contrary judicial interpretation. Such interpretations are so common we even have a name for them: *remedial* or *curative* legislation.

Consider the following story as related by one of the foremost scholars of statutory interpretation in the United States, Professor William Eskridge:

> [In the 1976 case of *General Electric Co. v. Gilbert*, the United States Supreme Court] held that an employer's exclusion of pregnancy-related disabilities from its employee disability plan does not violate title VII [of the Civil Rights Act of 1964]'s proscription against discrimination 'because of the individual's . . . sex.' . . .
>
> The political response to *Gilbert* was swift and furious. . . . Early in 1977, legislation was introduced in both chambers to overrule *Gilbert* by defining discrimination on the basis of gender to include pregnancy-based distinctions . . . The resulting Pregnancy Discrimination Act (PDA) is notable in part because the key legislative players rushed to declare, with unusual fervor, that the Court had misinterpreted title VII. The committee reports asserted that "the dissenting Justices [in *Gilbert*] correctly interpreted the Act." The statements of the PDA's sponsors were even stronger: "By concluding that pregnancy discrimination is not sex discrimination within the meaning of title VII, the Supreme Court disregarded the intent of Congress in enacting title VII. That intent was to protect all individuals from unjust employment discrimination, including pregnant women."[27]

There is no significant functional difference that I can see between the NPC's interpretation of the Basic Law issued in response to the *Ng Ka Ling* case[28] and the U.S. congressional interpretations of the Civil Rights Act issued in response to *Gilbert.* Both interpretations were issued in the form of validly enacted legislative instruments. Both were expressly promulgated as interpretations of law that overruled contrary court interpretations. Both had only prospective effect and did not effect the outcome of cases already decided under the old interpretation.

Since the end of the nineteenth century, the power or authority of the U.S. Congress to enact such legislation has never been in doubt.[29] If the Congress of the common-law United States can enact such legislation, one simply cannot claim that similar legislative interpretations of the Basic Law enacted by the NPC are contrary to the spirit of the common law simply because they represent a legislature rather than court interpreting the law.

Some might respond that the NPC interpretation of the Basic Law and the U.S. congressional interpretation of the Civil Rights Act in fact were not the same. In the American example, Congress was interpreting ordinary legislation, while in the *Ng Ka Ling* case, the NPC was interpreting what was effectively a constitution. In fact, it is well established in the United

States that both legislatures and executives have constitutional interpretative authority that exists independent of the courts.[30] However, this claim points us to another critical problem with the common-law essentialism of Hong Kong's constitutional discourse—its parochialism.

This parochialism has two debilitating aspects. The first, evinced by the previous argument, relates to it tendency to lull Hong Kong constitutionalism into a belief that China's constitutional framework is irrelevant to it. Interpretative arguments that hinge on a claim that Hong Kong's Basic Law is a "constitution" invariably overlook the fact that the term *basic law* is a well-established class of nonconstitutional, statutory legislation in the PRC's constitution. China has more than sixty "basic laws" in force at present, of which the Basic Law of the Hong Kong SAR is simply one. Contrary to what many in Hong Kong's interpretative community presumed, at least in the 1990s, simply calling the Hong Kong Basic Law a "Basic Law" did not endow it with some uniquely "constitutional" essence per se. Paying closer attention to China's own constitutional framework would have alerted the Hong Kong constitutional-interpretative community to this and allowed them to adjust their arguments accordingly.

This is not to deny that the Hong Kong Basic Law does not indeed possess some such constitutional essence. However, that essence comes, not from its title, but from the way it interacts with China's larger constitutional structure and principles. What gives the Hong Kong Basic Law its quasi-constitutional character is that it establishes and defines a core feature of China's emerging constitutional order—one country, two systems.

Viewed in this light, the Civil Rights Act of 1964, that legislation that the U.S. Congress "interpreted" *Gilbert* by passing the PDA, is no less "constitutional" in character than the Basic Law of Hong Kong. The passage of the Civil Rights Act was a defining moment in the U.S. civil-rights movement, which, according to noted constitutional law scholar Bruce Ackerman, represented a functional amendment of the U.S. Constitution (what he has famously termed a *constitutional moment*).[31] Indeed, the Civil Rights Act was expressly cast as a legislative "interpretation" of the Fourteenth Amendment to the U.S. Constitution.[32] As explained by Gerald Rosenberg, it was the enacting of the Civil Rights Act, rather than the much more famous constitutional interpretative moment of *Brown v. Board of Education*,[33] that really inaugurated the beginning of the passing of raced-based exclusions from American society.[34] Therefore, the real battle between Congress and the Supreme Court was indeed over a distinctly *constitutional* interpretation, just like that at issue in the NPC's interpretation of the constitutional implications of the *Ng Ka Ling* case.

Just as interpretations of the American Civil Rights Act of 1964 must take into account the American constitutional framework of which is it a part, so to must interpretations of Hong Kong's Basic Law take into account a larger constitutional framework, that of the PRC. Clearly, that framework grants to Hong Kong an extraordinary degree of autonomy. But that autonomy is not absolute; it is an autonomy that nevertheless is inevitably defined and circumscribed by its larger constitutional contexts, including the PRC Constitution. One simply cannot draw the boundaries of that that autonomy, no matter how broad and expansive that autonomy may be, without referent to that larger constitutional system that creates and inevitably defines it.

The confusion that surrounded the NPC interpretation of 1999 is a paradigmatic example of how Hong Kong's infatuation with common-law essentialism prevented it from effectively negotiating its own constitutional autonomy. Because of its Diceyian parochialism I suspect, Hong Kong's constitutional-interpretative community, in objecting to this interpretation, overlooked the fact that the process of NPC legislative interpretations is both defined and constrained by the PRC's own constitutional framework. Had they been more open to the implication of the PRC's own constitutionalism insofar as Hong Kong's constitutionalism is concerned, they might have recognized that such interpretations had to follow valid legislative procedure. And if they had recognized this, then they also may have recognized that in the case of the 1999 interpretation, these procedures arguably were not followed.

In fact, the 1999 interpretation was promulgated through a very abbreviated procedure that was arguably contrary to the spirit of the NPC's normative approach to legislative interpretation, if not its black-letter law. The interpretation process was significantly more opaque than was normal for NPC legislation of this sort. It did not appear to involve the range of consultations the NPC normally afforded similar kinds of legislative bills—the legislative process for the 1999 interpretation only took two weeks, as contrasted with the several months that NPC statutory interpretations would normally take.[35] But the Hong Kong constitutional interpretative community generally ignored these procedural shortcomings, focusing instead on the common law's alleged antipathy to legislative interpretation per se.

Would attention to these shortcomings have made a difference? Maybe, but maybe not. But it is worth noting that in the aftermath of the Tiananmen Square demonstrations in 1989, some Chinese scholars and parliamentarians had raised similar objections to the opaque procedures by which the State Council has declared martial law. This caused the NPC subsequently to issue legislation that clarified and rationalized these procedures, rendering them more transparent, more visible, and thus at least somewhat more susceptible to a wider field of political scrutiny.[36] If procedural criticism was able to accomplish this in the politically charged aftermath of Tiananmen, one wonders if a similar, procedurally focused critique of the NPC's 1999 interpretation could likewise have stimulated a more transparent, deliberative, and thus accountable process for NPC interpretations of the Basic Law.

The other debilitating aspect of Hong Kong common-law constitutional parochialism lies in the fact that it needlessly constrains constitutional insight. Constitutional systems routinely borrow ideas from one another in understanding and addressing new constitutional problems. The English (and American) idea of "judicial independence" came from the Baron de Montesquieu in France. The English idea of a civil service came from China. The German federalist structure came from the United States. Initial visions of America's New Deal constitutionalism came from Italy. Canada and Great Britain imported their ombudsman systems from Scandinavia.

In no case did any of these imported polities worry significantly about whether the imported feature was "common law" or "civilian" in its essence. The imports were adapted simply because they were perceived as the best solutions available for particular social or constitutional problems being experienced by the adopting constitutional system. (Indeed, I would argue that one of the strengths of the common-law system as it works in England or in the United States lies in its distinctive capacity to adopt and adapt foreign ideas into its cognitive framework—that is, to learn, from sources outside itself.) An interpretative project that denies the potential relevance of constitutional knowledge and experience simply because it comes from a system that is not "common law" simply wills its own ignorance.

Of course, the paradigmatic example of this is found in Dicey. One of the major motivations behind Dicey's quest to identify the constitutional essence of the common law was to inoculate English constitutional thought from the possible influence of French-style administrative law. This may have seemed wise in 1880, when the French system was indeed problematic. However, his effort to preserve a uniquely English common-law constitutional system ultimately caused that system to degenerate into insignificance insofar as Britain's continued political and social evolution was concerned.[37] And ironically, one of the major stimuli behind the reawakening of Britain's constitutional and administrative law system in the 1950s to 1970s turned out to be the pronounced success of that very system that Dicey had sought to insulate from English constitutional thought—the French administrative law system.[38]

Hong Kong has embarked (or has been embarked) on a constitutional arrangement for which there is no significant historical precedent. Whatever effective solutions it finds for addressing the many unresolved issues that will arise in the course of this experiment are highly unlikely to be discovered by some arbitrary, culturally defined vision of historical contiguity. They are, in other words, unlikely to be found in some historicist-essentialist reconstruction of the "common law." An interpretative methodology that requires it to look there and not elsewhere is a severe defect, not a source of strength.

Conclusion

In sum, nothing I have seen to date gives me any reason to suspect that the Diceyian common-law constitutionalism of Article 8 has been, is, or is likely to be any more supportive of the true, constitutional-democratic needs and concerns of Hong Kong today than it was of the true, constitutional-democratic needs and concerns of late-nineteenth-century England. In fact, I suspect that because Hong Kong's common-law system is more 'Diceyian' than the English common-law system that Dicey was working in, the interpretive politics of Article 8 are likely to be significantly more obstructive of Hong Kong's constitutional-democratic development than they were to that of Britain. In Hong Kong, in other words, the counterdemocratic tendencies of Diceyian common-law constitutionalism are much more likely to work as Dicey himself intended.

Hong Kong's legal-constitutional interpretive community needs to find ways of thinking creatively rather than archaically about Hong Kong's constitutional conditions. In doing so, it needs to invite, rather than ignore, the full diversity of Hong Kong's (and China's) unique constitutional experiences. And since a significant portion of these experiences is embedded outside the reach of the common law—in a population that speaks and experiences in Cantonese rather than English, for example, or in the evolving constitutional practices of the Chinese mainland—it needs to begin regarding this population, its language, and its culture as sources of empowerment rather than as a causes for embarrassment.

Notes

1. William Blackstone, *Commentaries on the Laws of England,* Book IV, 443. See also Quentin Skinner, "The State," in *Political Innovation and Conceptual Change,* ed. Terence Ball, James Farr, and Russell L. Hanson (Cambridge: Cambridge University Press, 1989), 90–131.
2. John Adolphus, ed., *A correct, full, and impartial report, of the trial of Her Majesty Caroline, Queen Consort of Great Britain, before the House of Peers, on the bill of pains and penalties: with authentic particulars, embracing every circumstance connected with, and illustrative of, the subject of this momentous event interspersed with original letters, and other curious and interesting documents, not generally known, and never before published, including, at large, Her Majesty's defence* (Buffalo, NY: Hein, 2001), 221.

3. See also Dror Wahrman, "Public Opinion, Violence, and the Limits of Constitutional Politics," in *Re-Reading the Constitution*, ed. James Vernon (New York: Cambridge University Press, 1996), 83–122.
4. On the participation of women in this debate, see Anna Clark, "Gender, Class, and the Constitution: Franchise Reform in England, 1832–1928," in ibid. See also Patrick Joyce, "The Constitution and the Narrative Structure of Victorian Politics," in ibid.
5. Adam Tomkins, "The Republican Monarchy Revisited," *Constitutional Comment* 19 (2002): 737.
6. See A. V. Dicey, *Lectures on the Relation between Law and Public Opinion in England during the Nineteenth Century* (New Brunswick, NJ: Transaction Books, 1981); Dicey, "Democracy in Switzerland—II," *The Nation* 41 (1886): 494–96.
7. See David Schneiderman, "A. V. Dicey, Lord Watson, and the Law of the Canadian Constitution in the Late Nineteenth Century," *Law and History Review* 16 (1998): 495–526; H. A. Tulloch, "Changing British Attitudes towards the United States in the 1880s," *The Historical Journal* 20 (1977): 825–40.
8. See William Wade and Christopher Forsyth, *Administrative Law, 9th ed.* (Oxford: Oxford University Press, 2004), 18–19.
9. See also Harold J. Laski, "On the Study of Politics," in *The Study of Politics: A Collection of Inaugural Lectures*, ed. Preston King (London: Frank Cass, 1977), 1, 13.
10. See Dicey, "Democracy in Switzerland—II."
11. See Maurice Keen, *English Society in the Later Middle Ages, 1348–1500* (London: Penguin Press, 1990).
12. See E. P. Thompson, *Whigs and Hunters: The Origin of the Black Act* (London: Allen Lane, 1975).
13. See Richard H. Helmholtz, "Origins of the Privilege against Self-Incrimination: The Role of the European Ius Commune," *New York University Law Review* 65 (1990): 962; E. P. Thompson, *The Making of the English Working Class* (London: Gollancz, 1963) (on the French influence on early industrial English constitutionalism); *Council of Civil Service Unions v. Minister for the Civil Service* [1985] AC 374, 410, HL (opinion of Lord Diplock) (importing French administrative law doctrine of proportionality into English common law).
14. Interview with Professor Hualing Fu of Hong Kong University Law Faculty.
15. Yash Ghai, *Hong Kong's New Constitutional Order: The Resumption of Chinese Sovereignty and the Basic Law* (Hong Kong: Hong Kong University Press, 1997); Peter Wesley-Smith, *Constitutional and Administrative Law in Hong Kong*, 2nd ed. (Hong Kong: Longman Asia, 1994).
16. See "Council Accepts IC Report, Resolves to End Bitter Turmoil in SLW," *City University Bulletin Issue*, no. 27 (December 1, 2002).
17. See The Law Society of Hong Kong, "Position on Legal Education and Training (September 2001), available at http://www.hklawsoc.org.hk/pub_e/news/submissions/20010924.pdf; Steering Committee on the Review of Legal Education and Training in Hong Kong, "Legal Education and Training in Hong Kong: Preliminary Review: Summary of Consultation Paper" (September 2000), available at http://www.hklawsoc.org.hk/pub_e/news/societyupdates/20010813a.asp (accessed October 23, 2006).
18. See *Re Cheng Kai Nam* [2002] 2 HKLRD 39, CFI.
19. See Larry Diamond and Leonardo Morlino, eds., *Assessing the Quality of Democracy* (Baltimore: Johns Hopkins University Press, 2005); Fareed Zakaria, "The Rise of Illiberal Democracy," *Foreign Affairs*, November/December 1997.

20. See, generally, Will Kymlicka and Alan Patten, eds., *Language Rights and Political Theory* (Oxford: Oxford University Press, 2004).
21. See James A. Epstein, *Radical Expression: Political Language, Ritual, and Symbol in England, 1790–1850* (New York: Oxford University Press, 1994); Larry D. Kramer, *The People Themselves: Popular Constitutionalism and Judicial Review* (Oxford: New York, Oxford University Press, 2004).
22. See Jon Elster, ed., *The Roundtable Talks and the Breakdown of Communism* (Chicago: University of Chicago Press, 1996).
23. See generally Kramer, *The People Themselves*. See also Gordon S. Wood, *The Radicalism of the American Revolution* (New York: A. A. Knopf, 1992).
24. A. W. Bradley and K. D. Ewing, *Constitutional and Administrative Law*, 12th ed. (London: Longman, 1997).
25. See Ghai, *Hong Kong's New Constitutional Order*. Compare with Samuel P. Huntington, *The Clash of Civilizations and the Remaking of World Order* (New York: Simon & Schuster, 1996).
26. See Albert Venn Dicey, *Introduction to the Study of the Law of the Constitution*, 8th ed. (London: Macmillan, 1915).
27. William N. Eskridge, Jr., "Reneging on History? Playing the Court/Congress/President Civil Rights Game," *California Law Review* 79 (1991): 613, 627–29. See also *General Electric Co. v. Gilbert*, 429 U.S. 125 (1976); *The Pregnancy Discrimination Act*, Pub. L. No. 95-555, 92 Stat. 2076 (1979) (codified as 42 U.S.C. § 2000e[k]).
28. *Ng Ka Ling & Others v. Director of Immigration* [1999] 1 HKLRD 315, CFA.
29. For more on the use of curative legislation by the U.S. Congress, see William N. Eskridge, Jr., "Overriding Supreme Court Statutory Interpretation Decisions," *Yale Law Journal* 101 (1991): 331.
30. See Kramer, *The People Themselves*.
31. See Bruce A. Ackerman, *We the People* (Cambridge, MA: Belknap Press of Harvard University Press, 1991).
32. See Office of the White House Press Secretary Press Release, "Special Message On Civil Rights" (February 28, 1963).
33. *Brown v. Board of Education* 347 U.S. 483 (1954).
34. See Gerald N. Rosenberg, *The Hollow Hope: Can Courts Bring about Social Change*? (Chicago: University of Chicago Press, 1991).
35. Compare the process the NPC used to issue its interpretation of the Basic Law in 1999, as described in Legislative Council of Hong Kong, Panel on Security, "Background paper prepared by Legislative Council Secretariat: Issue of right of abode in the Hong Kong Special Administrative Region of persons born in the Mainland to Hong Kong permanent residents," LC Paper No. CB(2) 946/01-02(01) (January 21, 2002) (available at http://www.legco.gov.hk/yr01-02/english/panels/se/papers/se0124cb2-946-1e.pdf) with the archetypical process as described generally in Michael W. Dowdle, "The Constitutional Development and Operations of the National People's Congress," *Columbia Journal Asian Law* 11 (1997): 70-85.
36. See, generally, Dowdle, ibid, 12.
37. See Wade and Forsyth, *Administrative Law*, 18-19.
38. See *Council of Civil Service Unions v. Minister for the Civil Service* (opinion of Lord Diplock).

CHAPTER 4

Interpreting Constitutionalism and Democratization in Hong Kong

Michael C. Davis[*]

Hong Kong's status as a Special Administrative Region of China has engendered considerable interest in its political development. Outside observers and Hong Kong people alike generally consider that greater democratization will mean greater autonomy and less democracy will mean more control by Beijing. This observation is founded on an appreciation of the fundamental role democratization plays in constitutionalism. Understanding the Hong Kong political reform debate is therefore important to understanding the emerging status of both Hong Kong and China. The Sino-British Joint Declaration and the Hong Kong Basic Law appear to require liberal human rights protection, the rule of law, and democratic rule in Hong Kong.[1] This chapter considers the politics of constitutional interpretation in Hong Kong and its relationship to developing democracy and sustaining Hong Kong's highly regarded rule of law.

High levels of popular support for democratic reform and human rights are a consistent feature of Hong Kong's political landscape, which is especially evident in electoral support for prodemocracy legislative candidates—typically running around 60 percent—and popular demonstrations over human rights and democracy.[2] These popular Hong Kong views on democracy and human rights have often confronted an antidemocratic stance of the Beijing government and its supporters. Beijing's resistance to democratic reform was first evident in the debates over the drafting of the Hong Kong Basic Law in the 1980s.[3] It has been evident at nearly every critical juncture, in

* Professor Davis would like to thank the Northwestern University Law School which hosted him as the J. Landis Martin Visting Professor of Law in 2005-6 during the preparation of this manuscript.

the pre-handover debate over political reform in the 1990s, in the exclusion of democrats at the handover, and in the recent debates over constitutional reform.[4] Does Beijing's resistance to democratization threaten the liberal constitutional agenda in both the Sino-British Joint Declaration and the Hong Kong Basic Law? [5]

How will Hong Kong fare in the face of this clash of political expectations and cultures? And how will the public, both local and international, come to view the Hong Kong project? This chapter will consider the intense debate over interpreting Hong Kong's path to democratic development. The next three sections consider the content of the Basic Law roadmap for democratization, interpretations of such Basic Law provisions, and the 2004 political debate over these requirements. I will then step back and consider how these factors and other developments may effect Hong Kong's constitutional development in its entirety, exposing a much deeper debate about the character of Hong Kong's political system and the quality of Hong Kong institutions.

The Roadmap for Hong Kong's Constitutional Development

To appreciate the centrality of democratic development in the Hong Kong political debate, it is important to consider the foundational democratic requirements spelled out in the Sino-British Joint Declaration, an international treaty properly ratified by both governments and registered with the United Nations as such, and the Hong Kong Basic Law. The 1984 Sino-British Joint Declaration put in play China's design of "one country, two systems." It signaled the democratic road ahead by providing that the legislature shall be chosen by elections and the chief executive by elections or consultations held locally. One country, two systems obviously aimed to encourage confidence in Hong Kong's "high degree of autonomy." Hong Kong people were encouraged to put their hearts at ease. As the subject of a great effort by China to garner international support, China also spoke to foreign governments, encouraging their reliance on the one country, two systems framework.

As stipulated in the Joint Declaration, the Basic Law takes up Hong Kong's democratic promise in Articles 45 and 68, supplemented by Annexes I and II, respectively. Basic Law Article 45 puts the democracy debate on the public agenda, indicating as follows: "The method for selecting the Chief Executive shall be specified in light of the *actual situation* . . . in accordance with the principle of *gradual and orderly progress*. The *ultimate aim* is the selection of the Chief Executive by *universal suffrage* upon nomination by a *broadly representative nominating committee* in accordance with *democratic procedures*" (Emphasis added).

Triggering the continuing reform debate, Basic Law, Annex I specifies election of the chief executive by a "broadly representative" election committee in the first two terms but provides in Annex I, Article 7 for changing the method of election, as follows: "If *there is a need* to amend the method for selecting the Chief Executives for the terms *subsequent to the year 2007*, such amendments must be made with the endorsement of a *two-thirds majority* of all the members of the Legislative Council and the *consent* of the Chief Executive, and they shall be *reported* to the Standing Committee of the National People's Congress *for approval*" (Emphasis added). Taking such action would move the system toward the specified "ultimate aim" of choosing the chief executive "by universal suffrage on nomination by a broadly representative nominating committee in accordance with democratic procedures."

Article 68 provides essentially the same process in relation to forming the Legislative Council (LegCo), except that there is no need for a nominating committee and the provision on changing the method in Annex II, Article III specifies that the change need only be reported to the Standing Committee of the National People's Congress (NPCSC) "for the record."[6] Under Basic Law Annex II, after several expansions of the number of directly elected seats in steps during the first ten years, by 2007, there will be thirty sitting LegCo members who were directly elected in 2004 and thirty members representing various functional constituencies—from business, social, and professional groups.

Interpreting the Basic Law

On April 6, 2004, the NPCSC reacted to calls for democracy in Hong Kong, issuing its own interpretation of Annex I, Article 7 and Annex II, Article III. This interpretation added new requirements to change the method of selection, essentially giving the central government complete control over initiating change. In its interpretation, the NPCSC specified in relevant part as follows:

> The Chief Executive of the Hong Kong Special Administrative Region shall make a report to the Standing Committee of the National People's Congress as regards whether there is *a need to make an amendment*; and the Standing Committee of the National People's Congress shall, in accordance with the provisions of Articles 45 and 68 of the Basic Law . . . , make a determination in the light of the *actual situation* in the Hong Kong Special Administrative Region and in accordance with the principles of *gradual and orderly progress*. The bills on the amendments to the method for selecting the Chief Executive and the method

> of forming the Legislative Council and its procedures for voting on bills and motions and the proposed amendments to such bills shall be introduced by the Government . . . into the Legislative Council. (Emphasis added.)[7]

Though the NPCSC wisely concluded that "subsequent to 2007" included changes for the method of selection in 2007 and 2008, by specifying that the chief executive would be required to issue a report to the central government as to the need for change the interpretation put power to initiate any reform in its own hands.

The PRC government had not always taken the view that it could intervene so readily in this democratic reform decision. In a comment in the *People's Daily* on March 18, 1993, then director of the Hong Kong and Macau affairs office, Lu Ping, stated, "As for how the legislature will be constituted after its third term, all that is needed is for two-thirds of legislators to approve, the chief executive to give his consent, and then report to the NPCSC for the record. There is no need for Central Government approval. How Hong Kong develops democracy in the future is entirely within the autonomy of Hong Kong."[8]

The April 6, 2004, interpretation was followed in just ten days time by a report by a government task force on constitutional reform and the indicated report by the Hong Kong chief executive specifying that there was a need to change the method for selecting the chief executive and forming the LegCo.[9] Nine conditions specified in the chief executive's report and elaborated in the task force report signaled to most members of the public that the change in methods of selection was going to be minimal. By specifying how the "actual situation" would be evaluated, the chief executive's report appeared to add to the Basic Law by specifying conditions and factors to consider that were in no way apparent in the text.[10] Both reports emphasized the lack of political maturity of politicians and political groups, the need for different sectors of society to be represented, and that "the pace should not be too fast." They also emphasized that any changes not have any adverse economic effect.

The April 26, 2004, response of the NPCSC to the chief executive's report sealed the doom for democratic reform, essentially barring any meaningful reform for the 2007/2008 elections by requiring continued use of the Election Committee (EC) for selecting the chief executive—though its membership could be increased—and specifying that the current 50-50 percentage ratio of directly elected to functional legislators be maintained.[11] The only reform options left open for the 2007/2008 elections was to increase the size of the EC and LegCo. In its October 2005 report, this was precisely what the government sought to do: double the EC membership to 1,600 and add five functional seats representing the District Councils balanced against five directly elected geographical seats.[12] Under the proposal, therefore, the democrats would have the same relative proportions in LegCo and an inability to win the post of chief executive, effectively maintaining the status quo. The democratic camp's outcry with respect to such limited reforms was expected.[13] With a two-thirds vote in LegCo needed to pass the "reform," LegCo's rejection of the reform proposals in December 2006 was also expected.

Beijing's continuing concerns over democratic reform in Hong Kong reflect its long-standing suspicions of liberal-minded democrats. The exclusion of key democrats from nearly all consultative roles before the handover, their expulsion from LegCo during the handover, and their continuing exclusion from Beijing bodies and even Beijing itself have long demonstrated Beijing's suspicions about the intentions of the democratic camp. Being ultimately accountable to Beijing, the Hong Kong government has generally joined in this suspicion, which is reflected in its own appointments and policies concerning democracy. The key difference in the 2004 episode is that the calendar had run out on Beijing's Basic Law strategy to defer democracy during the first ten years after the handover. At the same time, the July 1, 2003, mass demonstrations by a half-million people over the proposed national security legislation under Article 23 of the Basic Law surely put the government under pressure to abandon its resistance to popular demands.[14]

The 2004 Constitutional Debate

These interpretations and reports took place in an environment that conveyed the extreme hostility of the Beijing government toward democratization in Hong Kong—a hostility that met with considerable local and international objection. Before April 2004, Hong Kong democracy supporters had been subject to a two months barrage of severe criticism.[15]

Beijing, sometimes aided by its Hong Kong supporters, launched what was essentially a five-stage attack on the democratic camp. First, Beijing launched the so-called patriot debate, taking a swipe at foreign interference. Hong Kong was told that under any democratic reform "patriots must be the main body of those who govern Hong Kong."[16] Although Deng Xiaoping was cited for this requirement, Deng was frequently on record as indicating that one need not be pro-communist to be a patriot.[17] Categories of democracy activists who were labeled unpatriotic in this campaign included, as paraphrased in various media reports, those who are subversive of mainland authorities, those who support Taiwan independence, those who raise the flag of democracy but are in fact running dogs for Western forces, and those who opposed Article 23 national security legislation.[18] The patriot debate reached its zenith when the former Democratic Party Chair Martin Lee was criticized for testifying before a U.S. Senate hearing on Hong Kong.[19]

The second stage of the attack on democracy was to offer a steady diet of Deng Xiaoping statements arguing the meaning of "gradual and orderly progress."[20] As it became apparent that Deng's statements could be used on either side, this barrage slowed down. The NPCSC's interpretation of April 6 and the reports of the task force and chief executive offer little hint of what "gradual and orderly progress" means, other than to say it must not go too fast and that this depends on the actual situation. The rule of law would more clearly be served by reliance on the Basic Law text.

The third stage of this attack on democratic reform became even more aggressive when Beijing officials and the media started publishing threats to take emergency action. At this stage, NPC Vice Chairman Sheng Huaren delivered a long lecture on Beijing's power to declare a state of emergency in Hong Kong.[21] The *China Daily* hinted at the possibility that the central government would dismiss the LegCo if democrats gained more than thirty seats in the September 2004 elections,[22] warning that, "If those who try to use democracy to exclude the Communist Party of China and 'respect Taiwan self-determination' take the majority of seats in LegCo, Hong Kong's executive-led government will collapse and the central authority and national security will be severely challenged."[23] The local pro-Beijing newspaper *Wen Wei Po* quoted an unnamed Beijing official as saying, "I have a knife. Usually it is not used but now you force me to use it."[24] These statements were understood locally to threaten dissolution of the LegCo if pro-Beijing parties lost control in the 2004 election, which was a nearly impossible prospect under the existing electoral model.

The fourth stage in the crisis was for mainland experts to lecture Hong Kong on the "spirit" of the Basic Law and the demerits of "fake democracy." Hong Kong was told by mainland "legal expert" Xiao Weiyun that the spirit, not words, is the key to interpreting the Basic Law.[25] The spirit in question appeared to be a rather Mainland-regarding spirit and offered little regard to the assurances made long ago that Hong Kong people should put their hearts at ease and that the rest of the world might rely on Hong Kong's autonomy. The pro-Beijing business elite also weighed in on this spirit, worrying about a welfare state.[26]

The fifth and final stage in this effort to contain calls for democratic reform was embodied in the NPCSC interpretations and the ultimate "reform" the government put forward. Having used two months of vociferous attacks to push the goalpost back, Mainland officials then began to sound more conciliatory by mid-2004, even sending a Mainland official team to Hong Kong to explain the first interpretation. This more conciliatory attitude was surely calibrated in anticipation of the September 2004 election.

The September 2004 LegCo election did not prove to be the democratic landslide that had inspired so much hand-ringing in the pro-Beijing camp. With 60.63 percent of the popular vote, prodemocracy candidates performed more or less as they had in the past, though this was a slight improvement on the 57.16 percent they received in the 2000 LegCo election.[27] With an expansion of the number of directly elected seats and a slightly greater effort in regard to functional seats, democrats netted twenty-five of the total of sixty LegCo seats, well short of a majority. This broke down for the democrats to eighteen of the thirty directly elected seats and seven from functional constituencies. Given the makeup of the thirty functional seats, with many coming from well-disciplined business associations, it is not conceivable that the democrats could do better under the current model, effectively rendering them a permanent minority in LegCo, in spite of their majority popular support.

Political parties and their alignments are a noteworthy feature of the constitutional reform debate in Hong Kong. Hong Kong has around a half-dozen major political parties and the primary basis of alignment is the democratic reform debate. In the 2004 LegCo election, a new group of democrats emerged from the 2003 mass demonstrations over national security law proposals and the follow-on 2004 demonstrations over democracy. The Democratic Party, the historical flagship of the democratic camp, actually had fewer votes in the 2004 election—25.8 percent, down from 35 percent in the 2000 election—and their seat take was down to nine from the previous eleven.[28] The emergence of the Article 45 Concern Group (originally the Article 23 Concern Group), the group of lawyers and academics who had provided leadership in the 2003 and 2004 demonstrations, was an important consequence of Beijing's hard-line stance. The Article 45 Concern Group took four seats in the election but went on, with the participation of other democrats, to form the Civic Party, expected to be a major force in the next LegCo election. The 2004 debate over democracy predicts a similar debate in 2007-2008.

Alan Leong of the Civic Party represented the democratic camp in the 2007 chief executive selection. After a passionate effort in the small-circle election to the EC the democrats managed to secure 132 nominations, more than the 100 nominations needed for him to be a formal candidate. This status provided him the political wherewithal to demand and receive electoral debates with the current Chief Executive Donald Tsang. Though this was surely a futile effort in an EC process guaranteed to return the favored Beijing candidate, the core democrats judged this an opportunity to stir up public attention to this unfair process and promote the democratic cause. The final EC vote on March 25, 2007, was 649 to 123. Some democrats opposed democratic participation in this unfair election as merely lending credibility to a flawed election.

Hong Kong's Historical Path and Constitutional Theory

To assess Hong Kong's constitutional development, one must consider how constitutional institutions work and their relationship to democracy. Constitutionalists often overemphasize the constraints of constitutional government without sufficiently appreciating its positive empowering role.[29] In the first ten years of the HKSAR, Hong Kong officials have not lacked constraint as much as they have lacked a source of legitimacy and venues to mobilize support behind the many difficult choices they have had to make. They have often had to commit more energy to guarding their seemingly unwarranted powers and privileges than to finding imaginative solutions to pressing public issues.

The 1984 Sino-British Joint Declaration put Hong Kong on a visionary path to constitutional democracy. Although Chinese leaders offered creative solutions to the problem of Hong Kong's return, they may not have fully appreciated the constitutional implications of their vision. On a general level, it was understood that anything less than substantial constitutional democracy would fail to secure adequate confidence in Hong Kong's future. The elements of constitutional democracy typically include democratic elections, the protection of human rights and liberty, and the rule of law, especially constitutional judicial review, all of which are promised in some form in the Joint Declaration. The declaration also includes commitments to democracy and a panoply of liberal human rights norms, including the application of the international human rights covenants. The rule of law is expressly secured by the continued application of the common law, the independence and finality of the local courts, the supremacy of the Basic Law, and the right to challenge executive actions in the courts.[30] The latter right presumably includes constitutional judicial review, as is now widely accepted. These commitments were all stipulated for inclusion in the Hong Kong Basic Law.

The Basic Law faithfully incorporates most of the requirements of the Joint Declaration, but in three key areas the Basic Law sometimes comes up short, either in its text or in its interpretation. Malleability of existing institutions has put a high premium on democratic development to afford the highest level of public oversight. Disputes over Basic Law interpretation were evident in a variety of crises Hong Kong faced in the first ten years. Full direct election of the LegCo is promised but not provided. Liberal human rights guarantees are adequately provided but are put at risk by national security and public order provisions elsewhere in the Basic Law. Constitutional judicial review was long in doubt from the lack of explicit reference in the text. Although that doubt has been resolved favorably by judicial decisions, Beijing and pro-Beijing politicians at critical moments have sought to challenge such resolution. Actions of the government to overturn decisions of Hong Kong's courts as well as the various NPCSC interpretations have especially put the health of the judicial institution at risk. These developments are elaborated under three main headings in the discussion that follows.

Democracy

From Beijing's perspective, democratic development seems to pose the biggest threat to Beijing's control over events in Hong Kong. The Basic Law text, while ultimately favoring full democracy, in many respects reads like a roadmap on how to obstruct democratic development in Hong Kong. The level of distrust between competing supporters of authoritarian and liberal ideals is at its highest in the debate over democracy. Such obstacles on the road to full democratization are exacerbated by the lack of political commitment to democracy, both in the government and among its supporters. The local government does not, it appears, in any way challenge Beijing's efforts to control the process of democratization, a situation that demonstrates a weak sense of local autonomy. With the past failures at democratic reform, the undemocratic system of a select election committee choosing the chief executive in an uneven selection process and LegCo being dominated by progovernment and pro-Beijing legislators has continued and will be the subject of the next reform debate for the 2012 elections.[31] Confidence in government is not aided by the appearance of unfairness in an electoral system where a prodemocracy candidates for chief executive had no realistic chance and LegCo candidates from the prodemocracy camp won 60 percent of the popular vote but only netted a third of the seats. [32] Given the many obvious failures this system has engendered, it can be wondered how long the government and its supporters will insist on maintaining this system in the face of continuing calls for reform.

In addition to electoral shortcomings, a democratic deficit is in other ways built into the very fabric of the Basic Law. Basic Law Article 74 requires members of LegCo to obtain the chief executive's approval before they can introduce bills involving public expenditure or government policy. In addition, amendments to government bills and motions or bills introduced by individual LegCo members require majority approval by each of two different groups of legislators: the thirty from functional constituencies and the thirty directly elected members. The government has argued, so far unsuccessfully, in challenging the Legislative Rules of Procedure, that even amendments to government bills proposed by legislators require the chief executive's approval. This government position was reinforced in the NPCSC interpretation requiring that even amendments to the electoral laws under Annexes I and II must be introduced by the government. Though Basic Law Annex II, Part III would have allowed a change in "the procedures for voting on bills and motions," the final NPCSC response to the government's report disallowed this change as well. Avenues to amend the Basic Law are equally blocked. The general power to amend the Basic Law is vested in the NPC.[33] Even local legislative proposals for amendment require a two-thirds vote in the LegCo, the consent of two-thirds of the local (invariably "pro-China") NPC deputies and the approval of the chief executive.

Ordinary observers can appreciate the cost of such democratic deficit: at moments of crisis, this system tends to produce a legitimacy gap between those legislators who are directly elected and the officials and legislators who are not. With directly elected legislators in permanent minority under the current model, democrats are essentially left to the politics of shame to pressure officials in power or in the legislative majority to support popular initiatives. This situation tends to produce political crises when public outrage is at its highest, producing in Hong Kong government by expediency and often government by crisis management.[34] Such authoritarian government, in Jon Elster's terms, is unable to make itself unable to interfere when it is expedient to do so.[35]

The local government often attempts short-cut expedient measures to solve this credibility problem. In 2002, the Hong Kong government put in place a so-called ministerial system, seeking to offer up the "accountability" of nonelected "ministers." The government presumably aimed to offer this as an alternative to full democratization. The track record of this ministerial accountability has been less than satisfactory. Ministers still lack the capacity to mobilize public support for their policies, and their occasional ineptitude may simply serve to multiply the number of crises. In the face of its failings, Chief Executive Tsang appointed nearly all career civil servants to form his cabinet for his second administration in 2007. Government plans also now include proposals to expanded such appointments below the ministerial level to create politically appointed posts of undersecretaries and political assistants. Other expedient strategies have been evident in the SARS and bird flu crises where short-term issues were addressed with quarantines and the culling of birds but long-term solutions of public hygiene and the closing of open poultry markets were less forthcoming by a government concerned about vocal objections.[36] In late 2006, testimony before the government's Commission on Strategic Development's Committee on Governance and Political Development was reported to favor another such limited reform, recommending that when direct elections of the chief executive is eventually permitted, the required Nominating Committee should have the right to vet candidates to ensure acceptability to Beijing.[37] The capacity of the Nominating Committee to effectively block democratic candidates, either by vetting or by the majority vote of a largely unrepresentative nominating committee, will certainly be a contentious issue in the coming years. With the foundation for democracy largely in place, one can only question the wisdom of maintaining this flawed and system.

Human Rights

The Hong Kong Basic Law has a satisfactory chapter on human rights, which includes the various liberal rights specified in the Joint Declaration and requires that any restrictions on rights meet the standards of the international human rights covenants. As with democratic development, the chief obstacle to the realization of the liberal human rights guarantees promised in the Joint Declaration appears to be interpretation. Beijing's interpretive role, whether exercised in formal post-handover interpretations or in the numerous decisions respecting the acceptability of laws under the Basic Law during the handover, has generally been to restrict human rights—to which the local government offers no resistance. Two articles in Basic Law Chapter II on local-central relations especially raise concern: Article 18 allows for application of national law in cases of emergency or where the central government determines there is "turmoil" in the region; and Article 23 requires the enactment of local laws on subversion, secession, sedition, and state secrets. The Article 18 notion of "turmoil" was added to the Basic Law as a consequence of response in Hong Kong to the 1989 Tiananmen Square demonstrations. The Beijing government characterized the 1989 Hong Kong demonstrations as turmoil. There is certainly a risk that Article 18 will someday be invoked.

The government-proposed national security law advanced in late 2002 and early 2003 in respect of the Article 23 requirements[38] caused great public concern about potentially vague and overbroad standards. The arrogant and insensitive approach to promoting the legislation of government officials and progovernment supporters appeared to further outrage the public. The sense that Beijing and its supporters were pushing this legislation forward was also of concern. Although the government withdrew the legislative proposal in the face of such intense public opposition, the government's stance fomented a serious political crisis whose effects lingered in the subsequent debate over democratization. In the face of China's dramatically contrasting human rights tradition, the strength of local institutional commitment is especially important. For Chinese officials or their local supporters to seek to override the local security of human rights, whether through public pronouncements or formal interpretations, would profoundly undermine the one country, two systems formula. As was evident in the review and passage of legislation during the handover, Chinese officials and local pro-Beijing politicians have often appeared skeptical of strong human rights commitments.[39]

The most striking positive quality of the Hong Kong rights regime is its international character, a feature that contrasts sharply with China's approach to human rights.[40] The foundation for this international character was laid in the Joint Declaration, which included substantial human rights guarantees and maintenance of the international human rights covenants. The 1991 Hong Kong Bill of Rights Ordinance, which remains in force, copies the International Covenant on Civil and Political Rights (ICCPR) almost verbatim.[41] The ICCPR has therefore shaped the local courts' interpretations of Hong Kong's rights commitments. The government and LegCo, in the last years of colonial rule, reformed many nonconforming colonial laws to better protect human rights.[42] Basic Law Article 39 likewise incorporates the ICCPR and the International Covenant on Economic, Social and Cultural Rights, imposing the requirements of such covenants as a limit on any rights restrictions. These international rights guarantees have therefore been enforced by constitutional judicial review both before and after the handover.[43] The Chinese government has likewise continued to file reports on behalf of Hong Kong under the international human rights covenants. The application of international standards and international solicitude is certainly encouraged by these practices.

Rule of Law

The interpretations of the judiciary in exercising the power of constitutional judicial review will have a great bearing on whether the current system adequately protects human rights. Both the Joint Declaration and the Basic Law implicitly require the exercise of constitutional judicial review by the Hong Kong courts.[44] This power of constitutional judicial review in the local Hong Kong courts was acknowledged by the Hong Kong Court of Final Appeal (CFA) in the right of abode case.[45] The future vigor of this institution was challenged by the subsequent government attack on this judgment.[46] Since neither the Hong Kong government nor the NPCSC have explicitly sought to overturn the Hong Kong CFA's constitutional review power the challenge comes rather from the suggestions that disagreeable opinions may be overturned through referral. This position may tend to invite political attacks on the court and efforts to seek to go over its head. Rather than undermining the power entirely these referrals merely invite some challenge to the notion of finality of the courts' decisions and some efforts at political pressure. More so than the executive branch of the Hong Kong government, the court has so far appeared to defend its power of constitutional review, as reflected in its numerous decisions.[47]

The current system of government referral was by no means inevitable. Article 158 of the Basic Law offers the main guidance regarding interpretation of the Basic Law. Although it vests the power of interpretation in the NPCSC, it specifies that the Standing Committee authorizes local courts, when adjudicating cases, to interpret those provisions, which are "within the limits of the autonomy of the Region" and "other provisions." If the CFA is confronted with the interpretation of provisions that are the responsibility of the Central People's Government or concern local-central relations, then according to the text it must refer the matter to the NPCSC. Upon such referral, the NPCSC then interprets the provision with the advice of the Committee for the Basic Law.[48] The scope of these provisions are still to be worked out in local jurisprudence and related politics. It is certainly not too late for the Hong Kong Government and the NPCSC to adopt conventions of restraint regarding referral.[49]

Such restraint was not evident in the first referral, the "right of abode" case. In the right of abode case, the CFA embraced a purposeful and generous approach to interpreting the constitutional rights guaranteed in the Basic Law. The court explicitly accepted for itself the right to determine when to refer provisions respecting local-central relations or matters of central authority and concluded that referral was not required in the pending right of abode case. This decision was widely applauded in Hong Kong for its firm defence of human rights and the rule of law. However, the judgment attracted a harsh official response in two respects. Immediately after the judgment, the government, in a motion for clarification, attacked the *obiter dicta* (nonbinding aspect) of the judgment, where the court declared it had the right to "examine" acts of the NPC for conformity to the Basic Law—not necessarily a strategically wise claim by a court still feeling out its power. Pro-Beijing critics claimed the court was putting itself above the NPC. In its unprecedented clarification judgment, the court explicitly stated that it did not hold itself above the NPC or its Standing Committee, though the Court essentially restated its original position.[50] A second, more serious attack on the judgment and the rule of law occurred in May 1999. After the government issued a report claiming the judgment would produce a flood of 1.67 million migrants claiming the right of abode in Hong Kong, the government requested and was granted a reinterpretation of the relevant provisions by the NPCSC, effectively overturning portions of the CFA interpretation.[51]

From this process of referral, it seems that final judgments in Hong Kong, where constitutional rights are concerned, are not final, at least beyond the narrow application to named parties. The local government can potentially file a motion with the NPCSC to reinterpret the Basic Law and effectively overturn the court's decision. Given the general level of consensus between the Beijing government and its locally anointed officials, this may effectively amount to the local government having the right to overturn the judgment of the CFA, at least as to any other affected parties. The prospect of the government freely interfering with judicial finality has brought suspicion on the government in nearly every controversial legislative outing, where an assumption must be made that the courts may not be able to cure any legislative deficiency. This suspicion was especially apparent in debates concerning the government's proposed Article 23 national security legislation. Will the government someday avail itself of such referral in respect of interpreting the boundaries between national security and freedom in Hong Kong?

Conclusion

What the previous analysis tells us is not only how much democratic reform the Basic Law may allow in Articles 45 and 68 and Annexes I and II. At stake are larger issues of Hong Kong's constitutional development. Government by expediency and crisis and public action by shaming are an inherent feature of a constitutional system that cherishes liberty and the rule of law but fails to afford democracy. Such an authoritarian system may frequently put important constitutional institutions at risk, engendering public indignation and criticism. Such a political course is inherently unstable.

Pro-Beijing and progovernment leaders in Hong Kong frequently worry that democracy poses a risk to stability. The opposite may be true in Hong Kong. The lack of democracy in Hong Kong's liberal constitutional system may pose the greatest risk to stability, as the government veers from crisis to crisis. A system that undermines orderly constitutional channels for public action may simply encourage greater confrontation and disorder, as well as government by expediency and often by crisis management. The good news is that, except for direct elections and universal suffrage, most of the features for fully developing constitutional democracy are now in place.

Beijing's fear of Hong Kong democrats seems at odds with reality. No radical advocates of independence exist in Hong Kong and outside political control over local political actors cannot be substantiated. As evident in the 1989 demonstrations in Hong Kong, the democrats have long demonstrated an equal measure of concern for Hong Kong and China. The democrats thus pose no real threat to Chinese sovereignty. Efforts to change Beijing's attitude toward democrats have been resisted by a minority of unpopular pro-Beijing politicians and business elites. These elites have especially sought to poison the minds of Beijing officials concerning democrats in Hong Kong. But democracy clearly does not pose the threat about which these elites worry. Even most of their privileges will likely survive under democratic governance, as business typically does very well in a democracy. This essentially means that the chief risk of instability comes from the very Beijing officials and supporters that most often warn of instability from democracy.

Notes

1. Joint Declaration of the Government of the United Kingdom of Great Britain and Northern Ireland and the Government of the People's Republic of China on the Question of Hong Kong, September 26, 1984, 23 ILM 1371 (hereinafter "Joint Declaration"); Basic Law of the Hong Kong Special Administrative Region of the People's Republic of China, April 4, 1990, 29 ILM 1511 (1990) (hereinafter "Basic Law").
2. See Michael C. Davis, "Constitutionalism under Chinese Rule: Hong Kong after the Handover," *Denver Journal of International Law and Policy* 27 no. 2 (1999): 275–312; Hsin-chi Kuan and Siu-Kai Lau, "Political Attitudes in a Changing Context," in *Social Development and Political Change in Hong Kong*, ed. Siu-kai Lau (Hong Kong: Chinese University Press, 2000); Ming Sing, *Hong Kong's Tortuous Democratization: A Comparative Analysis* (London: Routledge Curzon, 2004).
3. See Michael C. Davis, *Constitutional Confrontation in Hong Kong* (London: Macmillan Press, 1990).
4. See Davis, "Constitutionalism under Chinese Rule"; Lau and Kuan, "Political Attitudes in a Changing Context"; and Sing, *Hong Kong's Tortuous Democratization.*
5. See Johannes Chan and Lison Harris, eds., *Hong Kong's Constitutional Debates* (Hong Kong: University of Hong Kong Centre for Comparative and Public Law, 2005).
6. Annex II, part III provides, "With regard to the method for forming the Legislative Council . . . and its procedures for voting on bills and motions after 2007, if there is a need to amend the provisions of this Annex, such amendments must be made with the endorsement of *a two-thirds majority of all the members* of the Council and the consent of the Chief Executive, and they shall be reported to the Standing Committee of the National People's Congress *for the record*" (emphasis added).
7. "The Interpretation by the Standing Committee of the National People's Congress of Article 7 of Annex I and Article III of Annex II to the Basic Law of the Hong Kong Special Administrative Region of the People's Republic of China" (Adopted by the Standing Committee of the Tenth National People's Congress at its Eighth Session on April 6, 2004), L.N. 54 of 2004 of the *Hong Kong Gazette*, L.S. No 2 to Gazette Ext. No. 5/2004

(reproduced in Chan and Harris, *Hong Kong's Constitutional Debates*), para. 3. (Hereinafter the "April 6, 2004, interpretation.")

8. See Frank Ching, "Be Consistent," *South China Morning Post*, March 30, 2004 (pointing out this earlier statement).
9. The Second Report of the Constitutional Development Task Force, "Issues of Principle in the Basic Law Relating to Constitutional Development, April 16, 2004 (reproduced in Chan and Harris, *Hong Kong's Constitutional Debates*) (hereinafter the "Second Task Force Report"); "Report on Whether There Is a Need to Amend the Methods for Selecting the Chief Executive of the Hong Kong Special Administrative Region in 2007 and for Forming the Legislative Council of the Hong Kong Special Administrative Region in 2008," a report of the Chief Executive, Hong Kong Special Administrative Region, Hong Kong, April 15, 2004 (reproduced in Chan and Harris, *Hong Kong's Constitutional Debates*). (Hereinafter the "Chief Executive's Report.")
10. The chief executive is currently selected by an 800-member Election Committee and so-called functional constituencies are currently used to fill half the seats in the sixty-member LegCo. The 800-member Election Committee is chosen mostly by similar functional categories of electors. The progovernment and pro-Beijing orientation of these categories is evident in that only one candidate was nominated in the second and third selection processes for the current chief executive and for his predecessor. Even where a democrat barely achieved nomination in the 2007 CE election, his defeat was preordained. The government can also nearly always count on the support of functional legislators.
11. "Decision of the Standing Committee of the National People's Congress on Issues Relating to the Methods for Selecting the Chief Executive of the HKSAR in the Year 2007 and for Forming the Legislative Council of the HKSAR in the Year 2008," April 26, 2004 (reproduced in Chan and Harris, *Hong Kong's Constitutional Debates*).
12. "The Fifth Report of the Constitutional Development Task Force," Package of Proposals for the Methods for Selecting the Chief Executive in 2007 and for Forming the Legislative Council in 2008, October 2005, available at http://www.cab.gov.hk/cd/eng/report5/index.htm, paras. 5.04 and 5.17. (Hereinafter the "Fifth Task Force Report.") For the Election Committee to choose the chief executive, the government recommended that 800 seats be added with approximately 500, including all members of the District Councils and the additional 300 seats coming from existing functional categories—with the details to be supplied later in a legislative amendment bill. For LegCo, all five new functional seats were to be elected by the District Councils, with the method of this likewise to be determined in subsequent legislation.
13. K. C. Ng and Philip Pan, "Hong Kong Democrats Blast Reform Plan," *Washington Post*, October 20, 2005.
14. See Hualing Fu, Carole J. Petersen, and Simon N. M. Young, *National Security and Fundamental Freedoms: Hong Kong's Article 23 under Scrutiny* (Hong Kong: Hong Kong University Press, 2005).
15. This barrage began with the visit of several elderly mainland legal experts in mid-January 2004. Gary Cheung, "Universal Suffrage in 2007 Flouts Basic Law," *South China Morning Post*, January 17, 2004, p. A1. A finger-wagging Xiao Weiyun even attacked constitutional judicial review by the courts and votes of confidence by LegCo. Jimmy Cheung, "Courts and LegCo 'Can't Interpret Basic Law,'" *South China Morning Post*, January 17, 2004, p. A3.
16. Ambrose Leung and Gary Cheung, "'Patriots Should Govern Hong Kong,'" *South China Morning Post*, February 11, 2004, p. A1.

17. Klaudia Lee, "'Selective' Quotes Skew Deng's Words," *South China Morning Post*, March 3, 2004, p. A2.
18. Gary Cheung and Ambrose Leung, "Xinhua Releases Criteria for Being True Patriot," *South China Morning Post*, February 25, 2004, p. A1.
19. An Min, a PRC vice minister of commerce and leading Mainland official attacked Martin Lee's father, General Li Yin-wo, a highly regarded KMT military officer who had fought in the resistance against Japan. Cheung Chi-fai, Gary Cheung, and Ambrose Leung, "Beijing Hits at US Over Democrats' Washington Trip, Senate Hearing on Democracy in Hong Kong Draws Fire," *South China Morning Post*, March 3, 2004, p. A1; Ambrose Leung, "An Min's Wrath Turns to Martin Lee's Father," *South China Morning Post*, March 8, 2004, p. A1.
20. See Lee, "'Selective' Quotes Skew Deng's Words." The "actual situation," more than just having popular support, includes a variety of innocuous legal factors, as well as "maturity of political talent and political groups." See "Second Task Force Report" and "Chief Executive's Report."
21. Gary Cheung, "Beijing Will Step in If Security Is Threatened," *South China Morning Post*, March 13, 2004, p. A1.
22. It is true that the Basic Law has provisions allowing for dissolution of the LegCo, but these only provide that the chief executive may dissolve the LegCo, after consultations, if it refuses to pass bills proposed by the chief executive. Basic Law, Article 50. Such provisions require a new election to form a new LegCo and specify that if the LegCo again refuses to pass such bill then the chief executive must resign. *See* Articles 52 and 70. It is seriously in doubt whether a nonelected chief executive under the current system would willingly subject himself to what amounts to a referendum.
23. Cannix Yau, "Democratic LegCo 'Will See Executive Collapse,'" *The Standard*, March 2, 2004, p. A1.
24. Edward Cody, "Hong Kong Reminded That China Is in Charge, Beijing Issues Warning against Direct Elections," *Washington Post Foreign Service*, February 19, 2004, p. A14.
25. Ambrose Leung and Louisa Yan, "'Spirit, Not Words,' Is the Key to Basic Law," *South China Morning Post*, March 16, 2004, p. A1; Louisa Yan and Ambrose Leung, "Democrats Are Accused of Betrayal," *South China Morning Post*, March 16, 2004, p. A2.
26. Wilson Wong, "Why Less Democracy Means More Free Lunches," *South China Morning Post*, February 16, 2004, p. A13 (responding to these various arguments by business elite).
27. Ma Ngok, "Democracy at a Stalemate, the September 2004 Legco Elections in Hong Kong," *China Perspectives*, no. 57(January/February 2005): 40–49, at 47.
28. Ibid., 48.
29. Stephen Holmes, "Precommitment and the Paradox of Democracy," in *Constitutionalism and Democracy*, ed. Jon Elster and Rune Slagstad (Cambridge: Cambridge University Press, 1988), 195–240; Bruce Ackerman, *We the People: Foundations* (Cambridge: Harvard University Press, 1991); Alexander M. Bickel, *The Least Dangerous Branch, The Supreme Court at the Bar of Politics*, 2nd ed. (New Haven, CT: Yale University Press, 1986).
30. Joint Declaration, para. 3(3), (5), (12), & Annex I, arts. I–III, XIII.
31. Basic Law, Annexes I and II. See Davis, "Constitutionalism under Chinese Rule," 275–312.
32. In the first post-handover Legislative Council election on May 24, 1998, various democrats received 64 percent of the vote but were able to secure only one-third of the sixty seats in the Legislative Council. "Record Turnout Poised to Give Democrats Sweeping Victory," *South China Morning Post*, May 25, 1998, p. 1; "Lessons of the Poll," *South China*

Morning Post, May 26, 1998, p. 18. As discussed previously, a similar voter outcome and seat distribution was evident in the September 2004 LegCo election. The Human Rights Committee under the International Covenant on Civil and Political Rights (ICCPR) has consistently challenged Hong Kong's democratic deficit as failing to conform to Hong Kong's obligations under the ICCPR.

33. Basic Law, Article 159.
34. Michael C. Davis, "A Vote for Democracy," *South China Morning Post,* November 26, 2003, p. A17.
35. Jon Elster, "Constitution-Making in Eastern Europe: Rebuilding the Boat in the Open Sea," *Public Administration* 71 (1993): 169–201, at 173.
36. See Michael C. Davis and C. Raj Kumar, "The Scars of SARS—Balancing Human Rights and Public Health Concerns," *The Hong Kong Lawyer,* May 2003.
37. Denise Hung, "Support for Plan to Vet Election Candidates," *South China Morning Post,* October 4, 2006, p. A3.
38. Art 23 of the Basic Law requires the Hong Kong government to enact "on its own" laws relating to national security. For an analysis of the rise and fall of the proposed legislation, see Fu, Petersen, and Young, *National Security and Fundamental Freedoms: Hong Kong's Article 23 Under Scrutiny.*
39. After the handover the Provisional Legislature enacted new laws regarding public order and societies to replace amendments made by the outgoing British administration, restricted the right of abode of Mainland children (later challenged in the well-known right of abode case), and froze legislation related to labor rights protections, among other changes. Margaret Ng, "Threat to Our Civil Rights," *South China Morning Post,* April 11, 1997.
40. See Michael C. Davis, "Adopting International Standards of Human Rights in Hong Kong," in *Human Rights and Chinese Values,* ed. Michael C. Davis (Oxford University Press, 1995); see also Petersen, Chapter 2 of this volume.
41. Hong Kong Bill of Rights Ordinance, No. 59 (1991) reprinted in 30 I.L.M. 1310 (1991); International Covenant on Civil and Political Rights, 6 I.L.M. 368 (1967). See Johannes Chan, "The Hong Kong Bill of Rights 1991–1995: A Statistical Overview," in *Hong Kong's Bill of Rights: Two Years Before 1997,* ed. George Edwards and Johannes Chan (Hong Kong: University of Hong Kong, Faculty of Law, 1995). When the Bill of Rights Ordinance was enacted, the colonial constitution, the Letters Patent, was also amended to include the ICCPR, a change that effectively implemented constitutional judicial review to enforce rights.
42. Amended laws included: (1) Societies Ordinance (1992); (2) Television Ordinance (1993); (3) Broadcasting Ordinance (1993); (4) Public Order Ordinance (1995); and (5) Emergency Regulations Ordinance (1995). The international character of the rights regime was enhanced by frequent judicial reference to overseas common law and European Union precedent. See *R v. Sin Yau Ming* [1992] 1 H.K.C.L.R. 127, at 141–42 (CA).
43. See also Petersen, Chapter 2 of this volume.
44. See Joint Declaration, Annex I, arts. 2, 3, and 13; Basic Law, arts. 2, 8, 17, 80–96, and 158. Such judicial role may be supplemented by other institutions that provide affordable avenues of complaint about public and private rights violations.
45. *Ng Ka Ling v. Director of Immigration* [1999] 1 HKLRD 315 (29 January 1999). Article 24 of the Basic Law provides that Hong Kong residents include "persons of Chinese nationality born outside of Hong Kong" of Hong Kong residents. The suit was brought by several children of Hong Kong residents claiming a denial of their basic right of residence under a newly enacted Immigration Ordinance that required them to apply on the Mainland for an exit permit, a process that could take several years.

46. See Mark O'Neill, "Beijing Says Abode Ruling Was Wrong and Should Be Changed," *South China Morning Post*, February 9, 1999, p. 1; Cliff Buddle, Angela Li, and Audrey Parwani, "Judges Asked to Clarify Right of Abode Decision," *South China Morning Post*, February 25, 1999, p. 1.
47. See also Petersen, Chapter 2 of this volume.
48. "Decision of the National People's Congress to Approve the Proposal by the Drafting Committee for the Basic Law of the Hong Kong Special Administrative Region on the Establishment of the Committee for the Basic Law of the Hong Kong Special Administrative Region under the Standing Committee of the National People's Congress," Adopted at the Third Session of the Seventh National People's Congress on April 4, 1990 (published with the Basic Law). The role of the courts and the NPC Standing Committee are addressed in Basic Law Articles 17, 19, and 158.
49. See also Lo, Chapter 8 in this volume.
50. *Ng Ka Ling v. Director of Immigration* [1999] 1 HKLRD 577 (February 26, 1999). The court concluded, "nor did the court's judgment question, and the Court accepts that it cannot question, the authority of the National People's Congress or the Standing Committee to do any act which is in accordance with the provisions of the Basic Law and the procedure therein."
51. See Chris Yeung, "Court Gives 1.67 m Right of Abode," *South China Morning Post*, April 29, 1999, p. 1. The government asked the NPC Standing Committee to reinterpret Articles 22 and 24(3) to overturn the CFA Final Judgment. Chris Yeung, "NPC Will Be Asked to Revoke Abode Rights for 1.5m Migrants," *South China Morning Post*, May 19, 1999, p. 1. The government sidestepped the problem of a lack of expressed power in the government to make such referral by seeking an endorsement from the Legislative Council and asking the State Council to make the referral on its behalf.

CHAPTER 5

Forcing the Dance

Interpreting the Hong Kong Basic Law Dialectically

Robert J. Morris

Article 158 provides an unambiguous delineation of the power of interpretation of the Basic Law: It lies in, and remains in, Beijing, with a small exception carved out for the courts of Hong Kong under certain carefully defined circumstances.[1] Indeed, this small exception was designed to be a check on the otherwise plenary power that the National People's Congress Standing Committee (NPCSC) has on the Mainland and was always so intended from the inception of the Basic Law. Attempts to obfuscate or finesse this straightforward declaration seem disingenuous.[2]

Articles 8, 18 and 160 of the Basic Law purport to entrench Hong Kong's common-law system, as well as the other "laws previously in force (原有法律)." Further, Article 18 assimilates the common law to "this Law" (i.e., the Basic Law). The power of interpretation of the Basic Law is similar to that set out in the PRC Legislation Law (中華人民共和國立法法), which reserves the power of legal interpretation strictly to the NPCSC, leaving the role of the Supreme People's Court and of other organs to that of merely requesting a legal interpretation. Article 47 of the Legislation Law states that legal interpretation adopted by the NPCSC "has the same effect as the laws enacted by it." This combines with Article 88 (power to amend and annul laws) to give the legislature total control over its own laws. These powers are reserved and defined in the statute on *legislation*, not judiciary. The exception carved out in the Basic Law for the Hong Kong Court of Final Appeal (CFA) has been reduced by successive NPCSC interpretations since 1997 under the aegis of Article 158, as the NPCSC has aggregated to itself greater powers, even *sua sponte* powers, than Article 158 provides. The central difficulty is Article

158 of the Basic Law, which provides that the Hong Kong courts sometimes interpret the Basic Law, and the NPCSC sometimes interprets the Basic Law. This Janus-like figure contemplates *both* judicial and legislative interpretation at once or sequentially, and this structure has caused no end of confusion and consternation.[3] One reason is that the rules of interpretation and therefore the assumptions and presumptions in the two systems are not the same: The People's Republic of China (PRC) is not a common-law jurisdiction.

Deng Xiaoping, the author and prime mover of the Basic Law, called it his "creative masterpiece"[4] and noted, as the preamble itself states, that it is the embodiment and enactment of "one country, two systems" (OCTS). Deng declared OCTS to be of international significance because it is "attributed to Marxist dialectical and historical materialism [辯証唯物主義, 歷史唯物主義]."[5] It is the quintessence of Mao Zedong Thought itself, summarized in the slogan, "Seek truth from facts (事實求是)."[6] "Who decides," he asked, "which of the classic international principles of communism are applicable to China?" We do, he answered. The party does.[7] That has never changed, so there is no exception in the Basic Law and therefore no deception in Article 158. But as Professor Xiao Weiyun has noted, "Only with sound understanding of this 'one country, two systems' principle can the Basic Law be implemented correctly."[8] Therein lies the rub because common-law commentators usually fail to take into account the implications for interpretation of "Marxist dialectical and historical materialism."[9] Many do this out of a naive belief that such things are now passé.

Deng Xiaoping's pronouncements might be viewed with skepticism at this late date; yet, as Thomas A. Metzger points out in his recent exhaustive study, Marxism, communism, and Leninist doctrine are very much alive in the PRC and must be taken into account in any analysis of Greater China.[10] Professor Yash Ghai notes that the Hong Kong Basic Law is a "socialist document."[11] Because I believe that we must take Professor Metzger's insistence seriously, these ideas, and many others like them, suggest the need to approach the interpretation of the Basic Law from the standpoint of its design and context: dialectics. Marx captured the idea nicely this way: "These petrified relations must be forced to dance by singing their own tune to them!"[12] Deng put forth the doctrine as a way to "harmonize" diversities among the Mainland, Hong Kong, and Taiwan, but "harmonize" in this context does not mean compromise or "meeting of the minds" in the common-law or social-contract sense. It means, rather, that as a "socialist document," the Basic Law itself operates dialectically. It is part of the dialectic.

This analysis raises the question—almost universally neglected in OCTS studies—of what will happen in 2047.[13] What will 2048 look like? Yet, this matter of 2047 is the *central question* in OCTS studies because it is the *endpoint of the dialectic*—the culmination of its work, the purpose for which it was designed. Furthermore, if Professor Metzger is correct, any treatise on OCTS and the Basic Law is perforce a treatise on Deng Xiaoping and his inflection of the socialist dialectic. This would cease to be true only if it were demonstrated that Deng Xiaoping Theory had been abrogated or amended. It has not. It is reasserted, reified, and affirmed in official dogma and practice at every turn, as indeed are many of the ideas of Mao and Marx, in the relationship between the periphery (Hong Kong) and the center (Beijing).[14] Hence, any legal and theoretical analysis of the purported operation and purposes of the Basic Law and OCTS must still consider these materials as not only primary sources in the historical sense but also as the *present, still efficacious drivers of the dialectic that undergirds the system.* Serious analysis cannot simply dismiss OCTS, as Chao Chien-min does, as a mere "propaganda gimmick designed by Beijing in the early 1980s to allure Taiwan back to the mainland fold."[15] It may indeed have been that as well,[16] but at the very least, perhaps a more accurate formulation of the OCTS reality would be "one country, one dialectic."[17]

If the Basic Law is indeed Hong Kong's "mini-constitution" that "enshrines the common law," as many common-law adherents are wont to say, then it above all other laws ought to behave as a constitution of the common law. It ought to constitute the common law, and it ought to constitute in the ways and methods of the common law, but it does not. It often does not behave as the common law.[18] This assertion requires explanation because by and large the courts of Hong Kong have attempted to treat it as a common-law document. OCTS has set up a world in which people are literally of two minds, and this is not merely the familiar "reasonable minds disagreeing" of the common law but a true multiplicity of *Weltanschauungen*. In this situation, both sides are perpetually amazed—and often allegedly stumped—that the other thinks the way it does. This is not so simple a matter as mere legal interpretation but of philosophy, of what Hans Kelsen and his interlocutors call the *grundnorm*.[19] In applying Kelsen (plus H. L. A. Hart and others) to Hong Kong's situation, Raymond Wacks deals with the "question of the continuity [and the discontinuity] of the legal system after the transfer of sovereignty in 1997."[20] After noting the idea that under the Basic Law, "Hong Kong's capitalist legal system is therefore to be sustained by a socialist one" (something that I will argue cannot be), he states: "This extraordinary duality must also be accounted for."[21] The idea of a "duality" is problematic because a duality is binary. The question of "whether a new legal system emerges from the womb of an old one" or is somehow "born again" in a fresh reincarnation, is part of this question of continuity.[22] Wacks concludes: "The validity of norms created by the Hong Kong SAR after 1997 will, in Kelsen's terms, depend upon the formulation of a basic norm. *This norm will impart validity to the Constitution of the PRC.*"[23] OCTS has in reality set up a Marxist[24] dialectic that is the true explanation of its operation.[25]

Peter Wesley-Smith similarly finds that "Hong Kong presents the intriguing picture of a common-law legal system *operating within* an alien framework," and then attempts to reason regarding the separation-of-powers doctrine based on common-law paradigms.[26] The argument does not entirely work—again because it is common-law reasoning applied to dialectics. OCTS and the Basic Law cannot be fully analyzed by Western common-law jurisprudence alone, if at all. The Basic Law does not establish a "separation of powers" but rather a *dialectic of powers*.[27] Professor Wacks assumes that the majority of Hong Kong's people regard the common law as worthy of support, that they regard OCTS "as, at the very least, satisfactory," and that the continuity of Hong Kong's legal system after 1997 "depends ultimately on the durability of the customs and traditions of the common law."[28] The reality is that under dialectical and historical materialism, out of which OCTS and the Basic Law arise, none of these assumptions is accurate or, more precisely, none of them matters. In Kelsenian terms, the wrong *grundnorm* has been assumed. Neither can OCTS be termed simply a formulaic synonym for "pragmatism." Professor Johannes Chan of the University of Hong Kong, who is critical of OCTS, argues, "'One country, two systems' is a journey without a destination. It is unclear whether the ultimate goal is to retain two equally thriving but different systems, or whether it is to assimilate Hong Kong into the mainland politically, legally, culturally and ideologically. As long as there is no clear destination, there will be tensions to maintain a separate liberal tradition on the one hand and to assimilate Hong Kong into the mainland on the other."[29]

I disagree with Chan because I argue that there *is* a destination for OCTS and that there has been from the beginning, and it is "clear" to those who have dialectic eyes to see it. The destination is indeed "to assimilate Hong Kong into the mainland politically, legally, culturally and ideologically," using force if necessary, at whatever place may exist there in 2047. Yet, it is not Chan's binary; it is, rather, the predetermined processes of dialectical materialism. The dialectic is not evolutionary—it is channeled to reach an inevitable historical outcome, being the assimilation of Hong Kong. Deng said, "If people understand our fundamental viewpoint and the basis on which we have put forward this concept [口号= slogan] and established this policy, they will be convinced that we are not going to change it [我们不会变 = we will not/cannot change]."[30]

It is crucial to understand what these words say and what they do not say. To say that "*we* will not change" or that "*we* will not change the policy" is not to say that the policy will not change. Deng is saying that *we will not change the dialectic*. We will keep dialectical and historical materialism intact as they are expressed and instantiated in OCTS. This is what will not change; but within the machinations of that dialectic, all will necessarily change toward its ends, for that is the quintessence of the dialectic.

How then can OCTS possibly mean, in Deng's promises to both Hong Kong and Taiwan, that once OCTS is implemented, there will be "no change"?[31] Either OCTS stands for a complete abandonment of dialectical materialism (which it does not), or the promises, like OCTS itself, are "too clever by half." There *will* be change during the first fifty years, and that change *will* be political absorption and assimilation to the PRC in a new, yet unknown, synthesis. Indeed, fifty years is metaphorical or symbolic, "only a vivid way of putting it (五十年只是一个形象的讲法)."[32] Otherwise, the dialectic has been abandoned. It is the dialectic itself that will not change and which is the one constant that remains amid ten thousand changes (萬變不離其宗). According to the proverb, "things at once oppose each other and complement each other (相反相成)." The whole point of striving to understand this dialectic is to be able to understand and *transform* or *change* the world. We study dialectics "for no other reason than to change this world, to change the age-old relationships in this world between humans, and humans and matter."[33] In addition, Deng said: "Everyone who enters the top levels at the Center has to stop being what he was before. . . . He has to change himself, including his personal style, and he has to change consciously."[34] Bertell Ollman, in discussing Marx's ideas of the "future development of anything and how it presents itself at this moment," states:

> Marx's naming practice here reflects the epistemological priority he gives to movement over stability, so that stability—whenever it is found—is viewed as temporary and/or only apparent, or, as he says on one occasion, as a 'paralysis' of movement. With stability used to qualify change rather than the reverse, Marx—unlike most modern social scientists—did not and could not study why things change (with the implication that change is external to what they are, something that happens to them). Given that change is always a part of what things are, his research problem could only be *how*, *when*, and *into what* they change and why they sometimes appear not to (ideology).[35]

Thus, the Basic Law reference to the "stability" (穩定) of Hong Kong means the stability of the dialectic and its operation in tension between the center and periphery. To know or change any reality of any kind, you must first personally participate in the practice and "direct experience" regarding it. "If you want to know the taste of a pear," Mao held, "you must change the pear by eating it yourself."[36] Dialectical logic resolves the "problem of the excluded middle" in formal logic (which includes Western law) because contradictory elements, which in Western logic remain static (*tertium non datur*), can be removed, negated, and resolved to become a third thing which is not-A and not-B but a new and higher thing or concept,[37] although some might argue that the new third is rather a *dilution* of both A and B. In any case, the reality that comes from this experience is higher than theory—theory only follows the employment of practice. Truth and facts are not "found" things, they are *made* things, manufactured things, things created by words and ideology. In this way, the dialectic is inimical to the separation of powers. Within the dialectic, there is no stasis or hiatus: This whole process exists *from beginning to end.*[38] "*Dialectics* is the teaching which shows how *opposites* can be and how they happen to be (how they become) *identical*—under what conditions they are identical, transforming themselves into one another."[39] Because the opposites are interconnected, interpenetrating and interdependent, "each of the contradictory aspects within a thing transforms itself into its opposite."[40] *Not to change* would be agnostic of the system and apostate of the imperative. The antithesis of this would be the image of permanently separated powers that forever tug and pull apart from each other in a kind of clockwork balance—the image of the American *Federalist Papers*. Thus (and this now describes Hong Kong), the bourgeoisie, through the collapse of its class, changes to the point where it comes under the rule of the proletarian state.[41] "Bourgeois democracy and proletarian democracy [the "dictatorship of the proletariat" or "democratic centralism"] are in opposition, but the former inevitably changes into the latter"[42] This is the ineluctable endpoint. Hence, "international peace treaties [contracts] are relative, while international struggle is absolute."[43] The Joint Declaration of 1984, the precursor of the Basic Law, was an international treaty agreed to between China and the United Kingdom.

The "law," in the common-law sense of a transcendent, uniform, independent, and fixed standard,[44] is not, therefore and never can be, enshrined in any constitutional system because the dialectic is, by definition, forever fluid—or rather, the mechanisms it motivates and powers are forever fluid. Suzanne Pepper demonstrates how the PRC communist leadership interferes in Hong Kong's "autonomy" through interlocking political directorates and refers to the "inevitable drift toward becoming one" that the Basic Law has designed as the inevitable goal of OCTS.[45] The final decision of the CFA in the flag-desecration cases (Flag III),[46] following as it does the earlier right-of-abode cases, stands for the premise that Hong Kong's "high degree of autonomy" is not an autonomous identity apart from the dialectic.[47] Pepper quotes Lee Wui-ting of Beijing's Xinhua News agency chiding Hong Kongers "for taking too literally the Basic Law's promise that they could maintain their own system 'for 50 years'. Some things, said Lee, must change."[48]

The dialecticization of a "fundamental" right obliterates its nature as fundamental. The dialectic, like the task of adhering to the socialist road (one of the Four Cardinal Principles), requires constant maintenance and vigilance for, as Deng knew, it was not like capitalism. In the struggle between socialism and capitalism, capitalism was *spontaneous*,[49] growing like a coral reef and hence does not require the dialectic to bring it to fruition. Socialism, however, is something "we decided upon" and therefore "must enforce."[50] This is not the compromise or harmonization familiar to the common law in which both sides "give a little, take a little."

For example, the tension that the Basic Law sets up between the CFA and the NPCSC regarding interpretation of the Basic Law can never be—is not intended to be—finally "settled."[51] They are in the perpetual tension of a dialectic, the foregone conclusion of which is that, in any contest between the two, the NPCSC must always prevail.[52] Hong Kong and the PRC are themselves brought into the dialectic.[53] As Professor Ghai points out, in the Basic Law there is no effective machinery to enforce the guarantee of autonomy because "one of the contestants is also the umpire."[54] Its implementation would make the Basic Law an important part of promoting the socialist modernization of the PRC.

Splitting adjudication from interpretation and switching the final authority of interpretation from the Privy Council to the NPCSC was not an innocent switch of title or location but rather was a fundamental sea change, as the NPCSC is anything but a common-law court, and it is not part of any "common law system."[55] It is not bound by the common law and does not operate within its parameters. This is coupled with the NPCSC's power to "return" to Hong Kong and therefore invalidate any law it finds to contravene the Basic Law or exceed its authority. In effect, the NPCSC has a truly "standing" power of legislative supervision over Hong Kong, despite the guarantee that Hong Kong "shall be vested with legislative power." We must recall Bishop Hoadly's famous truism: "Whoever hath an absolute authority to interpret any written or spoken laws, it is he who is truly the lawgiver, to all intents and purposes, and not the person who first spoke or wrote them."[56] The NPCSC does not work by precedent or *stare decisis*, and its *ratio decidendi* is usually stated perfunctorily or not at all.[57] Thus, we observe the absolute truth—and the absolute sophistry—in the statement of Xiao Weiyun, who cites Articles

18 and 84: "Hence, after 1997 the binding principle of precedent *shall be maintained in the courts of the HKSAR at all levels*."[58] The NPCSC is not one of the "courts of the HKSAR at all levels" and so is excluded from this command for all purposes. Xiao Weiyun statements are dialectics to him, but doublespeak[59] to common-law lawyers:

> Under the legal system of Hong Kong there is neither legislative interpretation nor executive interpretation as there is on the Mainland. Only the courts of Hong Kong have the right of legal interpretation . . . Therefore the courts of Hong Kong have the right of judicial interpretation.[60]
>
> There is a connection but also differences between the power of final adjudication and of interpretation . . . Logically, if there is a power of final adjudication, then there must be a power of final interpretation of the laws.[61]
>
> The judicial interpretation of the Court of Final Appeal of the HKSAR is the final interpretation . . . Final adjudication and interpretation is [sic] related . . . The final adjudication is the level of judgment, but not the interpretation of laws. The difference between the two is very clear. To properly clarify the relationship of the final adjudication and interpretation of the Basic Law and to allay concerns of some Hong Kong people, the principles of "one country, two systems" must be followed so as to protect the integrity and sovereignty of the state, and also to maintain prosperity and stability in the HKSAR and to protect its high degree of autonomy.[62]
>
> [Article 158] takes into due consideration the need for practicality and reasonableness in working with two different legal systems, as well as preserving the legal interpretation of laws by the NPCSC.[63]

These comments, occurring as they do within two pages of text, may be Marxist dialectic, but they are not common law. Such doublespeak allows Deng Xiaoping to make this kind of statement: "There will be *no changes* in my generation or in the next. And I doubt that 50 years after 1997, when the mainland is developed, people will handle matters like this in a narrow-minded way. So don't worry, there won't be any changes. *Or if there are*, they can only be changes for the better."[64]

Hence, Xiao, in the same vein, can say with complete dialectical honesty that the "high degree of autonomy" promised to Hong Kong in the Basic Law implies that the judicial power "is authorized to the [HK]SAR; the Central Government will not interfere with it."[65] But the wording that it is "authorized to" Hong Kong is significant, for like individual and human "rights" under the PRC Constitution, it is nothing inherent in Hong Kong or its people but originates from and within the central government.[66] It is a *grant* of autonomy only and as such may be "ungranted" at any time in any degree, even without notice or fanfare.

The Basic Law is not, as many common-law commentators have declared, a constitution or "mini-constitution" for Hong Kong. It is merely another law—a statute—enacted by the NPC.[67] It is subordinate to the PRC Constitution and does not occupy the entire field, as much of the PRC Constitution applies in Hong Kong as well.[68] Indeed, as Li Zaishun has argued, the PRC Constitution should be "integrated organically with the Hong Kong Basic Law to jointly form the constitution of Hong Kong."[69] This view of matters, including the courts, is a dialectical view, and it comports with Deng Xiaoping's intent regarding the Basic Law. As Li notes, "the Hong Kong Basic Law is a law that is primarily based upon the legal thinking of the continental law system while absorbing that of the common law system . . . Whether 'two systems' can be carried out properly is primarily the responsibility of the Mainland."[70]

This reality may be examined more clearly in the distinction between "court" and "judge." In many common-law jurisdictions, the two terms mean the same thing: the one is the other. Wherever the judge official is, there is the court. In Hong Kong, as Byron Weng points out, that has not necessarily been the case, and the distinction is made starker in Article 85 of the Basic Law. Thus, "independence of the courts and independence of the judges mean very different things." Weng notes the system of "judicial supervision" in the PRC and then describes how this assimilates the PRC system to the Hong Kong system: "This practice is bedded in the Chinese socialist ideology and built into the system. The courts must serve the revolution like other party and state organs. No one is supposed to be free from collective responsibility and party control, not even a judge." But then Weng adds the following:

> Evidence suggests that from the very first draft, Article 85 . . . of the Basic Law used the words "courts" instead of "judges." Hence, the use of the word "courts" was most probably deliberate and made for systematic as well as practical reasons. Was there an attempt to bring the SAR system closer to that of the PRC? Was it force of habit or mere negligence or a case of ignorance? There are good reasons to believe that the drafters were aware of the difference for it had long been in the constitutional law literature.[71]

This point is crucial, for as Li Zaishun holds, the Basic Law is primarily the "legal thinking of the continental law system" and judges are not to supersede it "with the legal concepts of equity or the western concept of 'legislation by judges'"[72]—despite the guarantee in Article 8 of the Basic Law that equity (平衡) is to be preserved in Hong Kong. The judges' "purely common law thinking" is something they must learn to "go beyond."[73] Hence, Weng's crucial question, "was there an attempt to bring the SAR system closer to that of the PRC?" must be answered yes. This is the purpose behind historical and dialectic materialism (OCTS in Hong Kong). This was no mere amendment of Article 158 but of the "common law system" and the "laws previously in force" structure of Articles 8, 18, and 160 of the Basic Law altogether. To all intents and purposes, the NPCSC now has taken unto itself the same plenary powers that it has elsewhere in the PRC. The implications of this for interpretation in Hong Kong are vast[74] and illustrate that OCTS is the "historical transition before this country [PRC] can thoroughly replace the capitalist system with a socialist system."[75]

Notes

1. See Section 4, Articles 80 through 96, of the Basic Law.
2. Hungdah Chiu, *The Draft Basic Law of Hong Kong: Analysis and Documents* (Baltimore: University of Maryland School of Law, Occasional Papers/Reprints Series in Contemporary Asian Studies, No. 5, 1988), 56–57.
3. A useful summary of the matter may be read at Yash Ghai, *Hong Kong's New Constitutional Order: The Resumption of Chinese Sovereignty and the Basic Law*, 2nd ed. (Hong Kong: Hong Kong University Press, 2001), 189–230.
4. Deng Xiaoping, *Selected Works of Deng Xiaoping (1982–1992)* (Beijing: Foreign Languages Press, 1994), 3:340.
5. Ibid., 3:107.
6. The ideas contained in the chapter are enshrined in the PRC Constitution. See Weiyun Xiao, *One Country, Two Systems: An Account of the Drafting of the Hong Kong Basic Law* (Beijing: Peking University Press, 2001), 4–6. Xiao is a professor of law at Peking University and an authority on PRC constitutional matters. He was educated in law at Leningrad University. He has written extensively on the Basic Law and is considered to be an authority. See, e.g., his co-authored article, "Why the Court of Final Appeal Was Wrong: Comments of the Mainland Scholars on the Judgment of the Court of Final Appeal," in *Hong Kong's Constitutional Debate: Conflict over Interpretation*, ed. Johannes M. M. Chan, H. L. Fu, and Yash Ghai (Hong Kong: Hong Kong University Press, 2001), 53–59. Jiang Zemin, Deng's successor, upheld Deng Xiaoping Theory as the "Marxism of present-day China." Quoted in Willem van Kemenade, "China, Hong Kong, Taiwan: Dynamics of a New Empire," *Washington Quarterly* 21 (1998): 105, 110.
7. See Deng, *Selected Works of Deng* Xiaoping,1: 239–40.
8. See Xiao, *One Country, Two Systems*, 1.
9. Ibid., 5. "Truth" in the formula 事實求是 is not the more usual "truth" 真理 in common parlance.

10. Thomas A. Metzger, *A Cloud across the Pacific: Essays on the Clash between Chinese and Western Political Theories Today* (Hong Kong: Chinese University Press, 2005), 335–44, 360, 475, 683, 688, 692–93.
11. See Ghai, *Hong Kong's New Constitutional Order*, 189, 191, 211, 229.
12. Marx, Karl, "Contribution to the Critique of Hegel's Philosophy of Law" in *Collected Works*, ed. Karl Marx and Frederick Engels (London: Lawrence & Wishart, 1975), 3:178. For a Chinese scholar's discussion of the Hegelian dialectic vis-à-vis the 道, see John C. H. Wu, "The Struggle between Government of Laws and Government of Men in the History of China," *China Law Review* 5 (1932): 53, 58. For a perhaps unintentional demonstration of the dialectic in Hong Kong's history, see Cindy Yik-yi Chu, "Back to the Masses: The Historiography of Hong Kong's Recent Political Developments and the Prospects of Future Scholarship," *American Journal of Chinese Studies* 10 (2003): 29. *See* also Chen-pang Chang, "The Dual Nature of Teng Hsiao-ping's Thought," *Issues & Studies: A Journal of China Studies and International Affairs* 25 (1989): 11, for an approach that deals with the subject as dialectic but does not overtly say so.
13. The Basic Law stipulates that Hong Kong's "previous capitalist system and way of life shall remain unchanged for 50 years," that is, until 2047.
14. One of the basic studies showing the direct influence of Marx on Chinese Marxism, Mao Zedong, and Mao Zedong Thought is Adrian Chan, *Chinese Marxism* (London: Continuum, 2003). H. L. Fu and Richard Cullen, "National Security Law in Hong Kong: Quo Vadis A Study of Article 23 of the Basic Law of Hong Kong," *UCLA Pacific Basin Law Journal* 19 (2002): 185, 190, allege that in China, the "market-based reforms of the last two decades have resulted in a rapidly waning *Marxist* influence, but *Leninist* approaches to governance and social control remain significant." A general overview of Marx and Marxism, with attention to dialectics, but not specifically to the Chinese situation, may be read in M. D. A. Freeman, ed., *Lloyd's Introduction to Jurisprudence*, 7th ed. (London: Sweet & Maxwell, 2001), 953–1039. See also Raymond Wacks, "Can the Common Law Survive the Basic Law?" *Hong Kong Law Journal* 18 (1988): 435 (the "interpreters" will be "party cadres" who will ensure that "they toe the party line"). Wacks did not see this as a necessary threat to the common law, justice, or democracy.
15. Chien-min Chao, "The Democratic Progressive Party's Factional Politics and Taiwan Independence," in *Essays on the Cheng Shui-bian Presidency: Taiwan in Troubled Times*, ed. John F. Copper (Hong Kong: World Scientific, 2002), 122.
16. In Mao's dialectic: "Strategically we should despise all our enemies, while tactically we should take them all seriously." Quoted in George W. Tsai, "Dynamic Stability in Beijing-Taipei Relations," in ibid., 128.
17. A key article in this regard is Anne Norton, "Transubstantiation: The Dialectic of Constitutional Authority" *University of Chicago Law Review* 55 (1988): 458.
18. Jordan, Ann D., "Lost in Translation: Two Legal Cultures, the Common Law Judiciary and the Basic Law of the Hong Kong Special Administrative Region" (1997) 30 *Cornell International Law Journal* 335, 349, interrogating whether the English "constitution" and the Chinese "憲法" are true cognates, even though they are routinely used to translate each other.
19. See, generally, Freeman, *Lloyd's Introduction to Jurisprudence*, 264–69, 284–89. I use *Weltanschauung* because it comes closer than *grundnorm* to the Chinese mind-set, as I understand it, expressed by Deng when he speaks of the "communist way of looking at the world" (*Selected Works of Deng Xiaoping*, 1:257) and the "communist world outlook" (2:126). Actually, I would prefer to opt for wholly Chinese categories such as the one Deng uses: 法制 legal system. This would prevent the imposition of foreign categories upon

Chinese thought and law. For a usage of "(dis)continuity" in a classic common-law sense, see Laurence Tribe, "Technology Assessment and the Fourth Discontinuity: The Limits of Instrumental Rationality," *Southern California Law Review* 46 (1973): 617, ("[policy] analysis is often intended not only to aid the decisionmaker in choosing a course of action, but also to help him in persuading others of the justifiability and wisdom of his choice").

20. Raymond Wacks, "'One Country, Two Grundnormen'? The Basic Law and the Basic Norm," in *Hong Kong, China and 1997: Essays in Legal Theory*, ed. Raymond Wacks (Hong Kong: Hong Kong University Press, 1993), 151, 153.
21. Ibid., 154.
22. Ibid., 171.
23. Ibid., 179; emphasis added.
24. Or "Marxian," depending on how one parses the words.
25. Such as the survival of many laws passed during the final years of Britain's colonial rule and the expected "through train" for sitting legislators. Beijing abolished the "through train." Hence, as I will elaborate later, the continuity was of *the dialectic itself*, not any particular common-law laws or practices subject to it. See J. M. Finnis, "Revolutions and Continuity of Law," in *Oxford Essays in Jurisprudence*, ed. A. W. B. Simpson, 2nd ser. (Oxford: Clarendon Press, 1973), 44–76.
26. Peter Wesley-Smith, "Judges and Judicial Power under the Hong Kong Basic Law," *Hong Kong Law Journal* 34, no. 1 (2004): 83. See also two recent attempts to reconcile similar problems, also using common-law analysis with resultant disjunctions: Simon N. M. Young, "Restricting Basic Law Rights in Hong Kong," *Hong Kong Law Journal* 34 (2004): 109; Kemal Bokhary, "Justice and the Law: The Evolving Role of the Lawyer," *Hong Kong Law Journal* 34 (2004): 133.
27. See, e.g., Deng, *Selected Works of Deng Xiaoping*, 3:195, 219.
28. Wacks, "'One Country, Two Grundnormen?'" 182.
29. Johannes Chan, "Civil Liberties, Rule of Law and Human Rights: The Hong Kong Special Administrative Region in Its First Four Years," in *The First Tung Chee-hwa Administration: The First Five Years of the Hong Kong Special Administrative Region*, ed. Siu-kai Lau (Hong Kong: Chinese University of Hong Kong, 2002), 116–17. Chan notes Hong Kong's *subservient culture* that is "eager to please" and to be "regularly second-guessing the wishes of Beijing." "The danger of subservient culture is that it is too easy to go beyond what the lord pleases in pleasing the lord" (114, 116).
30. See Deng, *Selected Works of Deng Xiaoping*, 3:107, 3:108–9. This must be compared with another of Deng's formulaic statements: Our policy will not change, 我们的政策是不会变的. Clearly, the focus in the quoted passage is "we."
31. Ibid., 3:80.
32. Ibid., 3:262.
33. Marx, "Contribution to the Critique of Hegel's Philosophy of Law," 125.
34. Andrew J. Nathan and Perry Link, *The Tiananmen Papers*, compiled by Zhang Liang (London: Little, Brown, 2001), 432. Compare this rendition with the rather different version in Deng, *Selected Works of Deng Xiaoping*, 3:292.
35. Bertell Ollman, *Dance of the Dialectic: Steps in Marx's Method* (Urbana: University of Illinois Press, 2003), 66; emphasis original.
36. Ibid., 137.
37. Ibid., 159–61.
38. Ibid., 166, 168, 200, 203; emphasis added.
39. Ibid., 187; emphasis original.
40. Ibid., 188–89.

41. Ibid., 189.
42. Ibid., 191.
43. Ibid., 197.
44. As described contrapuntally to Chinese law, tradition, and order in Thomas B. Stephens, *Order and Discipline in China: The Shanghai Mixed Court 1911–27* (Seattle: University of Washington Press, 1992), and in Stephens, "The Shanghai Mixed Court and the Ming Sung Umbrella Case 1926," *Australian Journal of Politics and History* 33, no. 2 (1987): 77.
45. Suzanne Pepper, "Hong Kong Joins the National People's Congress: A First Test for One Country with Two Political Systems," *Journal of Contemporary China* 8 (1999): 319, 343. See also Christine Loh, "The CCP and the Rule of Law in Hong Kong," *Hong Kong Law Journal* 25 (1995): 149, 153 ("Hong Kong remains culpably ignorant.").
46. The three flag-desecration cases are as follows: *HKSAR v. Ng Kung Siu & Anor* [1999] 3 HKLRD at 907 (Flag III); *HKSAR v. Ng Kung Siu & Anor* [1999] 2 HKC at 10 (Flag II). This case provides the record of the trial court (Flag I), especially for the report of the written decision of the Magistrate. *HKSAR v. Ng Kung Siu & Anor* [1999] 2 HKC 10 (Flag I).
47. 曾华群/Zeng Huaqun, "香港特别行政区高度自治权刍议/On the High Degree of Autonomy of the Special Administrative Region Hong Kong" 比较法研究 (季刊)/*Journal of Comparative Law*, no. 1 (2002, Quarterly Edition): 75, provides a useful discussion of this subject, with a comprehensive collection of sources, from the PRC standpoint.
48. Pepper, "Hong Kong Joins the National People's Congress," 340.
49. A point discussed and annotated in Anthony R. Dicks, "The Law-Making Functions of the Chinese Judiciary: Filling Holes in the Civil Law," *Comparative Law in Global Perspective: Essays in Celebration of the Fiftieth Anniversary of the Founding of the SOAS Law Department*, ed. Ian Edge (Ardsley, NY: Transnational, 2000), 258. See also Sujit Choudhry, "Globalization in Search of Justification: Toward a Theory of Comparative Constitutional Interpretation," *Indiana Law Journal* 74 (1999): 820; and Tatu Vanhanen, *Democratization: A Comparative Analysis of 170 Countries* (London: Routledge, 2003).
50. Deng, *Selected Works of Deng Xiaoping*, 3:214 *et seq.*
51. Benny Tai, "Is 'Final' Really Final?" *Hong Kong Law Journal* 32 (2002): 25; P. Y. Lo, "Master of One's Own Court," *Hong Kong Law Journal* 34 (2004): 47. See also Shiu-hing Lo, "The Politics of the Court of Final Appeal Debate in Hong Kong," *Issues & Studies* 29 (1993): 105, and David Faure, *Colonialism and the Hong Kong Mentality* (Hong Kong: University of Hong Kong, 2003).
52. That the NPCSC is subject to the party is demonstrated in Nathan and Link, *The Tiananmen Papers*, 349, 369, 386–87, 394, 403, 440.
53. Metzger, *A Cloud across the Pacific*, 127–28, 494, 666, 690; Edward J. Epstein, "China and Hong Kong: Law, Ideology, and the Future Interaction of the Legal Systems," in *The Future of the Law in Hong Kong*, ed. Raymond Wacks (Hong Kong: Oxford University Press, 1989), 56–57, note 112 and accompanying text. See also Johannes Chan, "Some Thoughts on Constitutional Reform in Hong Kong," *Hong Kong Law Journal* 34 (2004): 1—an example of good common law but not good dialectical, argument.
54. Yash Ghai, "Autonomy with Chinese Characteristics: The Case of Hong Kong," *Pacifica Review* 10 (1998): 7, 21.
55. Byron S. J. Weng, "Judicial Independence under the Basic Law," *Judicial Independence and the Rule of Law in Hong Kong, ed.* Steve Tsang (Hong Kong: Hong Kong University Press, 2001), 48, 60. Ominously, Weng notes a debate that took place during the drafting of the Basic Law, in which fears were expressed that the NPCSC would take to itself the

power to interpret the Basic Law "on its own initiative." See, e.g., Robert J. Morris, "The 'Replacement' Chief Executive's Two-Year Term: A Pure and Unambiguous Common Law Analysis," *Hong Kong Law Journal* 35, no. 1 (2005): 17. See Chan, Fu, and Ghai, *Hong Kong's Constitutional Debate*. See also the more recent Johannes Chan and Lison Harris, eds., *Hong Kong's Constitutional Debates* (Hong Kong: Hong Kong Law Journal, 2005). The NPCSC decision, June 26, 1999, "全国人民代表大会常务委员会关于《中华人民共和国香港特别行政区基本法》第二十二条第四款和第二十四条第二款第（三）项的解释/Interpretations of the Standing Committee of the National People's Congress to Paragraph 4 of Article 22 and Subparagraph 3 of Paragraph 2 of Article 24 of the Basic Law of the Hong Kong Special Administrative Region," may be found in the July 15, 1999 中华人民共和国全国人民代表大会常务委员会公报/*Gazette of the Standing Committee of the National People's Congress of the People's Republic of China*, 325, with additional explanatory materials following at pp. 327–31.

56. Frequently cited in histories of the common law as a "sermon preached before the King in 1717."
57. See, e.g., Albert H. Y. Chen, "The Interpretation of the Basic Law—Common Law and Mainland Chinese Perspectives," *Hong Kong Law Journal* 30, no. 3 (2000): 380. In 2005, the NPCSC rendered an interpretation of the Basic Law regarding the term of the chief executive who replaced the resigned Tung Chee-hwa. In doing so, the NPCSC published in *Gazette of the Supreme People's Court of the People's Republic of China* (中華人民共和國全國人民代表大會常務委員會公報), no. 4 (2005): 301, 302, 304, 307, and 308, five separate articles, including the interpretation itself, explaining what could be termed the *ratio decidendi* for the decision—being, as it was, much more purposive and reasoned that any past interpretations, which were more in the nature of fiat. In addition, members of the NPCSC and others met representatives of Hong Kong in Shenzhen to discuss the impending decision and engage in a "dialogue" regarding the process. None if this in any way vitiated the presence of the dialectic in this situation. This was not deliberation in the "deliberative democracy" sense because, by this point, the decision had already been made. The Shenzhen meetings were merely the announcement. The NPCSC decision was not a common-law process, and it maintained the superstructure of direction from Peking under Article 158 of the Basic Law.
58. Xiao, *One Country, Two Systems*, 351; see also 156.
59. See, e.g., Bruce Bueno de Mesquita, David Newman, and Alvin Rabushka, "Words Have Meaning—or Do They?" in *Red Flag Over Hong Kong*, ed. Bruce Bueno de Mesquita, David Newman, and Alvin Rabushka (Chatham, NJ: Chatham House, 1996), 49–67.
60. Xiao, *One Country, Two Systems*, 172.
61. Ibid.
62. Ibid., 173. Ghai, "Autonomy with Chinese Characteristics." A "high degree of democracy and high degree of centralism" is a phrase Deng attributed to Mao. See Deng, *Selected Works of Deng Xiaoping*, 1:310–11.
63. Ibid.
64. Ibid., 3:80.
65. Xiao, *One Country, Two Systems*, 96.
66. Ibid., 100–101.
67. Ibid., 54. Some in Hong Kong may dispute this. See pronouncements of the Hong Kong appellate courts in *HKSAR v. Ma Wai Kwan David* [1997] HKLRD 761, and *Chan Kam Nga and Others v. Director of Immigration* [1998] 1 HKLRD 142—issues beyond the scope of this study. But see *Yau Kwong Man v. Secretary for Security* [2002] 3 HKC 457 and *Lau*

Kong Yung v. Direction of Immigration [1999] 4 HKC 731, esp. the dissent of J. Bokhary, 775–77.

68. Xiao, *One Country, Two Systems*, 59, 84. Many, perhaps most, common-law lawyers and judges in Hong Kong would arguably resist this point, which has not yet been aired in the Hong Kong courts. The list of national laws that apply to Hong Kong as contained in Annex III of the Basic Law does not include the PRC Constitution. However, such inclusion may not be necessary or appropriate because (a) the Basic Law is a lesser law under the PRC Constitution and so would assume the Constitution's application to be an automatic given; (b) the Preamble of the Basic Law itself cites Article 31 of the PRC Constitution as the basis for the HKSAR's establishment as an "inalienable part" of the PRC and for the authority of the Basic Law itself; and (c) the PRC Constitution itself holds to the principle that China is "one country" of which the HKSAR and other "special" regions and zones are an integral part. Both documents espouse the central precept of "national unity." This would argue that the application of the constitution could not be excluded from any part of the "one country." Perhaps even more to the point, and pursuant to the thesis of this chapter, is that under Articles 82, 158, and 159 of the Basic Law, the powers of the NPC and NPCSC to interpret and amend the Basic Law may render irrelevant the opinion of Hong Kong common-law lawyers, judges, and courts on this point. Needless to say, this will be a point of interest to observe in the coming years.
69. Zaishun Li, "The Comprehensive Grasping of the 'One Country, Two Systems' Concept Is the Key to the Correct Implementation of the Hong Kong Basic Law," paper presented at the Constitutional Law Conference on Implementation of the Basic Law, Hong Kong, April 28–29, 2000.
70. Ibid., 7 passim. His use of the term *continental law* is problematic, as is the use of *civil law* by other authors to categorize Chinese communist law. The issue is of minor concern here but see John Quigley, "Socialist Law and the Civil Law Tradition," *American Journal of Comparative Law 37* (1989): 781; as well as Harold J. Berman, "What Makes 'Socialist Law' Socialist?" *Problems of Communism* 20 (1971): 24, 28; Carlos W. H. Lo, "Deng Xiaoping's Ideas on Law: China on the Threshold of a Legal Order," *Asian Survey* 32 (1992): 649; Lo, "Rejecting the Traditional Socialist Theory of Law," *China Information* 7 (1992): 1.
71. Weng, "Judicial Independence under the Basic Law," 53.
72. Li, "The Comprehensive Grasping of the 'One Country, Two Systems'," 10.
73. Ibid., 11. This echoes the argument made in Yan Gao, "Wo Guo Bu Yi Caiyong Panli Fazhi Du [It Is Not Suitable for Our Country to Adopt the Legal Precedent System]" *Zhong Guo Fa Xue* [*China Legal Studies*] 41 (1991): 43, with particular reference to Hong Kong and Taiwan. See also Zongling Shen, "Judicial Precedents in China Today: A Comparative Study of Law" *Asia Pacific Law Review*, special issue, 1 (1994): 109, arguing that case law is undemocratic and retrospective. But "judge-made law" is the quintessence and definition of the common law. Peter Wesley-Smith, *Constitutional and Administrative Law in Hong Kong*, 2nd ed. (Hong Kong: Longman Asia, 1994), 38.
74. See Martin S. Flaherty, "The Canons of Constitutional Law: Aim Globally," *Constitutional Commentary* 17 (2000): 205.
75. Chien-min Chao, "'One Country, Two Systems': A Theoretical Analysis," *Asian Affairs: An American Review* 14 (1987): 107, 110, 112.

PART II

Crossing the Border

CHAPTER 6

The Political Economy of Interpretation

*Yash Ghai**

Introduction

Decisions on the structure of the state and the allocations of powers are seldom made in accordance with principle or doctrine (whatever the invocations of Locke, Montesquieu, Marx, the Koran, or the Gita). Without wanting to discount the influence of legal and constitutional traditions, key decisions are made primarily in the interests of the decision makers, whether directly or through proxies. This applies as much to procedural issues as to matters of substance. In this chapter, I argue that, despite the explanation of conflict over the interpretation of the Basic Law of the Hong Kong Special Administrative Region (HKSAR) in terms of the differing traditions of the common law and the civil law, Article 158 (and its uses) is more realistically analyzed in terms of strategies of control.

To demonstrate my thesis, I begin, as background, with a study of the rise of two principal methods of constitutional interpretation, the legislative and the judicial. The former was initiated by the French National Assembly, which met in 1789 to draft and adopt a constitution in the progress of the Revolution, and the second was confirmed by the Federal Convention, which drafted the U.S. Constitution in 1787. The two processes were separated by only a few years, and among some members of the assembly and the convention, there was cordial friendship. The delegates to the assembly showed considerable

* I thank Sophia Woodman and Jill Cottrell for their assistance in the preparation of this chapter and the University of Hong Kong for the Distinguished Researcher Award which has facilitated my research on comparative constitutions.

interest in the bourgeois revolution of the United States as they were seeking their own path toward a similar class revolution. In particular, many of them were familiar with the proceedings and outcome of the Philadelphia Convention. The delegates of both the constituent assemblies were familiar with the works of Rousseau, Locke, and Montesquieu (which they frequently cited in their speeches during their deliberations). Both were strong proponents of people's sovereignty. Yet, on the critical issue of interpretation, their decisions were diametrically opposed.

Three Approaches to Interpretation

Judicial Interpretation

The U.S. Constitution is often credited with having invented and propagated judicial review (meaning in this context the authority in the courts to strike down legislation which, in the interpretation of the judges, violates the constitution). Sometimes it is Chief Justice Marshall who is credited, on the basis of that constitution, with having established this jurisdiction of the Supreme Court in the famous judgment of *Marbury v. Madison.*[1] The people of the thirteen colonies were of course familiar with the concept of judicial review as the Privy Council had reviewed colonial legislation for conformity with the charters of government granted by the English king. In that sense, the Privy Council, in its origin an advisory body to the king, was a powerful instrument of control, ensuring that each colonial administration kept strictly to the terms of its grant. But the legislatures that the Privy Council controlled in this way were subordinate bodies, and what was then being proposed for the United States was a sovereign legislature. Blackstone, well read by many members of the Federal Convention, strongly emphasized the supremacy of the English Parliament and the legal futility of trying to limit its powers. However, constitutions of some states since the overthrow of English rule had adopted judicial review.

So the idea was not novel to the members of the Philadelphia Convention, nor was much time taken up by the issue. However, it was not without controversy—to understand, it has to be appreciated that the convention saw as its task the making of a federal constitution (unlike France, which had strong unitary aspirations). Federal constitutions raise different kinds of judicial review issues from a unitary constitution, as the latter does not have to contend with the issue of the division of powers. The proponents of judicial review identified as a major deficiency of the Articles of Confederation that it provided a weak central authority by denying it its own judicial power. Several delegates, representing the larger states, argued for federal judicial power in view of the new powers given to the federal authorities and the division of powers between them and the states. Delegates of the smaller states were fearful that the courts would expand the powers of the federal authorities, eating into the authority of the states. However, it seems to have been accepted by both sides that the provisions of the draft constitution giving jurisdiction to federal courts implied the powers of judicial review (in the sense used here; see Article III of the U.S. Constitution).

This much is evident from the arguments for and against the adoption of the draft by state ratification conventions. The constitution had proclaimed its supremacy. A powerful case for judicial review was made by the "federalists," particularly by Hamilton in *The Federalist Papers*. He wrote that constitutional limitations on the powers of the legislature "can be preserved in practice no other way than through the medium of courts of justice, whose duty it must be to declare all acts contrary to the manifest tenor of the Constitution void. Without this, all the reservations of particular rights or privileges would amount to nothing."[2] He went on to say that the presumption that legislatures are judges of the limits of their own authority cannot be "the natural presumption," for in this way the intention of the representatives (agents) of the people (in the form of statute) will override the intentions of the people (in the form of the constitution).[3] "The interpretation of the laws is the proper and peculiar province of the courts."[4]

The importance of Hamilton's paper lies not only in its defence of judicial review. It is one of the best summaries (at the time) of the conditions under which a judiciary can operate independently. Calling the judiciary the weakest of the three departments of the state, he said, "though individual oppression may now and then proceed from the courts of justice, the general liberty of the people can never be engendered from that quarter: I mean, so long as the judiciary remains truly distinct from both the legislative and the executive. For I agree that 'there is no liberty, if the power of judging be not separated from the legislative and executive powers.'"[5] From this he deduced the fundamental principle of an independent judiciary: permanent tenure ("during good behaviour"), "since nothing will contribute so much as this to that independent spirit in the judges, which must be essential to the faithful performance of so arduous a duty."[6]

The case against judicial review was put most vociferously in an anti–Federalist Paper by "Brutus."[7] He argued that federal jurisdiction would allow courts "in the last resort" to determine the meaning of the constitution without being confined to "fixed or established rules."[8] Brutus goes on to say that "the judicial power of the United States, will lean strongly in favour of the general [i.e., the federal] government, and will give such an explanation to the constitution, as will favour an extension of its jurisdiction, is very evident from a number of considerations," including the general and broad language of the constitution. In another paper, he tried to show that the courts will interpret these provisions in favor of federal authorities and concluded that "that in proportion as the general government acquires power and jurisdiction, by the liberal construction which the judges may give the constitution, will those of the states lose its rights, until they become so trifling and unimportant, as will not be worth having."[9]

It was not until 1803 that the question of the validity of a federal legislation came before the courts in *Marbury v. Madison*. Even then, the issue was not necessary for the judgment of the Supreme Court. Apparently, Chief Justice Marshall used the occasion to emphasize the power of the court to invalidate legislation contrary to the constitution using arguments that were reminiscent of Hamilton.

Marshall also took the opportunity in *Marbury* to make a strong case for the rule of law. He said that the government of the United States "has been emphatically termed a government of laws, and not of men. It will certainly cease to deserve this high appellation, if the laws furnish no remedy for the violation of a vested legal right."[10] Perhaps the reason that Marshall took the initiative to reiterate the doctrine of constitutional supremacy and judicial review was to emphasize the rule of law as power passed from the party he had supported to the Republicans and perhaps also a reflection of his conservative bias as popular politics seemed to be emerging.

Legislative Interpretation

The idea of law emerged as central to the French polity after the National Assembly repudiated ancient privileges with laws reflecting differential statuses. "Laws common to all were to be source of equity and justice in the nation as well as unifying bond among citizens, so that law became paramount in the new regime's definition of itself."[11] This emphasized the role of the judicial system.

The National Assembly engaged in a wide-ranging reform of the judiciary; at one point, it decided to restructure the old system of justice in which the jurisdiction of tribunal and the rights of litigants depended on their status. As Fitzsimmons said, "The decision reflected the paramount importance that the National Assembly accorded to the judiciary as a critical element in its regeneration of France. Justice was now to be dispensed by the nation, guided by a sense of equity through the medium of laws common to all. Realizing that one of the greatest influences that a nation could have over its citizens was through the administration of justice, the deputies wanted the judiciary to reflect faithfully the new values of the nation."[12] The National Assembly considered the judiciary a linchpin of its new ideal of the polity.

Among the wide-ranging decisions that the National Assembly made was on the jurisdiction to interpret the constitution and laws (a constitution that was to herald a new France). The dilemma facing the National Assembly has been well captured by Eric Thompson. Those on the "left wing" (i.e., supporters of people's sovereignty) were suspicious of the judiciary, which had traditionally allied itself with the king and the nobility. They saw the legislative assembly, controlled by the Third Estate, as the embodiment of people's sovereignty. According to Thompson, they realized that as they had recently decided that the people's sovereignty over lawmaking was delegated to the national legislature and over executive functions to the king, people's sovereignty over the administration of justice should be delegated to judges—which would also be keeping in line with Montesquieu's principles of the separation of powers, which had profoundly influenced the assembly. He goes on to say, "But, on the other, it appeared clear to the deputies of the Left Centre and the Left Wing that there was a real danger to the political supremacy of the Third Estate in establishing a power which might impede the will of the Assembly, and partly through its power of interpreting the laws, and partly under the possible influence of subversive and reactionary elements in the State, might set up a will which could oppose the will of the legislative corporation."[13]

Torn between the reactionary forces around the king and the radicalism of the Paris crowds, they hesitated "to embody a judiciary which would be completely independent of the legislature."[14] Thompson writes, "Having taken steps to ensure that the 'representative general will,' theoretically reflecting the 'general will' of the sovereign people, should always be in accord with the will of the Third Estate, and having, to all intents and purposes, harnessed the executive power of this will, it appeared madness not to take all necessary steps to subordinate the judiciary to the 'general will' of the sovereign people, as reflected in the will of the Assembly."[15]

The right-wingers wanted either a completely independent judiciary or one that was part of the executive and appointed by the king.[16]

So strong was the will of the "leftist" forces[17] to maintain control over the judiciary that they insisted that judges should be appointed by the legislature and therefore did not need life tenure. Protected tenure, in their view, was important only if the appointing authority was to be the king, who could stay in power for a long period.[18] But for our present purposes, the most important decision of the National Assembly concerned its power to overrule decisions of courts "without making the power of quashing such decision too obvious an interference with the judicial power," as Thompson puts it.[19] One delegate advocated that the power to quash judgments, which might lead to attacks on the law itself, should be embodied in the legislature. With some sophistry, he said, "To quash a judgment is not to judge. Thus the right to quash a judgment should not belong to the judicial power; it emanates essentially from the legislative power."[20] At that time, there was no court of appeal in France and thus no judicial supervision of local tribunals. Some delegates suggested a court of appeal that would have the power to quash decisions of lower courts, as they felt that powers in the legislature to overturn judicial decisions would imperil the liberty of the individual.

The leftists, led by Robespierre, were not convinced. For them, the sovereignty of the "general will" implied that any doubt about the interpretation of this will in legal proceedings could be settled only by the representatives trusted by the people with such interpretation. He said,

> As the legislative assembly establishes only the general law, the strength of which depends on its exact observation, if the magistrate can substitute their own will they will be legislators. It will thus be necessary to have a power of supervision which will restore the courts to the principles of legislation. This power can only belong to the legislator, following principles which have been authentically recognised. It is for the legislator to interpret the law which he has made. It is thus necessary that the Assembly declare that to it alone belongs the right of maintaining legislation, and thus its own authority, be it by quashing of judgments or be it otherwise.[21]

The assembly did appoint a Court of Appeal, but its jurisdiction was restricted to violations of law and procedure and instructed in a decree "never go deeply into a case."[22] If the Court of Appeal had to decide a question of interpretation made by a lower court, it had to refer the question to the legislature, "which will make a decree declaratory of the law, to which the Court of Appeal shall be required to conform."[23] Thompson sums up his conclusion on the protracted debates and justifications in the assembly as follows: "The Assembly was chiefly influenced by the fear that a power might be established which would detract from the authority of the legislature. Its eyes were fixed rather on the preservation of bourgeois supremacy than on any strict separation of powers."[24]

The French Assembly did a magnificent demolition job; they tore apart, day by day, decree by decree, the foundations of the feudal, monarchical power, but they did not themselves succeed to state power. They had opened up the possibility of bourgeois rule, but they had not yet established it. Their own center of power was the assembly—and, they anticipated, future legislatures. Control of the legislature, and through it control of other institutions that retard their hegemony, was their central concern.

Comparing the U.S. and French Approaches

The French Assembly considered the option of vesting the courts (after appropriate reforms) with the competence to interpret the constitution and laws, but, despite recognizing the importance of laws to the new regime, they rejected it. In the United States, there was no significant opposition to giving courts this jurisdiction, exclusively, although delegates of smaller states, wedded to "state sovereignty," were apprehensive of the erosion of their own powers through the expansion of the powers of federal authority by the supreme court. In both countries, there were preexisting traditions of judicial review. The Privy Council, meeting in London, was the final court of the thirteen colonies, and one of its responsibilities was to maintain the integrity of the colonial charters by reviewing the laws and administrative decisions of the executive authorities. In England, the king's courts had gradually replaced feudal courts and other courts with special jurisdiction, and a uniform system, basically as an appendage of the central authorities, had developed. The colonial courts even more reflected this uniformity and dispensed a law that ultimately had its origins in the decisions of the central authorities, but, at the same time, had furthered the common-law rights of citizens. The common-law courts were generally regarded as the custodian of the rights of the people. The Americans justified their revolt against the English on the grounds that their common-law rights had been violated—at least the rights of the well off—and could no longer be protected by the British Parliament.

In France, the position was quite different. The provincial courts or *parlements* in France were "still bastions of aristocratic and provincial obstruction to royal authority."[25] Appointments to and preferment within *parlements* had strong elements of hereditary and dynastic principles. Egret observes, "Inspired by aristocratic pride and careful of their composition, several *parlements* demanded a fully acquired nobility for those candidates who were not the sons of judges."[26] Although for nearly two centuries, French kings were able to dispense with a legislative assembly,

> they were not able to suppress or to exert reliable control over these feudal courts. The *parlements* did conduct much routine judicial business, but they also had broader powers: royal decrees, for example, had to be registered with the *parlements* before obtaining legal effect and the *parlements* sometimes balked at endorsing measures they deemed improper.

> Beginning with Louis XIV, therefore, French kings had sought to build up a separate administrative machinery to circumvent the *parlements* and other provincial relics. Thus the French Revolution not only inherited models of centralised administrative organisation . . . but an association of courts with aristocratic privilege and provincial obstructionism. Because the revolutionaries still had to complete the work of eliminating feudal obstructions to national authority, they inevitably took a hostile view of courts as well as provincial authorities.[27]

Behind the choice of the courts or the legislature to interpret the constitution lies a complex reality. The Americans were content to retain common-law institutions and procedures because there were not true revolutionaries like their French counterpart. Their primary concern was the elimination of British sovereignty so that they—that is, the elite—could obtain political power, particularly over the regulation of the economy. The delegates in Philadelphia saw themselves as the elite, already well ensconced in the centers of political and economic power. For them, the rights of property were paramount, including as the basis of franchise. They emphasized continuity and stability; the English common law had already developed to nurture the market and rights.[28]

A great deal of their rhetoric of human rights and dignity was opportunistic. Its imperatives did not extend to Native Americans and the slaves, nor to, say, women and the poor (as is obvious from the Virginia Declaration of Rights of 1776). As the struggle against the British progressed, the elite became alarmed at the claims of the ordinary people for their rights and in particular demands for better working conditions and greater measure of social justice. Even as the constitution was being drafted, notions of "republican government" based on people's sovereignty and participation were being revised. Direct participation was downplayed and "representative democracy" became dominant. Even then, an active judiciary was regarded as a brake on populist initiatives, hence perhaps Marshall's intervention in *Marbury*.

The French Assembly had a much more ambiguous relationship with the masses, crowds, and mobs. They used them, both in Versailles where the assembly first met and then in Paris, to delegitimize the monarchy and the feudal order but were also scarred by their radicalism, spontaneity, and tendency toward violence.[29] The "left-wing" members depended greatly on the pressure from the crowds for the adoption by the assembly of radical proposals, even to the extent of the intimidation of members who opposed the proposals. We may contrast the open and participatory style of the French Assembly with the closed and secretive nature of the proceedings of the Philadelphia Convention as illustration of the openness to public pressure and scrutiny. Another factor that influenced the proceedings and outcome of the two bodies was the degree of cohesion among the delegates. The National Assembly was very disparate, including the nobility, clergy, and the general estate (mostly "middle class") in a membership of over a thousand delegates. The third category quickly established its dominance, but it was never fully united. The National Assembly was bitterly divided on several fundamental issues. On the other hand, the convention consisted of fifty-five members who came from largely the same class and most knew the others well. The differences between them were seldom of class; instead, they were about the interests of large states versus the interests of small states (which were largely resolved) and between the interests of slave-owning states and those without (which was not resolved—and led to a Civil War in the following century). The fact that thirty-four of the delegates were lawyers may also have facilitated agreement on legal structures and promoted a generally conservative attitude toward social issues and on judicial review.

Lawyers in the National Assembly, although not so numerous, also played a key role. According to Tackett, "Almost without exception, the most distinguished Jacobins in terms of Old Regime intellectual careers had been legal specialists . . . Nine of the eleven most active Jacobin orators were legal men by profession. In the National Assembly, as in the kingdom generally, it was often the men of law who represented the most important bastion of radicalism."[30] Unlike the American lawyer-delegates, the French lawyer-delegates were extremely critical of the courts and considered that they could not be reformed; the legal system had to be radically altered, with accountability to the legislature. Perhaps they saw a greater role for themselves in a reformed system.

Growing Convergence

Since the eighteenth century, the differences between the two systems have narrowed, so that Baudenbacher can say about the methods of civil courts that they are not far removed from the approach of common-law courts:

> The assertion that "purposive application of law is uncommon in the opinions of civil law judges" is untenable. In every civil law country, there are countless cases in which the purpose of the law at the time of its interpretation has been decisive . . . Civil law courts do not rule out any method of interpretation, and . . . no order of priority of the single elements of interpretation exists. That means that a court might in one case come to the conclusion that the right solution should be derived from the text of a provision. In another case the court may rely on the legislative history, on contextual interpretation, or on the purpose (the

> telos) of the provision. According to widespread opinion, courts should go through all the mentioned elements of interpretation. The balance, however, will often tip in favor of purposive interpretation. In following that approach, courts tend to take into account the social reality at the time of the application of the law.[31]

Even more striking has been the convergence on institutions charged with interpretation. France, cautious about judicial review since the time of the revolution, had no provisions to review legislation for conformity to the constitution until 1946. Then a constitutional committee of parliament was set up but proved ineffective. In 1958, the *Conseil Constitutionnel* (Constitutional Council) was established to examine the constitutionality of legislation. It is composed of former French presidents and nine judges appointed for nine years. It must automatically examine the constitutional validity of organic laws as well as parliamentary regulations. It must also examine other legislation if requested by the president, prime minister, the speaker of either house of parliament, or at least sixty members of parliament. Such review can take place only before the legislation is enacted. Despite these restrictions, Rene David says that the council can be considered a proper court, "in the light of the action it has taken which likens it to the constitutional courts existing in other countries."[32] It has played an active role in the protection of rights, defined the boundaries between the powers of the legislature and executive to make regulations, and held various draft statutes invalid.[33] The French model has been accepted in most of the former colonies in Africa and Asia, as well as Sri Lanka (although with some variations).

More radical departures have taken place in other civil law countries. Early departures were made in a number of important countries in Latin America, such as Argentina, Bolivia, Brazil, Chile, Colombia, and Venezuela, whose constitutions provided for the courts (or only the Supreme Court) to declare legislation invalid for nonconformity to the constitution.[34] But the more spectacular growth of judicial powers of review in civil-law jurisdictions occurred in Europe with the establishment of constitutional courts. The first of these was the constitutional court in Austria in 1920 (under the inspiration of Hans Kelsen). The constitution of that year continued the civil-law prohibition of judges reviewing legislation; but it set up a constitutional court to review the validity of national or regional (lander) legislation, at the instance only of the national or regional authorities. A subsequent amendment permitted supreme courts for civil and administrative matters to refer to the constitutional court, during the course of litigation, legislation whose constitutional validity is in doubt. The key characteristics of the constitutional court are that it exists apart from the regular court system (although referrals could be made to it by the regular courts), and its judges are not for the most part career judges and are drawn from universities and persons in public law. Judges have a twelve-year tenure so that frequent recruitment brings in judges who are attuned to social and political changes, more sensitive to political factors than ordinary judges. They are all specialists in constitutional law, unlike supreme courts of most countries, and more willing to engage with constitutional issues than traditional courts.[35]

The Austrian constitutional court proved very attractive as European and other states reorganized their constitutional systems after the Second World War (including Germany, Italy, Egypt, and Turkey). The most studied of these courts is the German constitutional court, closely based on the Austrian model, but with a more liberal access to the court. After the collapse of communism in the Soviet Union and Eastern Europe, the new constitutions have provided for constitutional courts that have played important, sometimes crucial, roles in the transition to democracy and the establishment of the rule of law.[36] The remarkable spread of judicial review to civil and socialist law jurisdictions (leaving as exceptions China, Vietnam, and Cuba) is an acknowledgment of the importance of separation of powers, the value of judicial review for the protection of rights, and the prevention of authoritarianism of the executive and of the legislature largely dependent on the executive. The critical issue is no longer what family of legal systems a country belongs to but its commitment to democracy, protection of rights, and the rule of law.[37]

The Marxist Approach

The Marxist approach is distinct from the previous two. Although it vests the powers of interpretation in the legislature, it is far removed from the civil-law tradition that followed the French Assembly. The authentic lineage of the People's Republic of China (PRC) rule of interpretation is not the civil law but the Leninist tradition of law and state power. The civil-law rule of interpretation by the legislature was based on a strict application of the separation of powers (most delegates expressed their commitment to Montesquieu's theory, but there was considerable debate in the French Assembly on the exact position of Montesquieu on this question).[38] However, the Marxist rule is based on the rejection of the separation of powers and the unification of all state power in the legislature ("people's assembly"—both Marx and Lenin were greatly impressed by the combination of legislative and executive power in the Paris Commune 1871, and the establishment of a supreme body, which they regarded as a model of a communist political order). The dictatorship of the proletariat (as expressed by the Communist Party) and party and state centralism were essential to the communist state as established by Lenin.[39] We need to compare the essential principles of civil-law jurisdiction constitutions (starting with the French Assembly) of democracy, rule of law, limitation of state powers, and accountability mechanisms with the communist constitutions with their emphasis on dictatorship of the Communist Party, the subordination of state organs, including the judiciary, to the party, supremacy of policy over law, highly controlled electoral systems, and weak institutions of accountability, to realize that we are talking of very different legal, constitutional, and moral traditions.

A leading Hungarian scholar writing in the heyday of communism in his country said, "It follows from the principle of popular sovereignty that the National Assembly is as for authority superior to any other existing or potential organ, it has a kind of established primacy which does not tolerate even a state of balance between the supreme legislative organ and other agencies."[40] He goes on to say that the arrangement in a bourgeois state, where under the doctrine of the separation of powers, parliament could be subject to some external supervision, is inconceivable in a socialist country.[41] He quotes another Hungarian scholar, Beer, to the effect that in a socialist state a constitutional court would conflict with the "primacy of the supreme organs of state power, the absoluteness of their competence."[42] This absolute competence was at the disposal of the Communist Party. These attitudes are also consistent with the Marxist-Leninist attitude to the law, as subordinate to politics, and as purely instrumental to the achievement of socialist objectives.

Legislative interpretation in civil law was concerned to interpret the original will of the legislature, not to expand the scope of the law (to do the latter would be inconsistent with the rule of law to which the civil law systems were committed from the eighteenth century onward). In China, however, there seems to be no sharp distinction between construction and expansion of the law.[43]

For a true understanding of the origins of the NPC's power to interpret the constitution and laws, we do not need to turn to the civil law (although it has become customary both in Hong Kong and China to refer to its civil-law heritage in discussions of the powers of interpretation). Sophia Woodman has argued in this volume that the first constitution in communist China was prepared under the influence of Stalin's Soviet constitution (which had provided for interpretation by the Presidium of the USSR Supreme Soviet).[44] Even before the 1954 Constitution, the Organic Law of the Central People's Government of the People's Republic of China (1949) had provided for the Committee of Central People's Government to both enact and interpret the law. There was very little of the civil law about that Organic Law, as indeed there was very little of the civil law about the 1954 Constitution.

This is acknowledged in the very first article of the 1982 constitution, which describes China as a socialist state under the people's democratic dictatorship and describes the socialist system as the basic system of the People's Republic. The preamble states that the country is governed under the leadership of the Communist Party and the guidance of Marxism-Leninism and Mao Zedong Thought. The National People's Congress is the "highest organ of state power" (Article 57), and it is obvious from the elaboration of its powers (in Articles 62–63) that it supervises all state organs so that there is no separation of powers, which is a fundamental principle of most civil law systems. Its power and that of its Standing Committee (NPCSC) are part of this scheme, to emphasize the aggregation of state power in this body. The essential nature of the constitutional order of the People's Republic becomes clearer when we turn to the Constitution of the Communist Party of China (1992). The basic principle of the Party is democratic centralism, which effectively means that the decisions of the highest party organ are binding on all persons and institutions, including institutions of the state.

China justifies these overriding powers for Mainland audiences in terms of socialist legal traditions and communist political theory; but in Hong Kong by reference to civil-law traditions (which they perceive are less threatening and more acceptable to Hong Kong people and foreigners alike).

Basic Law Provisions on Interpretation

Although rooted in the Chinese constitution, the NPCSC's interpretation powers were probably intended to perform a different kind of function in Hong Kong. In the Mainland, the government has various methods to carry out its policies: laws, directives, acts under the hegemony of the local party mechanisms, *nomenklatura*, subordination of the judiciary, and so on. It seems not to matter which method is applied, as there is no challenge to any policies of the government or the party. Most of these methods are not possible in relation to Hong Kong (although China exercises decisive control over the chief executive). Given the importance of the ideology of the rule of law, China had to devise a method of control that would be seen to be "legal" and reasonable. It was on the one hand essential to keep intact many of the provisions about the independence of the judiciary and the principles of the common law—as well as the previous expansive jurisdiction of the Hong Kong courts. On the other hand, the Hong Kong legal system, especially in the jurisdiction of the Court of Final Appeal (CFA), had to be subordinated to Beijing. For this purpose, the NPCSC's power of interpretation could be tailored, justifying by reference to civil-law traditions and the system of adjudication in the EU—although these analogies are quite inappropriate.

Although much of the discussion on interpretation has focused on Article 158, it is necessary to note that other parts of the Basic Law also provide for an interpretative role by Beijing authorities, attesting to its importance. The NPCSC had to decide at the birth of the HKSAR which colonial laws would be repealed for inconsistency with the Basic Law (Article 160). When a Mainland law is extended to Hong Kong, there must be a determination that the law relates to defense or foreign affairs or other matters outside the autonomy of Hong Kong (Article 18). Law passed by Hong Kong's legislature may be reviewed by the NPCSC for consistency with the Basic Law and declared invalid when inconsistent (Article 17). Questions of interpretation would also arise in relation to the last paragraph of Article 159, dealing with amendments of the Basic Law, for no amendment may contravene the "established basic policies of the People's Republic of China." In this case, the final power of interpretation would be that of the NPC itself.

Thus, the power of interpretation is intertwined deeply in the relationship between Beijing and Hong Kong; it is not simply about the meaning of laws but about power relationships. The Basic Law is primarily about control and not autonomy, as is obvious in the provisions about Beijing control over the chief executive, senior public servants, and the Legislative Council. But the independence of the judiciary and the total unacceptability of a role for the Mainland courts meant that the Hong Kong courts could not be so easily subordinated. The power of interpretation plugs this gap and of course performs other functions as I show later.

The importance that Beijing attached to the NPCSC's power of interpretation is evident from the history of the drafting Article 158. Apart from the controversies about the political system, the most contentious issue during the drafting of the Basic Law of the HKSAR concerned the power to interpret the Basic Law. The issue was not directly addressed in the Joint Declaration, although the formulation, "the power of final judgment of the HKSAR shall be vested in the court of final appeal in the HKSAR"[45] might have given at least the Hong Kong public the impression that the final power to interpret the Basic Law would be with the Hong Kong courts (as would be the case under common law, which was intended to be the underlying law of Hong Kong). Although the Basic Law was to be the supreme law in Hong Kong, the Joint Declaration makes no mention of any powers of the NPCSC regarding the interpretation of the Basic Law for resolving conflicts between Hong Kong laws and the Basic Law. In the transition, final judgment in the Joint Declaration turned into final adjudication in the Basic Law.

There were clear and fundamental differences between Hong Kong and Mainland members of the Basic Law Drafting Committee on the question of the jurisdiction of the Hong Kong courts and the power of the NPCSC to interpret the Basic Law. Various proposals were considered by the Drafting Committee. Some said that there should be no limit on the powers of the Hong Kong courts. Others were prepared to accept that NPCSC could interpret any provision of the Basic Law, but with retrospective effect, although others feared that this would erode the power of final adjudication given to the Hong Kong courts in the Joint Declaration. Martin Lee proposed that the final power of adjudication in respect of all provisions of the Basic Law should vest in Hong Kong courts, but with power in the NPCSC to override prospectively interpretation of provisions outside the autonomy of the SAR.

One Mainland member's reasons for limiting jurisdiction of Hong Kong courts, as related in the records of the Drafting Committee was that "since Hong Kong courts have been given the power of final adjudication, there was concern that the courts of the SAR might be 'wrong' in their interpretation of the Basic Law, in which case the matter could not be corrected"[46]—thus assuming the infallibility of the NPCSC![47] Some reacted to this by saying that it was extremely unwise to "drill a small hole" (as one Mainland member had described it) into the power of final adjudication of the SAR in order to remedy what the Central People's Government considers to be a "wrong interpretation" in relation to only one or two cases—for then "the price would be too great."[48] Most members were concerned to find a compromise between the common-law position and the Chinese position. Few Hong Kong members understood the scope or the dynamics of the Chinese method of interpretation. The expression interpretation is not defined in the constitution. In 1955, the NPCSC issued a Resolution on the Interpretation of Law. This resolution made clear that, where the limits of articles and decrees needed to be further defined or additional stipulations needed to be made, the NPCSC should provide the interpretation or additional provisions by decree. Thus, the distinction between clarification and making of law—a distinction central to most legal systems—was blurred.[49] There was little reference during the drafting of the Basic Law, as far as one can tell, to the power of the NPCSC to change the law by interpretation (although at that time the 1955 Resolution was still valid).[50]

In this way, fundamental conceptual differences were largely ignored. Martin Lee correctly saw Mainland proposals as threatening the independence of the judiciary (and thus ultimately the autonomy of Hong Kong). He concluded that "The Mainland members have not made any concession at all; on the contrary they have succeeded in making sure that the CPG will be able to exercise very firm control over the courts of SAR."[51]

It is true that the different constitutional context of Hong Kong is recognized in some rules. Unlike the Mainland courts, Hong Kong courts have been given some constitutional jurisdiction by Article 158 and implicitly by Article 8, which maintain the system of the common law. Article 159 prescribes the method and scope of the amendment of the Basic Law and rules out amendments that are inconsistent with China's basic policies regarding Hong Kong as stipulated in the Joint Declaration, suggesting that amendments cannot be made through interpretations. Finally, a committee, the Committee for the Basic Law, composed of an equal number of Mainland and Hong Kong members is established under the NPCSC, which the NPCSC has to consult before making an interpretation.[52] As I will show, these modifications have had little impact on the behavior of the Mainland authorities.

Interpretations by the NPCSC

The Standing Committee has made five interpretations of the Basic Law or law relating to the Basic Law. The first was before the Basic Law came into force; it was made under its authority in the Chinese constitution and involved the interpretation of the Chinese Nationality Law in its application to Hong Kong. The second was made at the commencement of the Basic Law to determine the validity of previous laws under Article 160. The remaining three were made under Article 158(1). There was also a "proxy" interpretation made by the Court of Final Appeal in February 1999, at the behest of the HKSAR government but effectively on the instruction of Beijing. The interpretations of the NPCSC, and indeed the very choice of issues on which interpretations were made, were driven by political motives. Unfortunately, because of a lack of space, I cannot consider them in detail.

Chinese Nationality Law

The interpretation of the Chinese nationality legislation (applicable in Hong Kong by virtue of Annex III) extended the right to those not entitled to it, on a natural meaning of Article 24. Many Hong Kong Chinese, unsure of their future on the resumption of Chinese sovereignty, left the territory before July 1, 1997, to settle abroad (primarily in the United Kingdom, Canada, the United States, and Australia). Many took the nationality of these countries and established their homes there. Many of them subsequently changed their minds and wanted to return to Hong Kong. But they wanted to return with the right of abode, so they could enjoy the full rights of citizenship, including holding public office. However, under the Basic Law, they could not resume the right of abode, as they could not bring themselves under any of the categories in Article 24—the two most favorable to them being categories in subsections (1) and (2), Chinese citizens born in Hong Kong or Chinese citizens who have ordinarily resided in Hong Kong for a continuous period for seven years. Because the returnees had lost Chinese citizenship on acquiring foreign citizenship and settling abroad, they had ceased to be Chinese citizens (under Article 9 of the Chinese Nationality Law).

Unlike the children stranded in the Mainland, most returnees were persons of wealth and influence whom China was anxious to cultivate. The Preliminary Working Committee (many of whose members held foreign passports) recommended (without any legal basis) that if a returnee returned before July 1, 1997, he or she would be treated as having the right of abode—a view accepted by the Hong Kong and Macau Affairs Office in Beijing. However, the Preparatory Committee broadened the recommendation and removed the July 1, 1997, deadline (without, it would seem, any serious analysis of the Basic Law). It proposed that if a migrant or indeed an ethnic Chinese resident in Hong Kong with a foreign passport did not declare his or her foreign nationality to the Immigration Department in Hong Kong (and if they did not use the foreign passport for entry to and exit from the HKSAR or any other part of the PRC), they would be regarded as Chinese nationals and would retain their right of abode. But the corollary is that they would have to give up their right to foreign consular protection—something China had been particularly eager to ensure. The NPCSC adopted an interpretation of the Nationality Law to give effect to this recommendation on May 15, 1996 ("Interpretation on Several Questions Relating to the Implementation of the Nationality Act of the PRC in the Hong Kong Special Administrative Region"). However, the same generous treatment was not given to those Hong Kong Chinese who were granted British citizenship under special British legislation in the wake of Tiananmen Square.[53]

Decision on Previous Laws

On February 23, 1997, the NPCSC adopted a decision under Article 160 on existing laws that would not be adopted as the law of the HKSAR because they were inconsistent with the Basic Law.[54] As with the previous interpretations, the NPCSC followed the recommendations of the Preparatory Committee and paid little regard to the provisions of the Basic Law. A considerable number of laws were made in the final years of British rule, in part to introduce political and legal reforms. These were initiated by Governor Chris Patten, against the wishes of the Chinese authorities, who used the opportunity provided by Article 160 to curb or repeal the most important of these. The Chinese had intended to repeal the Bill of Rights, which was passed in 1991 (but were dissuaded from doing so, including by this author). However, four sections were repealed, dealing with the status of the Bill of Rights, guidelines on its interpretation, and its relationship with other ordinances. In the end none of them had any serious negative effect, for with the repeal, the gap was filled by common-law principles, which also suggests that those who recommended the repeal did not really understand the common law. But what is obvious is the intense dislike by the Chinese authorities of the Bill of Rights, despite that both the Joint Declaration and the Basic Law require a strong protection of human rights and their attempts to downgrade it.

The reforms in the rights of association, assembly, and demonstrations were also removed, creating gaps and confusion in the law but paving the path for the Provisional Legislative Council, firmly under Beijing's control, to introduce restrictive legislation. Also repealed was the entire corpus of legislation on elections, doing away with the Patten reforms toward universal franchise and again clearing the path for the Provisional Legislative Council to reintroduce discredited elements of the colonial system (which continue to plague Hong Kong politics to this day).

In making these decisions, the NPCSC clearly exceeded its jurisdiction, which was confined to removing laws that were inconsistent with the Basic Law. It removed several recent laws that were more consistent with the Basic Law than the older colonial laws. Beijing undid all that, showing its preference for restrictive colonial laws over the reforms that carried forward the Basic Law provisions. Also, by modifying or adding to laws, the NPCSC went beyond declaring laws invalid and thus usurped the responsibility of the HKSAR legislature. In no case did the NPCSC give any reasons or justifications for the decisions.

The Right of Abode

The first interpretation by the NPCSC after the coming into force of the Basic Law concerned the right of abode. The interpretation was made at the request of the chief executive. The request was made following a decision of the Court of Final Appeal on the right of abode (i.e., to the status of a permanent resident of Hong Kong) of children on the Mainland born to a person with the right of abode in Hong Kong. A Hong Kong law, passed by the Provisional Legislative Council,[55] restricted the right of abode of a child in the Mainland born to a parent who had the right of abode in Hong Kong, by making that child subject to the Mainland procedures (and approval) for entry into Hong Kong. It also specified that to be entitled to the right of abode by virtue of a parent's right of abode, the child had to be born during the period when the parent had a right of abode. The CFA held that the right of a child born to parents with the right of abode was not subject to Mainland law on entry into Hong Kong. It also held that a child had the right of abode even if the child was born before the parent acquired the right of abode.

The HKSAR government did not like the ruling as it feared that a large number of children in the Mainland, at least 1.7 million, would seek to enter and settle in Hong Kong and create acute social problems.[56] So it requested the State Council to interpret the Basic Law, which amounted to an appeal to the NPCSC against the decision of the CFA.[57] It rejected the possibility of seeking an amendment of the Basic Law because it would take too long; as the NPC meets once a year for a short period, and a preliminary process under Article 159 would have to be followed. In justifying a reinterpretation of the Basic Law, it was at pains to state that an interpretation was not an amendment[58] (as it was customarily understood on the Mainland, and as indeed was the case with the interpretation of the Nationality Law in May 1996). From the rather torturous reasoning of the government, it was obvious that an interpretation was seen as a way out of what it regarded as a difficult situation, quite regardless of the legal niceties. The whole tone of its statements implied that the interpretation would deliver what the government sought.

Beijing duly obliged. The NPCSC stated that the Mainland laws regulating the entry of a Mainland person to Hong Kong applied to children entitled to a right of abode under the Basic Law. It also held that the legislative intent was to extend the right of abode to a child only if at the time of the child's birth a parent had acquired the right of abode. In fact, this question was not resolved in this way until August 10, 1996, by the NPC following a recommendation of a preparatory committee—six years after the enactment of the Basic Law! It also chastised the CFA for not having referred the first matter to the NPCSC for a ruling before its decision, in accordance with Article 158, as it concerned the relationship between Hong Kong and the Central People's Government.

Beijing was also upset at the CFA decision for implying that Mainland laws inconsistent with the Basic Law would not be enforceable in Hong Kong. Four eminent Mainland scholars, advisers to the Mainland authorities and associated with the drafting of the Basic Law (generally referred to in Hong Kong as "Guardians" of the Basic Law) mounted a spirited attack on the CFA.[59] They asserted that Hong Kong courts had no authority to declare invalid the acts of the NPC or its Standing Committee, the highest organs of state power. Indeed, it had no constitutional jurisdiction. In typical fashion, others joined in the attack and the Hong Kong government was pressured by Beijing to seek a "clarification" from the CFA of its judgment (widely interpreted as a move to humiliate the CFA[60] and perhaps as a warning to rein in the CFA). In an unusual proceeding, the CFA clarified that part of its judgment, which related to the NPC and the NPCSC. Although much subdued, and with the help of some ambiguity, the CFA held its position, and certainly its statement would not have satisfied the Guardians. It said that it could not question the interpretations of the Standing Committee and had to follow them. It went on to state, "Nor did the Court's judgment question, and the Court accepts that it cannot question, the authority of the National People's Court or the Standing Committee to do any act which is in accordance with the provisions of the Basic Law and the procedure therein." However, much was made later of this acknowledgment when the request to the NPCSC was made for the interpretation of the provisions relating to the right of abode.

Interpretations on Constitutional Reform

One of the most contentious issues during the drafting of the Basic Law was the political system, with considerable support for universal franchise and one person one vote. This would have ended the system of functional and appointed members of the legislature and an executive elected by the people. This view was resisted by Beijing and many Hong Kong delegates who feared a democratic system in which their own privileged position would be undermined. A compromise of sorts was reached, under which the Basic Law guarantees as the "ultimate aim the selection of the Chief Executive by universal franchise" although on the nomination of a committee (Article 45[2]). A similar promise for the election of all members of the Legislative Council is included (Article 68[2]). However, in both cases the "ultimate aim" is subject to the "principle of gradual and orderly progress."

Annex I set out the method for the election of the chief executive and Annex II for the Legislative Council until 2007. After that if "there is need to amend," the methods for either of them, the amendments must be made with "the endorsement of a two-thirds majority of all the members of the Legislative Council and the consent of the Chief Executive" (para. 7 of Annex I and section III of Annex II, respectively). However, in the case of amendment to the election of the chief executive, the approval of the NPC is necessary but not in the case of the Legislative Council.

As the 2007 elections for the chief executive and the 2008 elections for the Legislative Council came closer, there were renewed calls for universal suffrage or at least significant progress toward it (as well as resistance to any change). But brakes on the movement for reform were swiftly applied by Beijing in collaboration with the Hong Kong administration. During Chief Executive Tung Chee-hwa's "duty" visit to Beijing in December 2003, Chinese President Hu Jintao informed him of "the serious concerns and principled position of the Central Authorities regarding Hong Kong's constitutional development"[61] (presumably in reaction to Hong Kong demands for democracy).

On January 7, 2004, the chief executive set up a Task Force on Constitutional Development consisting of the chief secretary, the secretary for justice, and the secretary for constitutional affairs. Its tasks were to "examine in depth the relevant issues of principle and legislative process in the Basic Law relating to constitutional development, to consult the relevant departments of the Central Authorities, and to gather the views of the public on the relevant issues." The first report of the task force was issued in March 2004, which contained its analysis of the relevant provisions of the Basic Law and views of the public. Its second report issued a month later contained the recommendations on the criteria for constitutional progress.

The ground for the NPCSC's insertion in the decision-making process on future developments was laid in its interpretation on April 6, 2004. It clarified that reforms could commence in 2007 (and thus settled the controversy whether reforms had to wait until after the 2007 elections). Second, it ruled that there was no inevitability about reforms in 2007, as the formula that "if there is need" assumes that there may in fact be no need. Third, it set out the procedure for initiation of the reform process. The chief executive was to make a report to the NPCSC whether there is need for amendments to the electoral processes. Based on the report, the NPCSC would make a determination "in the light of the actual situation in Hong Kong and in accordance with the principle of gradual and orderly progress."

The NPCSC also ruled that it is up to the chief executive to introduce legislative bills for amendments into the Legislative Council, and pending amendments, the existing system would continue.

The chief executive made his report on April 15, 2004. He reiterated the recommendations of the task force, which he described as government policy. The recommendations, though based on the conclusion that amendments should be made, were extremely restrictive and conservative. They included giving complete veto to the Central Authorities, confining Hong Kong initiatives to the chief executive, undiminished Chinese control over appointment and powers of the chief executive, and much more, such as that any proposed amendments must not bring about any adverse effect to the systems of economy, monetary affairs, public finance, and others as prescribed in the Basic Law.[62] The proposals would not have represented any significant progress toward full electoral democracy. On April 26, the NPCSC made its determination. This was not strictly speaking an interpretation but a "decision" made, as the NPCSC stated, after wide consultations including with the Committee for the Basic Law, under the framework set out in the previous interpretation. Nevertheless, its effect is that of an "interpretation" for it purports to establish the framework for determining when and to what extent reforms would be allowed.

The NPCSC adopts the general, conservative principles in the chief executive's report. The NPCSC rules out universal suffrage unless there is consensus on it (which gives a veto to the conservative elements or other protégés of Beijing) and ruled out any significant changes.

On the basis of this decision, the task force produced its third report in May 2004, which set out the amendments that could be made within the parameters established by the NPCSC and seeking public comments or endorsement of them. The possible amendments seemed of little consequence. Its fourth report recorded the views of the public (based on 480 submissions), which predictably showed no consensus, even on the rather unimportant options that were offered to the people. Its fifth and final report was published in October 2005 in which the task force offered its own recommendations and proposed a timetable for implementation, with the introduction of the necessary bills by the government by early 2006. Its recommendations were very conservative (with the exception of a larger role for District Councillors both in the Election Committee and in the Legislative Council, devoting all new functional constituencies to them). It was the general view of commentators that they represented no significant advance toward democracy. In these circumstances, it is not surprising that its proposals failed to win sufficient support in the Legislative Council. It marked, at least for the time being, the end of the movement for constitutional reform.

Although Annexes I and II appeared to give the initiative to the people of Hong Kong for constitutional reforms within the terms of Articles 45 and 68 (and in the latter case, not giving a veto to the NPCSC), as a result of its own interpretation, the NPCSC placed itself in the driving seat (despite a conflict of interests). As between Hong Kong institutions, it gives the preeminent role to the chief executive in a way that is not obvious from the Basic Law. There is also considerable evidence of collusion between Beijing and the Hong Kong administration; the latter seems unable or unwilling to take a position independently of Beijing—underscoring the point that Hong Kong institutions enjoy little autonomy. The introduction of the criteria for democratization by the NPCSC significantly changes the framework for progress on democratization. This is a serious derogation from the provisions and promises in the Basic Law. The interpretation has given Beijing a key role in the reform process that the specific provisions of the Basic Law do not. The process was intended to start in Hong Kong, and as regards the elections for the Legislative Council, the NPCSC was given no role other than to be informed that an amendment had been made. Under the interpretation, the NPCSC can prevent even the initiation of the process. Thus, the NPCSC's power of interpretation has turned out to be crucial, a huge reservoir for self-interested and arbitrary decisions to further Beijing's agenda in contravention of "Hong Kong people ruling Hong Kong."

Interpretation on the Term of the Office of the Chief Executive

In April 2005, the NPCSC, on the request of the Chinese government, made an interpretation of Article 53(2) on the length of the term of a chief executive who assumes office before the full term of his or her predecessor has been completed. The issue arose when Chief Executive Tung Chee-hwa resigned on the grounds of "ill health," although it was widely believed that he was forced out by Beijing as he had proved to be inefficient and misread the public mood—and had become a liability to Beijing.

For once Hong Kong opinion, among lawyers and politicians, whether "anti-" or "pro-" China, was that his successor would have a term of five years as stipulated in Article 53. However, in the face of this unanimity, the NPCSC ruled that the new chief executive would hold office for the remainder of the term of the predecessor. It based this decision on the grounds that Annex I assumes that the method of election could be altered in 2007, which would not be possible if the new chief executive had five years. This is an example of the tail wagging the dog. In addition, it flies in the face of the decision Beijing took in 1997 to disregard the Basic Laws provisions on the formation of the first legislature when it was dissatisfied with the Patten political reforms.[63] An uncharitable interpretation of Beijing's position was that it wanted to keep Tung's anointed successor, Donald Tsang, on a short leash—he had to prove his loyalty before he enjoyed a full term.

Conclusion

My purpose in this chapter has been to demonstrate that choices about legal forms, in this instance the mode of interpretation, are based on considerations of political advantage. It is not to comment on all aspects of the scheme for the interpretation of the Basic Law, such as the difficulties of integrating Hong Kong and Chinese laws insofar as necessary for the operation of the Basic Law or to maintain Hong Kong's autonomy. I hope I have demonstrated that the issue of interpretation in Hong Kong is not whether it is to be governed by common-law or civil-law principles. China's political system is not governed by civil law. The care with which Beijing ensured that the NPCSC would have the final say was motivated by more than the concern for a true interpretation of the Basic Law.

The NPCSC is primarily a political body under the direct control of the Communist Party and ensures that its policies are implemented. It is not its function to maintain the rule of law. It has no juridical techniques geared toward principled interpretation. Its proceedings are not open to the public and the process of reaching a decision is confined to a small number of officials.

Interpretations of the Basic Law have violated its framework. The Committee on the Basic Law has been co-opted and subordinated to the Central Authorities, most of its members, from the Mainland as well as Hong Kong, acting as the chorus for Beijing, and taking positions on interpretation well before the NPCSC formally takes jurisdiction. Its procedures are secretive, and it has lost all confidence among the people of Hong Kong. The provisions for the amendment of the Basic Law have been rendered nugatory by NPCSC's interpretation on democratization, which has assumed absolute power under the guise of interpretation. Through the exercise of the power of interpretation, Beijing has changed fundamentally the framework and contours of the Basic Law, eliminating the autonomy of Hong Kong when and where that autonomy matters.

Notes

1. *Marbury v. Madison*, 5 US 137 (1803).
2. Alexander Hamilton, "Federalist Paper No. 78." The references are to its reprint in Alexander Hamilton, James Madison, and John Jay, *The Federalist Papers* (New York: New American Library, 1961).
3. Ibid., 466.
4. Ibid., 467.
5. Ibid., 466.
6. Ibid., 469.
7. XI, January 31, 1788, reprinted in Ralph Ketcham, ed., *The Anti-Federalist Papers and the Constitutional Convention Debates* (New York: Penguin Putnam, 1986; repr. 2003), 293–98.
8. Ibid.
9. XV March 20, 1788, ibid., 304–9.
10. *Marbury v. Madison*, 163.

11. Michael P. Fitzsimmons, *The Remaking of France: The National Assembly and the Constitution of 1791* (Cambridge: Cambridge University Press, 1994).
12. Ibid., 100.
13. Eric Thompson, *Popular Sovereignty and the French Constituent Assembly 1789–91* (Manchester: Manchester University Press, 1952), 86.
14. Ibid.
15. Ibid., 86.
16. The National Assembly did however accept that it was improper for the judges to be involved in matters of administration because their proper function was to adjudicate on relations between citizens (the origin of the French rule under which legal issues about the administration and its relations with citizens were determined by special courts as part of the administration).
17. *Leftist* is a relative term; after all, the French Revolution was a bourgeois revolution. The true test of the commitment of the left to people's sovereignty came when the National Assembly debated whether to prescribe jury trials; the left rejected the proposal that juries might decide on evidence in civil cases, fearing that a popularly elected jury would not be up to the complexities of civil litigation. As Thompson says, there was a "foreboding that in the interests of business and professional classes, it would be undesirable to hand over too much power to the masses as far as civil jurisdiction was concerned"; ibid., 95.
18. Ibid., 94.
19. Ibid., 95.
20. Ibid.
21. Ibid., 96.
22. Ibid.
23. Ibid.
24. Ibid., 97.
25. Jeremy Rabkin, "Revolutionary Visions in Legal Imagery: Constitutional Contrasts between France and America," in *The Legacy of the French Revolution*, ed. Ralph E. Hancock and Gary L. Lambert (Lanham, MD: Rowman and Littlefield, 1996), 224–25.
26. Jean Egret, "Was the 'Aristocratic Revolt' Aristocratic?" reprinted in *The French Revolution: Conflicting Interpretations*, ed. Frank A. Kafker and James M. Laux, 4th ed. (Malabar, FL: Robert E. Krieger, 1989). Both quotations appear on page 39.
27. Rabkin, "Revolutionary Visions in Legal Imagery," 225.
28. Very similar conclusions are reached by Rabkin, who says that "the revolutionaries in America had many reasons to be legal conservatives"; ibid.
29. See Timothy Tackett, *Becoming a Revolutionary: The Deputies of the French National Assembly and the Emergence of a Revolutionary Culture (1789–90)* (Princeton, NJ: Princeton University, 1994), for a wonderfully vivid account of the role of crowds and mobs in the operations of the National Assembly.
30. Ibid., 287. Jacobins were among the most radical of assembly factions, led by Robespierre who was to play a key role in the violence that erupted after the assembly. Tackett says that of the top eleven among the Jacobins, only two were not trained in the law. Forty-seven of the Jacobins were lawyers, thirty-three were magistrates, eighteen were other kinds officeholders, three were law professors, and six held other miscellaneous professions probably entailing a law degree: a total of 107 of 185 (58 percent).
31. Carl Baudenbacher, "Some Remarks on the Method of Civil Law," *Texas International Law Journal* 34 (1999): 345–46, footnotes omitted. On page 337 he writes, "The codes of Austria, France, Italy, and Spain even contain rules providing guidance to judges on how

to proceed in the case of a gap. The Swiss Code expressly grants judges the authority to develop judge-made law in certain circumstances."

32. Rene David, *Sources of the Law*, Vol. 2 of *The Legal System of the World and Their Comparison and Unification, World Encyclopedia of Comparative Law* (The Hague: Martinus Nijhoff, 1984), ch. 3.
33. Ibid., 39. Its approach is illustrated by a decision in 1988, whose spirit is captured by Favoreu as follows, "[If] the law does not conform to the Constitution, it is not the expression of the general will. A majority of elected deputies cannot defeat what has been established in favor of a much larger consensus. The will of the majority equals the general will only if it follows the path marked by the Constitution. And it is no longer a question of leaving to Parliament itself the responsibility for limiting itself and respecting the Constitution; the *Conseil Constitutionnel* is responsible for the control of constitutionality, the purpose of which is to assure conformity of the exercise of legislative power to the Constitution" (a statement reminiscent of Chief Justice Marshall in *Marbury*). Louis Favoreu, "Constitutional Review in Europe," in *Constitutionalism and Rights: The Influence of the United States Constitutional Abroad*, ed. Louis Henkin Albert J. Rosenthal (New York: Columbia University Press, 1990), 305–6.
34. David, *Sources of the Law*, 40–41.
35. Growth of constitutional courts resulted partly because in civil-law jurisdictions when judges were given review powers (Weimar Republic and Italy 1848–1956), they were reluctant to exercise it due to earlier traditions of nonjusticiability. See ibid., 43–45.
36. See, for example, Schwartz, Herman, *Struggle for Constitutional Justice in Post Conflict Europe* (Chicago: University of Chicago Press, 2000).
37. David quotes a Polish scholar, Rozmaryn, to the effect that "one cannot extend to the level of constitutional law those categories which suit the level of private law"; *Sources of the Law*, 46. In both South Africa and Sri Lanka, although regarded formally as part of the Roman-Dutch legal system, their public law is derived largely from the common law.
38. As Baudenbacher says, "The French prohibition on interpreting the written law, coupled with an obligation to call in the parliament in cases of doubt that was based on a rigid understanding of the separation of powers, was abandoned as early as the nineteenth century"; see "Some Remarks on the Method of Civil Law," 303.
39. This is not to deny that noncommunist systems may not also have preferred legislative interpretation because of the wish for the centralization of state power. Lin et al. say that while legislative interpretation "originates from a long and well-established tradition of the civil law system," it "reflects not only the jurisprudential theory of a legislature creating the 'will of the state,' but it is also inseparable from the need to understand the role that state centralism plays as part of a particular era." See Laifan Lin et al., "An Analysis of the Legislative Interpretation System in the PRC," *Hong Kong Lawyer* (August 1999): 56-61, which can be found at http://www.hk-lawyer.com/1999-8/Default.htm. (Visited on 27 August 2007).
40. Otto Bihari, *Socialist Representative Institutions* (Budapest: Akademiai Kiado, 1970), 175. He notes that both Yugoslavia and Czechoslovakia had initiated constitutional courts but attributes this to their federal character. Woodman makes a similar point about the fusion of power in Chapter 11 of this volume. Eyula Eorsi, one of the most distinguished legal scholars of communist legal systems, an outstanding comparativist and rector of Budapest University used to tell me that the techniques of law are determined by tradition, but its values are determined by ideology. Socialist law, arising first in continental Europe, adopted the technique of civil law to achieve the values and goals of communism.
41. Ibid., 176.

42. Ibid.
43. Elsie Leung, then secretary of justice in Hong Kong, tried to make this distinction in 1999 in her speech to the LegCo (Legislative Council)—but it was also clear that it was up to the legislature to decide whether the text was unclear and so required interpretation or it was clear but required amendment.
44. See Chapter 11 in this volume.
45. Article 3(3) and Part III of the Annex.
46. The account here relies principally on Martin Lee, "A Tale of Two Articles," in *The Basic Law and Hong Kong's Future*, ed. Peter Wesley-Smith and Albert Chen (Butterworths: Hong Kong, 1998).
47. This is a strange claim since the science of interpretation is little developed where as the common law as practiced in Hong Kong has a well-developed corpus of principles and doctrines of interpretation.
48. Lee, "A Tale of Two Articles," 318–19.
49. It has been suggested that these broad powers of interpretation were acquired to ensure the flexibility of law. Dr. Kong Xiaohong says that this attitude comes both from the realization that, with rapid economic and social changes, the laws have to be flexible, as well as from the low priority given to law, its essential purpose being seen as serving the Communist Party's political objectives—suggesting a highly instrumental view of law. She writes, "Such an attitude proves that, contrary to the legislators in the West, Chinese legislators do not intend to treat the exercise of the interpretation power as a very sensitive matter"; page 498 in her article, "Legal Interpretation in China," *Connecticut Journal of International Law* 6 (1991): 491.
50. It can be argued that this broader view of the scope of interpretation is incompatible with the Basic Law, given Article 159 of the Basic Law (restricting the power of the NPC to amend the Basic Law).
51. Lee, "A Tale of Two Articles," 324.
52. The committee has also to be consulted when the NPCSC declares a Hong Kong law invalid, a Mainland law (except an emergency law) is extended to Hong Kong, and an amendment to the Basic Law is introduced. Its precise consultative role has not been defined. It is possible that at first a larger role for it was intended, as it was said to be based on the Nordic autonomous model; see Yash Ghai, "Resolution of Disputes between the Central and Regional Governments: Models in Autonomous Regions" *Journal of Chinese and Comparative Law* 5 (2001): 1–20. Albert Chen, an original member of the committee, thinks that it was "intended to be a mediating and arbitral organ for resolving differences of opinion between the central authority and the SAR." He also proposed vesting the Basic Law Committee with the authority to mediate in conflicts between the State Council and SAR after the SAR has made a complaint to the NPCSC; see Albert Chen, "The Relationship between the Central Government and the SAR," in *The Basic Law and Hong Kong's Future*, 138–39.
53. This paragraph is based on a lengthy discussion in Yash Ghai, *Hong Kong's New Constitutional Order: The resumption of Chinese Sovereignty and the Basic Law*, 2nd ed. (Hong Kong: Hong Kong University Press, 1999), 167–72.
54. For a detailed commentary on the decision, see the first edition of Yash Ghai, *Hong Kong's New Constitutional Order* (Hong Kong: Hong Kong University Press, 1997), 492–98.
55. The Provisional Legislative Council was set up by Beijing when it repealed the last Legislative Council before the transfer of sovereignty, in apparent disregard of the Basic Law (ibid., 63–64, 78).

56. A detailed account of the events leading to the interpretation is to be found in J. M. M. Chan, H. L. Fu, and Yash Ghai, eds., *Hong Kong's Constitutional Debate: Conflict Over Interpretation* (Hong Kong: Hong Kong University Press, 2000).
57. Neither the Basic Law nor other Mainland laws gives the chief executive of the HKSAR the right to refer a matter to the NPCSC for interpretation. The provisions of the Basic Law, which were invoked by the chief executive to refer the matter to Beijing and seek its assistance, did not really bear the interpretation placed on them by him.
58. In a paper tabled at the Legislative Council House Committee (May 18, 1999), entitled "Right of Abode: The Solution" (reprinted in Chan, Fu, and Ghai, *Hong Kong's Constitutional Debate*, 310–19).
59. Their views are reprinted in ibid., 53–59.
60. Johannes Chan, "What the Court of Final Appeal Has Not Clarified in Its Clarification: Jurisdiction and Amicus Intervention," in ibid., 180–81.
61. "Chief Executive's Report on Constitutional Development to the State Council" (April 15, 2004), 2.
62. For the recommendations of the chief executive, see his April 15, 2004, report, ibid., and for a detailed analysis, see the "Second Report of the Constitutional Development Task Force: Issue of Principle in the Basic Law relating to Constitutional Development" (April 2004).
63. On which see Ghai, *Hong Kong's New Constitutional Order*, 63, 78.

CHAPTER 7

One Term, Two Interpretations

The Justifications and the Future of Basic Law Interpretation

Lin Feng and P. Y. Lo

Introduction

Following the resignation of the first chief executive (CE) of the Hong Kong Special Administrative Region (HKSAR) in the middle of his second term, a controversy arose over whether his successor would serve the remainder of the outgoing CE's second term or a new term of five years. A judicial review application was filed with the Court of First Instance (CFI), seeking a declaration that "the true effect of Article 46 of the Basic Law is that the term of office of the CE shall be five years, whether or not the vacancy in the office of the CE arises otherwise than by reason of expiry of term of office."[1] Before the court could make a decision on the application, the question was resolved by an interpretation issued by the Standing Committee of the National People's Congress (NPCSC), which states that "prior to the year 2007, when the CE is selected by the Election Committee with a five-year term of office, in the event that the office of CE becomes vacant as he fails to serve the full term of office of five years as prescribed by Article 46 of the Basic Law, the term of office of the new CE shall be the remainder of the previous CE."[2]

This chapter will first briefly set out the background of the controversy over the term of the CE and will analyze the justifications on each side of the legal debate. The analysis will show that a sharp contrast exists between scholars trained in the common law and those trained in Mainland Chinese law. We examine the factors that have caused such differences in interpretation and argue that differences in the method of constitutional interpretation may not be the key factor underlying the debate. The determining factor seems to be the different legal and constitutional contexts in which a provision is interpreted.

The Background to the Controversy

On March 10, 2005, the Central People's Government (CPG) of the People's Republic of China (PRC) accepted the resignation of the Hon Tung Chee-hwa, the first CE of the HKSAR. Pursuant to Article 53 of the Basic Law,[3] a new CE had to be elected within six months.[4] Otherwise, the HKSAR would face the constitutional crisis of having no CE. Before the election of the new CE on July 10, 2005, one highly controversial and contentious issue was whether the term of the new CE should be a full term of five years or the unserved remainder of Tung's term, that is, two years. The controversy lay in the diametrically opposed answers given by Hong Kong lawyers trained in the common law and Mainland Chinese legal academics rooted in the civil law system as practiced in the PRC. Furthermore, the HKSAR government abandoned its original common-law–based views and preferred the views of the Mainland scholars.

Several Mainland legal scholars who were perceived as official guardians of the Basic Law publicly expressed their views that the term of office of the new CE should be the remainder of his predecessor's term and that it was unnecessary and undesirable to seek another interpretation of the Basic Law from the NPCSC. The Legislative Affairs Commission (LAC) of the NPCSC issued a detailed statement that reached the same conclusion. The CPG's intention was clear: if possible, it wanted to avoid another interpretation. By early April 2005, however, two applications for leave to apply for judicial review had already been filed with the CFI,[5] raising for the CFI's consideration the legal issues concerning the term of the new CE.[6] The HKSAR government was concerned that the pending legal proceedings might not be concluded in time to enable a timely election for the new CE on July 10, 2005.[7] The government therefore decided on April 6, 2005, to resolve the controversy by submitting a report to the CPG, asking for an NPCSC interpretation of Article 53. The NPCSC on April 27, 2005, issued its third interpretation of the Basic Law, putting an end to the debate over the term of the new CE.

The question of the length of the term of office of the new CE depended on the proper interpretation of Articles 45, 46, and 53 and Annex I of the Basic Law. Article 46 of the Basic Law provides that "the term of office of the CE of the HKSAR shall be five years. He or she may serve for not more than two consecutive terms." Those people who favored a term of five years for the new CE primarily relied on the clear wording in Article 46. However, those commentators favoring the remainder of the term of the former CE argued that other provisions in the Basic Law, especially Articles 45 and 53 and Annex I, were also relevant. Qiao Xiaoyang, the deputy secretary-general of the NPCSC, said that it was really about whether Article 46 or Article 53 applied.

In addition to the six months time limit, Article 53 provides that the selection of the CE is to be in accordance with the provisions of Article 45 of the Basic Law.[8] Article 45 sets out two requirements for the method of selecting the CE: (1) The method is to be specified in light of the actual situation in the HKSAR, (2) the method must follow the principle of gradual and orderly progress.[9] Article 45 also states clearly that the ultimate goal is to select the CE by universal suffrage upon nomination by a broadly representative nominating committee in accordance with democratic procedures.[10] The specific method for selecting the CE is laid down in Annex I of the Basic Law. In addition to setting out the composition of the Election Committee and its term of office (five years), Annex I also states in paragraph 7 that "if there is a need to amend the method for selecting the CE for the terms subsequent to the year 2007, such amendments must be made with the endorsement of a two-thirds majority of all the members of the Legislative Council and the consent of the CE, and they shall be reported to the Standing Committee of the National People's Congress for approval."

Although the NPCSC interpretation resolved the debate at hand, how those provisions of the Basic Law should be interpreted and what lessons could be learned from the third interpretation are issues worthy of further academic debate and analysis. The next part of this chapter will examine the justifications both for and against the view that the term of office of the new CE should be the remainder of his predecessor's term.

Analysis of the Justifications

The advocates of the view that the term of the new CE should be the remainder of the term unserved by the former CE were mostly those trained in Mainland Chinese law. The HKSAR government, on March 12, 2005, changed its position and agreed to the view held by Mainland scholars. The secretary for justice at the time, the Hon Elsie Leung, stated that she had changed her view after taking into account: (1) the views of Mainland scholars; (2) the constitutional practice in the Mainland; (3) the original intent underlying the design of the CE election system, including the arrangements for the Election Committee; (4) the drafting history of Article 53; (5) the context of the Basic Law, including other Articles and Annex I; and (6) a later decision made by the NPCSC on April 26, 2004, on interpreting the provisions of the Basic Law on the election of the CE in 2007 and formation of the Legislative Council in 2008.[11] The position taken by the HKSAR government was endorsed by the LAC of the NPCSC in its statement issued on the same day, though the LAC's reasoning was more profound than that of the secretary for justice.[12] The reasons relied on by the secretary for justice were challenged and rejected by several commentators in the HKSAR.[13]

A detailed examination of all the arguments made in support of the view that the term of the new CE should be the remainder of the term of his predecessor will show that there were two categories of reasons. The first was political. Several scholars from the HKSAR held the view that political expediency was the primary factor that influenced the decision of the CPG to go ahead with the interpretation of Article 53 of the Basic Law.[14] Undeniably, the crucial factor prompting the HKSAR government to seek an interpretation and the NPCSC to agree to do so was the political concern that the new CE be selected by July 10, 2005. Qiao openly admitted this on one occasion and said that a new CE must be selected on July 10, 2005, and any other factors had to give way to this primary consideration.[15]

Political considerations certainly influenced the interpretation, but legal justifications also existed for the NPCSC to interpret the Basic Law for the third time. The NPCSC articulated its approach to statutory interpretation, "original legislative intent," when it first interpreted the Basic Law in 1999 and applied the approach in its second and third interpretations. Also, Qiao referred to the method in his speech, and the spokesman of the LAC alluded to it in its statement issued on March 12, 2005.[16]

The approach alone is not enough. Specific rules are needed to find out the "original legislative intent" of the Basic Law. Although Mainland Chinese scholars are generally of the view that the literal meaning of a specific provision, its context and drafting history, as well as the Mainland political and legal systems should be taken into account, no well-established, articulated, and widely accepted rules exist which can be applied to discover the original legislative intent of any national legislation in the Mainland.

The Legislation Law ("*Li Fa Fa*") specifies two circumstances in which the NPCSC can interpret a national law, one of which is that the exact meaning of a statutory provision needs to be further clarified.[17] The Legislation Law, however, does not supply the means to determine whether the meaning of a particular statutory provision is clear and to make the choice between looking at the literal meaning of a statutory provision alone or also taking into account the context of a statutory provision.

Contextual Approach

The NPCSC alluded to two methodologies for identifying the original legislative intent of a provision of the Basic Law in its third interpretation: a contextual approach and the use of *travaux préparatoires*. The LAC's statement of March 12, 2005, foreshadowed the application of those two methodologies. The contextual argument was that the meaning of Article 46 should be interpreted "in the context of" other provisions of the Basic Law, especially Article 53 and Annex I. Qiao expressed the view that it was an issue of whether Article 46 or Article 53 applied.[18] Professor Lian Xisheng, one of the two legal scholars whose views was sought and relied on by the secretary for justice, noted in his opinion that a contextual approach should be adopted to "further define the meaning of a provision that seems to be clear on its face" and to fill a gap in that provision (presumably referring to Article 53).[19] This comment suggested that whether or not the exact meaning of a provision in the Basic Law was clear also depended on the "context" of that provision.

The contextual approach is also used widely in common-law jurisdictions, including the HKSAR. In the case of *Director of Immigration v. Chong Fung Yuen*, the Court of Final Appeal (CFA) states that a provision of the Basic Law should be "considered in the light of its context and purpose . . . The exercise of interpretation requires [the identification of] the meaning borne by the language when considered in the light of its context and purpose. This is an objective exercise."[20] The Bar Association in its statement dated March 10, 2005, also used the contextual approach and concluded that the context did not support "the contention that the new CE selected in accordance with Article 45 of the Basic Law of the HKSAR as a result of the office becoming vacant serves not a term of office of five years as specified in Article 46, but the remainder of the term of his predecessor-in-office."[21]

Scholars and practitioners trained in the common law pay even more attention to the language of a statutory provision than to its context. Chief Justice Li outlined the common-law approach to interpreting the Basic Law in *Chong Fung Yuen*: "to construe the language used in the text of the instrument in order to ascertain *the legislative intent as expressed in the language* . . . It is the text of the enactment which is the law and it is regarded as important both that the law should be certain and that it should be ascertainable by the citizen." Context and purpose may throw light to the meaning of the language used in the instrument in the objective exercise. "Whilst the courts must avoid a literal, technical, narrow or rigid approach, they cannot give the language a meaning which the language cannot bear."[22] Thus, clear and unambiguous provisions should be interpreted according to their literal meaning. Only when the provisions are unclear or ambiguous will the methodologies ascribing legislative intention need to be considered.[23] In the eyes of many Hong Kong scholars and practitioners, including the Bar Association,[24] "the CE selected under Article 53 is a new CE returned under a fresh election held in accordance with the provisions of the Basic Law." The provisions of Article 46 are unambiguous, and their meaning is clear. Therefore, it is incorrect to apply any meaning to its provisions other than what is readily apparent. The HKSAR government also adhered to this approach when it introduced electoral law governing elections for the CE in 2001 and reiterated it in May 2004 in its written response to a question raised by the Legislative Council.[25]

Accordingly, despite the recognition and application of the contextual approach by scholars and practitioners trained in the common law and scholars trained in Mainland Chinese law, each group arrived at a different interpretation of Articles 46 and 53.

The Use of Travaux Préparatoires

The second methodology revealed by the NPCSC's third interpretation was the use of *travaux préparatoires* in the interpretation of some phrases in the Basic Law such as "a new CE." Professor Lian wrote that the term of the CE under Article 53 was not a substantial issue, though it was raised during the drafting process. Any proposed changes to Article 53 were not mainstream views, did not draw sufficient attention, and hence were not adopted.[26] Some Mainland Chinese scholars and also the secretary for justice relied on the change of wording in Article 53(2) of the draft Basic Law from "a CE of the new term" to "a new CE" to support the argument that the legislative intent of Article 53 was that a CE returned in a by-election was not to be a CE for a new term.[27]

One Hong Kong commentator argued that Article 46 was originally drafted to include the phrase "each term of office of the CE," which was later replaced by the present wording "the term of CE." Article 53, he argued, does not use phrases such as "by-election," "substituting"/"succeeding" CE and only emphasizes that a new CE will be selected according to the normal selection procedure as set out in Article 45. His view was, therefore, that the clear legislative intent is that the provisions and arrangements relating to by-elections of different positions of mainland governmental organs should not be applicable to the selection of the CE.[28]

The Bar Association came to the conclusion that the drafting history is "neither determinative nor conducive to the resolution of the present question of interpretation."[29] Again, no consensus could be reached by referring to the drafting history of the Basic Law.

Constitutional/Institutional Convention

Professor Lian said that to the Mainland members of the drafting committee of the Basic Law, it was obvious that in the political and legal systems of Mainland China the new CE, returned in a "by-election" by an Election Committee with a term of office, should be the successor of the original CE, and, accordingly, his term of office should be the remainder of his predecessor's term.[30] This view is supported by the opinion of the other scholar, Professor Xu Chongde, whose opinion was also relied on by the secretary for justice. Professor Xu considered that the practice in the Mainland showed that none of its political organs determined the term of office by referring to the appointment or departure of a particular individual but rather by the term of office of the respective organs as provided for in the Chinese Constitution. He suggested that the term of the CE and his election was drawn up with reference to the practice adopted in the Mainland and accordingly the term of the next CE should be the remainder of the term of his predecessor.[31] According to these scholars the Mainland Chinese drafters were of the view that Article 53 clearly meant that the term of the CE returned in a "by-election" should be the remainder of the term of the former CE.

Professor Wang Zhenmin from the School of Law of Qinghua University made a similar point from a slightly different angle, saying that the Basic Law is a national law enacted under the Chinese Constitution and is an extension of the Chinese Constitution in the HKSAR. Accordingly, it should not be detached from the Chinese Constitution and allowed to develop in a completely different way. Given that the CE is a government position established under Chinese legislation, there was, according to Professor Wang, no doubt that the same principle as adopted in the Mainland should be applied in interpreting the term of office of the CE.[32]

The secretary for justice also accepted the three scholars' views in terms of the context of the institutional framework in the Mainland.[33]

Some HKSAR commentators in favor of a new term of five years challenged the relevance of the context of the institutional framework and rules of statutory interpretation of the Mainland to the interpretation of the Basic Law. They argued that conventions under Chinese constitutional law should not be applied to the interpretation of the Basic Law because the political system in the HKSAR is different from the Chinese constitutional system.[34] Furthermore, the drafters from Hong Kong, especially those trained in common law, might also have believed that the meaning of Articles 53 and 46 was clear: the term of the CE should be five years.

When Articles 46 and 53 of the Basic Law were drafted, drafters on both sides may well have thought that the meaning of the provisions was clear, but in fact, they were thinking of different meanings.

Differences in Methodologies?

Several scholars have examined whether the statutory and constitutional interpretation rules in a common-law system differ from those in the civil-law system as practised in the Mainland. One view was that there is no difference, as the legal text under both systems is always the basis of interpretation.[35] Another view was that no systematic rules of statutory and constitutional interpretation exist in the Mainland system, and if there are any, they are a mere *ipse dixit*.[36] Alan Hoo S. C. thought that the civil-law system as practiced in the Mainland places a greater emphasis on original legislative intent.[37]

The previous discussion reveals a semblance of an "original legislative intent approach" to statutory and constitutional interpretation in the Mainland. Several methodologies associated with that approach can be identified from the interpretations already given by the NPCSC, such as literal interpretation, contextual approach, and the use of *travaux préparatoires*.[38] However, the approach is by no means systematic or well developed. The methodologies said to have been applied to find out the original legislative intent are by no means different from those used in the common-law system as practiced in the HKSAR to identify the purpose of a statutory provision, including a constitutional provision such as Article 46 or Article 53 of the Basic Law. Furthermore, the arguments in favor of the new CE serving the remainder of Tung's second term are just as convincing as the arguments in favor of a new term of five years.

Determining Factor

Although Morris argues that even by using common-law rules of statutory and constitutional interpretation, the term of office of the next CE should be the remainder of the unserved term of the second term of Tung,[39] the majority of HKSAR practitioners and scholars, especially the Bar Association and the Law Society, were of the opinion that the term of the new CE should be five years. However, most Mainland scholars were of the view that the term of office of the new CE should be the remainder of the term of his predecessor. What is the factor that caused this difference in stance?

If the argument made in the previous discussion that the interpretation methodologies are quite similar in the Mainland and the HKSAR is accepted and the political factor is excluded from our discussion, then the only possible factor seems to be the difference inherent in the two different political and legal systems. On the Mainland, the people's congress system and its constitutional or institutional practice with regard to the term of all kinds of governmental organs and their officials, led Mainland scholars to the only possible conclusion.[40] However, a person trained in common law cannot reach this conclusion without an ingrained understanding of the "system" in Mainland China.

Can the context of a legal system lead to such a great difference in the interpretation of the same statutory provision? The Privy Council tackled this issue in *Ming Pao Newspapers Ltd v. Attorney General*,[41] declining to invalidate, on the pleaded ground of protecting fundamental human rights, Hong Kong legislation enacted to restrict freedom of expression in order to combat corruption. The Privy Council observed:

> Given that local conditions of parties to the International Covenant [on Civil and Political Rights] are likely to vary far more widely than conditions in states who are contracting parties to the European Convention their Lordships consider that the situation in Hong Kong must be of considerable importance in determining the proportionality of the means adopted to achieve the aim.
>
> . . .
>
> The position is accordingly this. First, the Legislative Council has decided that notwithstanding the provisions of the Bill [of Rights Ordinance] s 30(1) is necessary to preserve the integrity of investigations into corruption. This is a policy that cannot be described as "so unreasonable as to be outside the State's margin of appreciation." . . . Secondly, the court with its knowledge of local conditions in Hong Kong has endorsed the decision. In these circumstances their Lordships could see no reason to interfere.[42]

So, the highest judicial (and under the common-law doctrine, interpretive) authority of the sovereign permitted a local court to interpret a limit on a fundamental human right in a way conceivably different from the way it would have interpreted the provision—despite both being common-law systems. The current sovereign of the HKSAR, the PRC, and the HKSAR have completely different legal systems. Different interpretations will inevitably be given to the same provision of the Basic Law by the interpreters in their respective constitutional context.

The Relevance of the Mainland's Interpretation Approach

Some commentators have argued, correctly, that the interpretation methodologies or rules as applied in the Mainland, if there are any, should not be applied in the HKSAR. The CFA has developed a mature approach toward the interpretation of the Basic Law. On the one hand, the court has acknowledged that the NPCSC has a freestanding power to interpret the Basic Law. On the other hand, it has expressly stated that the courts in Hong Kong will adopt a common-law approach to the interpretation of the Basic Law. This approach is the best way to safeguard the common-law system and tradition in the HKSAR without risking direct confrontation with the NPCSC. The Bar Association and many others therefore were justifiably concerned when the secretary for justice changed her position by adopting the interpretation suggested under Mainland legal system and conventions.[43]

Nonetheless, some commentators may have been overreacting when they argue that "if the Mainland practices were to be conclusive in determining the length of the term of office of the CE, it would be very difficult to assert that Hong Kong still enjoys in a real sense the promised 'high degree of autonomy.'"[44] The Basic Law gives the final power of interpretation to the NPCSC; it is a constitutional reality that the NPCSC enjoys such authority.

The CFA has asserted autonomy by applying the common-law approach to interpreting the Basic Law and has not been challenged on this point by any person or governmental organ in the Mainland. That the HKSAR government did not consistently follow the same line is disappointing. The enjoyment of a high degree of autonomy does not and cannot in any way deny the authority of the NPCSC to interpret the Basic Law. Nor does it require the NPCSC to refrain from interpreting the Basic Law according to the statutory interpretation methodologies and values of their own legal and constitutional context and experience. The legal system on the Mainland could be said to be underdeveloped and not based on the rule of law, and Hong Kong's experiences may well influence the development of the mainland legal system. However, the NPCSC undeniably has the authority to interpret the Basic Law according to its own constitutional and institutional conventions.

The Future

What then will the future be? Neither the HKSAR government nor the CPG is willing to undertake that they will refrain from seeking an interpretation from the NPCSC, indicating that the possibility of further NPCSC interpretations cannot be completely ruled out. One commentator argued that this attitude is "a classic Beijing tactic of undermining the express words of the Basic Law."[45] Allegedly, political expediency influenced the decision of the CPG to go ahead with the interpretation of Article 53 of the Basic Law.[46] As discussed, one motivation for seeking the interpretation in 2005 was indeed the political decision to remove any uncertainty to ensure that a new CE could be properly selected by July 10, 2005. Perhaps it was not a tactic on this occasion. Professor Rao Geping, one of the Mainland legal scholars advising the Central Authorities on the Basic Law, hinted that a term of five years might suit Mainland China better, and their real intention on this occasion was to ensure that the true "original legislative intent" should be implemented.[47]

Although the Legislation Law sets out the grounds on which the NPCSC can interpret a national law, it does not prescribe rules that the NPCSC will use to interpret a national law. An official statement on the methodologies that the NPCSC and its LAC will use in the process of identifying and searching for original legislative intent would be helpful. The adoption of a legislative intent approach or a purposive approach to replace the "original legislative intent approach" for statutory and constitutional interpretation in the Mainland also has merits.[48]

The third interpretation of the Basic Law would not have been avoided if the Mainland had adopted these practices. The difference in interpretation was caused by the different constitutional contexts and experiences in the Mainland and the HKSAR rather than by the methodologies of statutory interpretation. This determining factor will presumably be better appreciated if the Mainland authorities responsible for the interpretation of laws openly state their approach in the task of statutory interpretation and the methodologies they may adopt in carrying out that task.

Notes

1. See *Chan Wai Yip Albert v. SJ* (HCAL 36/2005).
2. Interpretation of Paragraph 2, Article 53, of the Basic Law of the Hong Kong Special Administrative Region of the People's Republic of China by Standing Committee of the National People's Congress (Adopted at the Fifteenth Session of the Standing Committee of the Tenth National People's Congress on April 27, 2005); see Laws of Hong Kong (Looseleaf Edition) Vol. 1, 7C/1–2.

3. Basic Law of the Hong Kong Special Administrative Region of the People's Republic of China (Adopted at the Third Session of the Seventh National People's Congress on April 4, 1990) 29 ILM 1511.
4. See Article 53(2) of the Basic Law.
5. Apart from the Honorable Chan Wai Yip, a member of the Legislative Council, Ching Lok Suen Carl also filed an application for judicial review that raised a similar issue, but he was later content to have his case heard at the same time with the Chan's case (see note 1); see also "Challenge to Voting Committee Rejected," *South China Morning Post*, April 23, 2005, page 2.
6. See the Statement of the Hong Kong Bar Association on "The Acting Chief Executive's Request for NPCSC Interpretation of Article 53 of the Basic Law of the HKSAR," April 14, 2005, para 2, available at http://www.hkba.org/whatsnew/submission-position-papers/2005/re_New_CE_20050414_E.doc.
7. The Hong Kong Bar Association noted the point (ibid., para. 5).
8. Article 53(2).
9. Article 45(2).
10. Ibid.
11. See "Statement by the Secretary for Justice on the Term of the New Chief Executive," March 12, 2005, available at http://www.doj.gov.hk/eng/archive/pdf/sj20050312e.pdf; hereinafter SJ's Statement of March 12, 2005.
12. See "The Statement of the Legislative Affairs Commission of the NPCSC on Term of Office of the Chief Executive Returned at a By-election upon the Occurrence of a Vacancy," issued on March 12, 2005, available at http://www.legco.gov.hk/yr04-05/english/bc/bc56/papers/bc560414cb2-1278-1e-scan.pdf (LC Paper CB(2) 1278/04-05[01]); hereinafter LAC's Statement of March 12, 2005.
13. For example, see Benny Y. T. Tai, "A Tale of the Unexpected: Tung's Resignation and the Ensuing Constitutional Controversy," *Hong Kong Law Journal* 35 (2005): 7-16.
14. Ibid.; see also Yash Ghai and Jill Cottrell, "The Politics of Succession in Hong Kong," *Hong Kong Law Journal* 35 (2005): 1-6.
15. See Qiao Xiaoyang, "Xin Teshou Chanshen Mianlin Maodun, Shefa Shi Weiyi de Banfa" ("The Selection of the New Chief Executive Faces Controversy, Interpretation is the Only Solution"), available at http://www.fmcoprc.gov.hk/chn/zt/zzfz/t192757.htm.
16. Ibid.; see also LAC's Statement of March 12, 2005.
17. See Article 42 of the Legislation Law.
18. See Qiao, "Xin Teshou Chanshen Mianlin Maodun, Shefa Shi Weiyi de Banfa."
19. See the legal opinion prepared by Professor Lian Xisheng, in the "Background Material on the Drafting of Article 53 of the Basic Law," available at http://www.legco.gov.hk/yr04-05/english/hc/papers/shc0315background-index-e.pdf;hereinafter Lian's Legal Opinion.
20. See 4 HKCFAR 211 (2001), per Li C. J., 223–24.
21. See the Statement of the Hong Kong Bar Association on "Legal Issues out of the Resignation of the Hon. Tung Chee Hwa from the Office of Chief Executive of the HKSAR, dated March 10, 2005, available at http://www.hkba.org/whatsnew/submission-position-papers/2005/20050311_e.pdf; hereinafter HKBA's Statement of March 10, 2005.
22. 4 HKCFAR 211 (2001), per Li C. J., 223–24.
23. See also Young, Chapter 1, in this volume.
24. See HKBA's Statement of March 10, 2005.
25. See SJ's Statement of March 12, 2005, para. 2.
26. See Lian's Legal Opinion.

27. Ibid. See also the legal opinion prepared by Professor Xu Chongde, in the "Background Material on the Drafting of Article 53 of the Basic Law," available at http://www.legco.gov.hk/yr04-05/english/hc/papers/shc0315background-index-e.pdf: hereinafter "Xu's Legal Opinion." See also LAC's Statement of March 12, 2005, para. 8.
28. See Eric Cheung, "Renqi Zhengyi, Wang Zhenmin De Fali Luoji Miuwu" ("Debate on Term of Office, the Logical Mistake in Wang Zhenmin's Reasoning"), *Ming Pao*, May 5, 2005.
29. See HKBA's Statement of March 10, 2005, para 9.
30. See Lian's Legal Opinion.
31. See Xu's Legal Opinion.
32. See Wang Zhenmin, "Xianggang Teshou Buxuan Renqi Fei Wu Nian de Fali Genji" ("The Jurisprudential Grounds on Why the Term of Office of the New Chief Executive Returned in a By-election Should not Be Five Years"), available at http://www.fmcoprc.gov.hk/chn/zt/zzfz/t189596.htm.
33. See SJ's Statement of March 12, 2005.
34. See Tai, "A Tale of the Unexpected," 2–3.
35. Ibid., 4.
36. See Robert Morris, "The 'Replacement' Chief Executive's Two-Year Term: A Pure and Unambiguous Common Law Analysis," *Hong Kong Law Journal* 35 (2005): 17-28, at 23.
37. See "Gangzhuanjia: An Jibenfa He Xianfa Lijie Xingzhengzhangguan Renqi" ("Experts from the HKSAR: to Understand the Term of Office of the New Chief Executive Returned through By-election according to the Basic Law and Constitution"), available at http://hm.people.com.cn/GB/42273/3265582.html.
38. See also Young, Chapter 1, in this volume.
39. See Morris, "The 'Replacement' Chief Executive's Two-Year Term."
40. That is, possibly, what Professor Wang Zhenmin meant when he argued that the Basic Law is an extension of the Chinese Constitution to the HKSAR, and there cannot be a different interpretation. The length could only be the remainder of the term. See Zhenmin, "Xianggang Teshou Buxuan Renqi Fei Wu Nian de Fali Genji."
41. [1996] AC 907.
42. Ibid., 103.
43. See the Statement of the Hong Kong Bar Association on "Secretary for Justice's Statement on the Term of the New Chief Executive of the HKSAR," issued on March 17, 2005, available at http://www.hkba.org/whatsnew/submission-position-papers/2005/20050317_e.pdf. However, the secretary for justice seemed to be in a difficult position. On the one hand, she was bound by the judgments of the CFA and had to adopt a common-law approach in the interpretation of the Basic Law. On the other hand, the interpretation of the term of the next chief executive strictly following the common-law approach was almost certainly not to be accepted by the CPG and would lead to a direct confrontation with the CPG.
44. See Tai, "A Tale of the Unexpected," 4.
45. See Yash Ghai and Jill Cottrell, "The Politics of Succession in Hong Kong," 2.
46. Ibid.; see also Tai, "A Tale of the Unexpected."
47. The point was made by Professor Rao to Dr. Lin Feng.
48. For example, see Lin Feng, "The Constitutional Crisis in Hong Kong—Is It Over?" *Pacific Rim Law & Policy Journal* 9 (2000): 311–13.

CHAPTER 8

Rethinking Judicial Reference

Barricades at the Gateway?

P. Y. Lo

The power of final adjudication of the Hong Kong Court of Final Appeal (CFA) is qualified by Article 158 of the Basic Law of the HKSAR,[1] which on the one hand authorizes the HKSAR courts to interpret provisions of the Basic Law,[2] and on the other hand requires the CFA to seek an interpretation from the Standing Committee of the National People's Congress (NPCSC) of provisions of the Basic Law concerning affairs, which are the responsibility of the Central People's Government, or concerning the relationship between the Central Authorities and the HKSAR, where such interpretation will affect the judgment on the case.[3] The CFA has been asked on several occasions to make such a "judicial reference" of Basic Law provisions to the NPCSC for interpretation. An examination of the CFA's judgments on these applications indicates that the CFA has taken an uncompromisingly autonomy oriented approach toward the question of judicial reference, trying, on the one hand, not to be placed in a position to countenance the question if possible, and tacitly resisting, on the other, the filling up of constitutional space by NPCSC interpretations, and the consequential snuffing out of its freedom to interpret the Basic Law.

The first part of this chapter highlights the CFA's record of confronting issues concerning judicial reference. The second part contains a reflective comparison of judicial reference with Article 158's "prototype," the preliminary reference mechanism under the legal system of the European Union (EU), which allows and, in the case of final appellate cases, obliges national courts of EU Member States to make references to the European Court of Justice (ECJ) for preliminary rulings concerning the interpretation of EU measures. The final part outlines the ways in which the HKSAR courts can respond to a request for judicial reference, and how it may shape, within the framework of the Basic Law, its institutional agenda in relation to the institutions of the HKSAR, and of the Central Authorities (particularly the NPCSC).

Of Requests and the Odd Omission: A Critical Review of CFA Jurisprudence

The CFA considered three requests for judicial reference between 1997 and 2005. It declined to act on two and did not deal with the other. This, however, is not the complete score sheet: one other case befitted judicial reference.

The respondent in the case of *Ng Ka Ling & Ors v. Director of Immigration* made the first request.[4] The CFA explained its understanding of Article 158 at the outset of its judgment. According to the CFA, the constitutional authorization in Article 158(2) for the HKSAR courts to interpret Basic Law provisions that are within the limits of the HKSAR's autonomy "on its own" is indicative of the HKSAR's high degree of autonomy and the independence of its courts.[5] These attributes of Hong Kong's separate system are so essential that the CFA found that it must seek to protect them in its formulation of the test for judicial reference.[6]

The CFA found that Article 158(3) obliged it, when the prescribed conditions are satisfied, to make a judicial reference to the NPCSC for interpretation of provisions concerning the affairs which are the responsibility of the Central People's Government or concerning the relationship between the Central Authorities and the HKSAR (which it called the *excluded provisions*").[7] The CFA identified those conditions (which it called the *classification condition* and the *necessity condition*) and devised the test for determining whether they were satisfied.

The CFA then held, on a view accepted by both parties, that "it is for the Court of Final Appeal and *for it alone* to decide, in adjudicating a case, whether both conditions are satisfied. It is for the court, *not* the [NPCSC], to decide whether the classification condition is satisfied, that is, whether the provision is an excluded provision."[8] The consensus of views before the CFA may be unsurprising, given the clarity of the language of Article 158(3); it is for the HKSAR courts, in adjudicating cases, to seek an interpretation from the NPCSC. Nonetheless, to reach the consensus, the language of Article 158(3) must have been read, understood and *interpreted*.[9] In order for the CFA to comply with the jurisdictional limit placed on it by Article 158(3), which the court itself recognized, it would have to assess whether Article 158(3) was an excluded provision (that is, the court would have to apply the classification condition). If the court had found the provision to be excluded from its jurisdiction, which is a plausible conclusion, then the CFA would have had to consider whether there was a need to interpret an excluded provision in the very first case in which it was called upon to exercise its constitutional jurisdiction and formulate the test for judicial reference; and whether such interpretation would affect the judgment on the case (the necessity condition). Answering these two questions in the *absence* of consensus could have compelled the CFA to make its first judicial reference that of the very Basic Law provision having to do with judicial reference. The symbolic impact of such a move on confidence in Hong Kong's separate system would have been significant. The CFA's consensus building thus avoided the unsavory situation of finding its hands tied or exposing its hands to be tied in this crucial case, a situation that may have ensued from proper articulation of its reasoning. Instead, the court's bold assertion of its *Kompetenz-Kompetenz*[10] boosted the institutional prestige of the CFA.

The CFA also emphasized that the subject of a judicial reference must be a specific Basic Law provision, as opposed to "the question of interpretation involved generally."[11] It considered that Article 158(3) "does not require a reference of the question of interpretation involved generally when a number of provisions (including an excluded provision) may be relevant to provide the solution of that question."[12] Denis Chang SC, who argued the case before the CFA for the right of abode claimants, subsequently acknowledged that this point was "emphasized very much in argument and has found a place in the judgment itself."[13] If, then, a case involves a provision that modifies or limits another provision, only the "predominant provision" will be referred to the NPCSC for interpretation.

This narrow scope for judicial reference appeals to the CFA's sense of being obliged to preserve the autonomy of the independent judicial institution in the HKSAR, as it concedes as little as possible to the NPCSC for decision. The CFA was persuaded to adopt the "predominant provision test,"[14] as the "test the Court should apply in considering whether the classification condition is satisfied."[15]

The "predominant provision test" and its rationale immediately attracted doubt[16] and criticism.[17] The CFA, after applying the test to decline to refer Article 22(4) to the NPCSC for interpretation, proceeded to interpret that article itself in adjudication[18]—the act that according to the language of Article 158(3), it must not do "on its own."[19]

Chang defended the CFA's test, emphasizing the fluid and dynamic nature of the adjudicatory process and the fact that "*[excluded] provisions do not carry identity cards.*" The problem of "classification" necessarily arises if counsel argues that a Basic Law provision interpreted "in its context" disposes of the case in a particular way. If it is contended that a provision of the Basic Law must be interpreted in its context and that such context would include other Basic Law provisions, the question that naturally arises is "what as a matter of substance is the predominant provision which has to be interpreted in the adjudication of the case." This question "cannot be considered in isolation from the issues in the case."[20]

Chang received some support from Ghai, who indicated that "a careful and creative reading of the entire Basic Law" was required to "determine where a particular power belongs."[21] Judges engaging in a "dynamic adjudicatory process" where "context is everything"[22] may well be persuaded to muddy the distinction between interpretation and adjudication, in spite of the language of Article 158(3), and to heed the words of Roscoe Pound: "It is as clear as legal history can make it that interpretation apart from judicial application is impractical, that it is futile to attempt to separate the functions of finding the law, interpreting the law and applying the law."[23]

In spite of Chang's persuasive arguments, the "predominant provision test" does not withstand scrutiny. The determination, as a matter of substance, of the predominant provision that is to be interpreted in the adjudication depends on the proponent's point of view. As Lord Mustill shrewdly observed: "[quite] often the benefits of a 'purposive approach' are illusory, since the purpose which is used as a point of reference merely reflects the contention of one or other of the parties about what the words ought to mean."[24]

In other words, a suggestion that provision X qualifies, limits or modifies provision Y can legitimately be reformulated as one that provision Y qualifies, limits or modifies provision X. If either suggestion can be more than reasonably argued, then it must be recognized that the interpretation of both provisions X and Y will affect the judgment in the case. If one of the two provisions is an excluded provision, the judicial reference requirements must apply.

The *Ng Ka Ling* judgment was blown to the four winds. Its interpretation of Articles 22(4) and 24(2)(3) lost its precedential value as a result of the NPCSC Interpretation of June 26, 1999.[25] The CFA's test for judicial reference was thrown into doubt by the speech of Qiao Xiaoyang, the Deputy Secretary of the Legislative Affairs Commission, NPCSC, explaining the draft interpretation to the NPCSC session on June 22, 1999. Qiao said that:[before] making its judgment, the Court of Final Appeal did not seek an interpretation of the NPCSC *in compliance with* the requirement of Art 158(3) of the Basic Law. Moreover, the interpretation of the Court of Final Appeal is not consistent with the legislative intent.[26]

The CFA soon faced the second "request" for judicial reference. On October 21, 1999, during the hearing of *HKSAR v. Ng Kung Siu & Anor*,[27] counsel for the appellant asked the CFA to consider making a judicial reference.

Counsel handed up a sheet of paper to the bench, seeking clarification of the following issues:

Whether BL18 and Annex III, which provide for the application of certain PRC national laws in the HKSAR, have, consistent with the Basic Law—(a) imposed a legal obligation on the HKSAR, and further or in the alternative; (b) empowered the HKSAR legislature, to implement Article 19 of the PRC National Flag Law, an Annex III law, by making it a criminal offence for a person in the HKSAR to desecrate the national flag by publicly and wilfully defiling it.[28]

One of the two principal issues in the Flag Desecration Case was the validity of an ordinance[29] enacted locally to implement a national law included in Annex III of the Basic Law by the NPCSC. The appellant contended that the local implementing ordinance was, by virtue of its pedigree, immune from challenge for inconsistency with other provisions of the Basic Law.

The CFA responded heatedly to the suggestion that the matter be referred. Ching PJ was heard to have observed: "To refer this question would make us look like a bunch of clowns. There is simply no question, as far as this present case is concerned, of that nature."[30] Counsel for the appellant wisely submitted that the *question* was only raised for consideration. The CFA critically questioned the contention, probing the extent of the alleged constitutional immunity.[31]

No part of the exchange and discussion described above found its way into the CFA's judgment in the Flag Desecration Case. The CFA did not make any determination on judicial reference. Its unanimous judgment instead focused *solely* on the other principal contention of the appellant, namely the question of whether the two offences of flag desecration under scrutiny before it[32] passed muster under Article 19 of the International Covenant on Civil and Political Rights[33] as permissible restrictions on the freedom of expression guaranteed under that article on the ground of public order (*ordre public*).[34] The CFA held that they were and upheld the two offences.[35] The challenge to the lawfulness of the convictions having fallen away, it was "unnecessary to deal with other arguments that were canvassed."[36]

The reference question was touched on again in the final appeal in *Lau Kong Yung & Ors v. Director of Immigration*,[37] which the CFA heard one week after it heard the Flag Desecration Case. The central questions put before the CFA concerned the nature and effect of the NPCSC Interpretation of June 26, 1999. The chief justice, giving the principal judgment,[38] recognized that the NPCSC Interpretation was made pursuant to the general and unqualified power to interpret all provisions of the Basic Law under Article 158(1) and was binding on all HKSAR courts. Accordingly, the CFA performed the "painful duty"[39] of declaring that the Immigration (Amendment) (No 3) Ordinance 1997[40] "is and has since 1 July 1997 been constitutional."[41]

The chief justice, in addition, acknowledged that the Preamble to the NPCSC Interpretation of June 26, 1999, indicated that the NPCSC did not support the CFA's interpretation of Article 158(3). The chief justice continued: "the Court may need to re-visit the classification and necessity conditions and the predominant test in an appropriate case."[42]

The HKSAR government apparently took the hint[43] and asked the CFA to reexamine the test for judicial reference in *Director of Immigration v. Chong Fung Yuen.*[44] The director of immigration, seeking to overturn the lower court's interpretation of Article 24(2)(1) of the Basic Law, contended before the CFA that Article 24(2)(1) was an excluded provision and since it was necessary in the adjudication to interpret that provision to decide the final appeal, the CFA was *duty bound* to make a judicial reference. The right of abode claimant disputed the director of immigration's new formulation of the classification condition.[45]

The CFA did not find the *Chong Fung Yuen* case to be the occasion to reexamine the "predominant provision test" since it was common ground that the "question of interpretation involved generally" was concerned with the interpretation of only one provision of the Basic Law.[46] The director of immigration attempted to change the complexion of the classification condition, focusing on the "implementation" of the provision of the Basic Law in question.[47] The CFA rejected those submissions. Pointing out that the NPCSC Interpretation of June 26, 1999, did not contain an interpretation of Article 158(3), it proceeded to interpret Article 158(3) using the common law approach, on the basis of the provision's language when read in the light of its context and purpose, apparently assuming that the provision was *not* an excluded provision.[48] The CFA observed that Article 158(3), in describing the excluded provisions, focused "on the provision in question. It does not refer to the effect of its implementation. In our view, Article 158(3) . . . cannot be *interpreted* to prescribe, as the test whether a provision is an excluded provision, the factual determination of the substantive effect of its implementation." Focusing on the "provision in question" instead required the CFA to consider the "character" of the provision.[49] The CFA declined to make a judicial reference of Article 24(2)(1) because the character of that provision was not one which concerned affairs which were the responsibility of the Central People's Government or the relationship between the Central Authorities and the HKSAR.[50]

The NPCSC shortly thereafter issued a statement that the CFA's interpretation of Article 24(2)(1) was inconsistent with the legislative intent and expressed concern. The statement did not comment on whether the CFA had been correct in declining to make a judicial reference, however. Nor did it comment on the interpretation the CFA applied to the NPCSC Interpretation of June 26, 1999. Chen considered the CFA to be undoubtedly correct in rejecting the director of immigration's arguments on judicial reference, saying that the events resulted in a "win-win" situation through the restraint of the Central Authorities and the courageous action of the CFA.[51]

The NPCSC's statement was a form of *biaotai* (an expression of their stance). It was made in full recognition that the CFA's acceptance in the *Lau Kong Yung* case of the binding effect of an NPCSC interpretation under Article 158(1) remained valid and that the NPCSC, if it so wished, could have issued the counter-measure necessary to neutralize the recalcitrant court's interpretation point blank and to reinstall its own understanding of the Basic Law as the "final" interpretation. The NPCSC's response would have to be directly on point given the approach of the CFA in the cases of *Chong Fung Yuen* and *Tam Nga Yin* that it would interpret, or to put it mildly, read a NPCSC interpretation narrowly to minimize impact of, or to avoid acceptance of arguments based on analogies based on, the terms of the interpretation.[52]

The last case in the review is the odd omission: the right-of-abode case of *Ng Siu Tung & Ors v. Director of Immigration*, in which the CFA had to grapple with more than 5,000 applications for judicial review.[53] In dealing with one set of issues arising under the case, the majority of the CFA judges made explicit that "the answer to the applicants' argument depends on the *effect* of Article 22(4) [. . .], having regard to the [NPCSC] Interpretation [of 26 June 1999]."[54] They went on to hold that Article 22(4) was prospective in effect.[55] The majority accordingly interpreted Article 22(4) *on their own* to reach the holding in favor of the relevant appellants.

The controversy of this holding was that many commentators believed Article 22(4) was an excluded provision,[56] although neither the NPCSC Interpretation of June 26, 1999[57] nor the CFA[58] could be taken as having firmly decided the issue. That provision arguably qualifies as an excluded provision under the current "character of the provision" test propounded by the CFA in *Chong Fung Yuen*. No judicial reference was suggested or made. The NPCSC did not issue any statement after the handing down of the judgment.[59] The CFA had played a volley close to the line and the linesmen did not object.

The review of jurisprudence above reveals an institutional reluctance on the part of the CFA to make judicial references. The CFA relied on past consensus and argumentative devices to avoid classifying any provision of the Basic Law as an excluded provision, including Article 158(3). Avoiding such a decision is now more difficult, however, given the "character of the provision" test the court adopted in *Chong Fung Yuen*. The CFA passed over a reconsideration of the proper order or approach for evaluating a request for judicial reference and the "predominant provision test." The court also declined to make judicial references, maintaining that the matter was clear, even though in one case there was a strong argument that the provision of the Basic Law concerned was an excluded provision.

These results contrast significantly with the phenomenal success of the model on which Article 158(3) was based, namely the treaty based system for the ECJ to make preliminary rulings on the interpretation and validity of EU measures, on reference from national courts of Member States of the EU, to which this chapter will turn.

EC Treaty Article 234: The Engine for European Legal Integration, A Lesson for Hong Kong?

The mechanism for making judicial references of Basic Law provisions was modelled on[60] the preliminary rulings procedure to the ECJ,[61] which was itself "inspired by similar systems [for reference between different systems of courts] in the legal systems of the original Member States."[62] Lord Denning MR compared the EEC Treaty with "an incoming tide . . . [flowing] into the estuaries and up the rivers. It cannot be held back."[63] In the United Kingdom, the law which flowed into the legal system pursuant to the European Communities Act 1972 has enriched the development of English law. Will Article 158(3) of the Basic Law provide for a similar flow, leading to a level of legal integration like that which the preliminary ruling procedure has encouraged in Europe?

A 1986 report by Dorothy Liu[64] noted that the implementation of the "one country, two systems" principle in Hong Kong would create a differentiation between the institution exercising the power to interpret the Basic Law (the NPCSC) and the institution applying it (the courts of the HKSAR).[65] She contended that a way must be found for the satisfactory resolution of "conflicts of legal interpretation" arising out of the possibly contrasting legal traditions of Mainland China and Hong Kong.[66]

Liu's report provided a starting point for this resolution by referring to the judgment of Lord Denning MR in *H P Bulmer Ltd v J Bollinger SA*,[67] especially the distinction made between the task of interpreting the EEC Treaty and the task of applying it; and the separation of the final authority to perform each of those two tasks.[68] *Bulmer v Bollinger* contains a rich discussion of the preliminary ruling procedure to the ECJ and how the courts of the Member States operated it at the time. Wang found the preliminary ruling procedure "worthy of consideration" because, in his mind, the Central-HKSAR relationship and the EU-Member States relationship were "the same in that the power of interpretation and the power of final adjudication are not vested in the hands of one and the same institution."[69]

The preliminary ruling procedure is provided under Article 234 of the EC Treaty:

> The Court of Justice shall have jurisdiction to give preliminary rulings concerning:
> (a) the interpretation of the Treaty;
> (b) the validity and interpretation of acts of the institutions of the Community and of the ECB;
> (c) the interpretation of the statutes of bodies established by an act of the Council, where those statutes so provide.
>
> Where such a question is raised before any court or tribunal of a Member State, that court or tribunal may, if it considers that a decision on the question is necessary to enable it to give judgment, request the Court of Justice to give a ruling thereon.
>
> Where any such question is raised in a case pending before a court or tribunal of a Member State, against whose decision there is no judicial remedy under national law, that court or tribunal shall bring the matter before the Court of Justice.

Important features of the procedure set out in this article are found in Article 158(3) of the Basic Law, such as the necessity for judgment condition for requesting ECJ preliminary ruling; and the mandatory requirement on the part of the court of final adjudication of a Member State to "bring the matter before" the ECJ when a case raising a question on, for example, the interpretation of the EC Treaty is pending.

Article 158(3) of the Basic Law also contains features peculiar to the implementation of the principle of "one country, two systems." The mandatory requirement is limited to making a judicial reference of an excluded provision, thus requiring a demarcation between excluded provisions and non-excluded provisions within the same constitutional document. The HKSAR courts would have to develop their own jurisprudence on this "classification condition."

The subject of the preliminary ruling procedure is the question of interpretation of EU law. The jurisprudence of the ECJ indicates, however, that it does consider the facts of the case as found by the national court and strives to provide an answer to the question of interpretation in the specific context of the case. Schermers and Waelbroeck provide a few examples, such as the *LTM* case, where the ECJ responded in the following terms to a submission that the question before it was not an abstract question and in reality one of application:

> Although the court has no jurisdiction to take cognizance of the application of the Treaty to a specific case, it may extract from the elements of the case those questions of interpretation or validity which alone fall within its jurisdiction. Moreover the need to reach a serviceable interpretation of the provisions at issue justifies the national court in setting out the legal context in which the requested interpretation is to be placed. The court may, therefore, draw from the elements of law described by the *Cour d'Appel*, Paris, the data necessary for an understanding of the question put and for the preparation of an appropriate answer.[70]

In the *Cristini* case, the ECJ looked at the facts and answered the question posed in the specific context of the case in spite of its general and abstract formulation, stating that it "may . . . provide the national court with the factors of interpretation depending on Community law which might be useful to it in evaluating the effects of such provision."[71]

The CFA has taken a more restrictive approach to the subject of a judicial reference. Contrasting the CFA's approach with the ECJ jurisprudence quoted above tends to confirm the observations above of the CFA's institutional reluctance, if not avoidance, of judicial references. By insisting on referring only the excluded provision, the CFA may succeed in requiring the parties before it to formulate the subject for judicial reference into an abstract and general form so devoid of context and factual basis that it would be able to turn round and refuse to refer on the ground that the answer was "absurdly clear"![72]

Analysts of the EU system have celebrated the role of the preliminary ruling procedure in European legal integration. The twin pillars of the European legal order, namely, "direct effect" and "supremacy of EU law," were pronounced and developed by the ECJ in preliminary rulings.[73] Weiler considered the preliminary ruling procedure to be a "protective shelter" that enabled the ECJ and the national judges to have a partnership that both empowered one another (*vis-à-vis* other governmental authorities) and increased the effectiveness of EU law for private actors.[74] Stone Sweet pointed out that the indeterminate or open-ended nature of norms in the EU measures as well as the extreme difficulty of reversing an interpretation of the ECJ contributed to the phenomenon of a fluid and dynamic process of adjudication in which judges possess "meaningful discretion over the legal norms they interpret and apply."[75]

Professor James Crawford SC does not agree that the reference process in the Basic Law and the EC Treaty are comparable, however. He observes that the preliminary ruling procedure "might have given someone an idea, in some respect a clever idea, but the position is quite different."[76] Under the EU arrangement, "the national courts retain the power of final adjudication within the European Union, in form and to a large extent in substance." By contrast, under the Basic Law respect of the power of final adjudication is counterbalanced by the power of interpretation of the NPCSC, subject only to "judgments previously rendered" being preserved under Article 158(3). This situation "reduces the power of final adjudication to a rather formal matter, not much more than *res judicata*."[77]

Crawford may have in mind the NPCSC's plenary power to interpret all provisions of the Basic Law, which can and indeed has been exercised to rob a CFA judgment of its precedential value. In so doing, however, the NPCSC displaces an interpretation as opposed to applications of that interpretation, and invalidates a judgment of the CFA only in so far as that judgment contains a Basic Law interpretation, while not affecting the disposition of the case in that judgment.[78] This is a necessary consequence of committing to two institutions the power of interpretation of the same constitutional document under a hierarchical relationship; the higher-order institution controls the exercise of that power by the lower order institution.

The ECJ's interpretative jurisdiction is plenary in a similar sense and must be so, given that the ECJ does not adopt any formal doctrine of precedent.[79] When, for example, in a subsequent preliminary ruling from another national court, the ECJ decides to interpret a provision of the EC Treaty differently, the new interpretation would surely be the norm to be applied by *all* the national courts and it is up to the national legal systems to determine the extent of the effect of the new interpretation on previous and pending cases. The difference between the two arrangements, as Crawford stresses, is the inability on the part of the ECJ to invalidate judgments of national courts that do not interpret an EU measure consistently with the ECJ and other Member States. This illustrates a cooperative relationship—the essence of the European venture of sovereign states.[80] However, ways exist to ensure uniform interpretation. The national legal system is capable of rectifying anomalies and litigants enthusiastically rely on ECJ judgments to secure for themselves the protection of an EU measure. Compliance with an EU measure may also be enforced by the European Commission under Article 226 of the EC Treaty.[81]

Crawford seems to suggest that the power of final adjudication of the CFA is somewhat barren in the light of the NPCSC's power of interpretation. The same point can in fact be said of the power of final adjudication of national courts in the EU in the light of the ECJ's power of final interpretation of EU measures, since like constitutional litigation in Hong Kong, litigation raising an EU issue before a national court is concerned with the compatibility of a national measure with an EU measure with direct effect and having supremacy. Although, as Judge Mancini of the ECJ indicated, the ECJ's jurisdiction is limited in the sense that if asked whether "national rule A is in violation of Community regulation B or Directive C," the court would answer that "its only power is to explain what B or C actually mean," the ECJ often "went on to indicate to what extent a certain type of national legislation can be regarded as compatible with that measure. The national judge is thus led hand in hand as far as the door; crossing the threshold is his job, but now a job no harder than child's play."[82]

Judges of the CFA apparently do not wish to be led or to be shown the door by the NPCSC, which, as Ghai and others remind us, is a political body taking instructions from the Central People's Government and ultimately the Chinese Communist Party. Given that the Central Authorities are "frequently protagonists in differences and disputes" and that they are using the NPCSC to resolve Central-HKSAR political disputes through interpreting the relevant provisions of the Basic Law,[83] the CFA understandably and instinctively applied various techniques to "take the Basic Law away from the NPCSC"[84] or to adjudicate the case before it without reaching for the Basic Law. The next and last part of this chapter outlines these techniques systematically in the light of the earlier review of jurisprudence.

The Strategems of Autonomy

The Central Authorities approach the implementation in Hong Kong of the principle of "one country, two systems" not as the divine watch-maker of eighteenth century deism who creates the machinery and then allows it to run on its own, but rather in accordance with the precepts of theism, where the higher power intervenes regularly to ensure the fruition of the divine plan.[85] Since that intervention from on high could occur before, during, and after adjudication,[86] the CFA has a precarious hold on its independent judicial power and therefore on the autonomy of the HKSAR. The CFA will also have to ensure that the HKSAR courts adjudicate the causes before them robustly and effectively, especially where guaranteed rights and freedoms are pleaded.

The CFA knows that judges at the appellate level face choices and that "the higher they go the more numerous and more difficult are the leeways for choice."[87] The interpretation of the Basic Law presents more, and more open, choices. The court is authorized to interpret the nonexcluded provisions of the Basic Law on its own, and relies on the *Kompetenz-Kompetenz* to decide on whether to make a judicial reference. Subject only to any interpretations issued by the NPCSC, the CFA exercises the power of constitutional interpretation, acting as a check upon measures taken by other institutions of power under the Basic Law.

The CFA has to manage the tensions of these constraints and liberties. The approaches and responses outlined are particularly meaningful in the context of managing the court's encounters with judicial reference.

Avoidance

In the Flag Desecration case[88] the CFA passed over the controversial task of assessing the status of a local law implementing a national law listed in Annex III of the Basic Law. It instead decided conclusively, and sufficiently for disposition, the less controversial issue of the compatibility of the local legislation with the guaranteed freedom of expression. Logically, though, the more controversial status question should have been the first to be decided.

Courts formulate rules of restraint on the basis of judicial experience, so the question of the constitutionality of a piece of legislation will only be decided where the decision is strictly necessary for the adjudication of the matter before the court:[89] Courts will not "anticipate a question of constitutional law in advance of the necessity of deciding it." Nor will they pronounce on "a constitutional question although properly presented by the record, if there is also present some other ground upon which the case may be disposed of."[90] In addition, when formulating a rule of constitutional law, courts will not "formulate a rule . . . broader than is required by the precise facts to which it is to be applied."[91] Such rules of restraint are consistent with the authority of the HKSAR courts to interpret provisions of the Basic Law in the *adjudication* of cases.

The CFA, however, seems to be exercising restraint against deciding an issue of constitutional law when it suits its purpose. It has not barred the taking of cases that are academic between the immediate parties if it perceives "a sufficiently great public interest to be served."[92] It has responded to a "waterfront" approach to making submissions by stating its opinion on all the issues raised, even though strictly speaking the favorable holding in relation to one issue disposed of the appeal and did not require a ruling on the constitutional issue.[93] In another case, a majority of CFA judges pronounced their views on the constitutionality of the part of a statute raised by the appellants in the final criminal appeal before it, even though the validity of those provisions had nothing to do with the safety of the convictions of the appellants, which were ultimately upheld.[94]

The court must identify "the circumstances for action and the occasions for restraint."[95] The CFA seems to be keen on expounding its views on the Basic Law especially where guaranteed rights and freedoms are involved. It will no doubt continue to do so as long as no arguably excluded provision intrudes into the discussion, in which case it would be likely to avoid the issue in a show of restraint.[96]

Deference

The CFA said in the Flag Desecration Case that it would give "due weight" to the view of the HKSAR's legislature that the enactment of the Flag Protection Ordinances was "appropriate" when the court considered whether it was necessary to criminalize flag desecration.[97] With these remarks, the CFA introduced the language of deference.[98]

Academic discussion of the concept of deference is legion and can often be confusing.[99] The relevant legal scene in Hong Kong is no less disordered. Article 19(3) of the Basic Law removes from the jurisdiction of the Hong Kong courts "acts of state such as defence and foreign affairs."[100] The CFA considered in the *Ng Ka Ling* case that this provision was an example of restrictions on the jurisdiction of the HKSAR courts imposed by the legal system and principles previously in force.[101] Outside of the rubric of "act of state," there may be questions of such a political nature that the HKSAR courts should decline jurisdiction. The suggestion seems to be arguable, as it has been said that "Courts are not concerned with political matters. They are solely concerned with issues of law."[102] Yet, the HKSAR courts have not formulated for themselves any doctrine of "political questions."[103]

If the courts of the HKSAR had established a doctrine of "political questions," then perhaps there may have been no need for the CFA to become flustered over the classification of provisions of the Basic Law and thus judicial reference to the NPCSC. The doctrine could be expanded to exclude from the purview of the HKSAR courts the questioning of decisions on matters committed under the Basic Law to be the responsibilities of the Central Authorities.[104] Expansion of the doctrine in this way may be meaningful, since it would involve consideration of the substantive question, as opposed to the present contorted manner of looking into the character of provisions for the purpose of making a judicial reference.

The CFA is unlikely to embark on such an adventure, however, as it would bring in via the back door the kind of derogation of the HKSAR's autonomy that the CFA, in the cases discussed earlier, sought to reject at the front door.

Defiance/Compliance (or acte clair/acte éclairé)

In 1999, Chen introduced Hong Kong readers to the European legal concept of *acte clair*, where a national court of final adjudication may decline to refer the question of interpretation of a EU measure to the ECJ on the ground that the meaning and effect of the provision in question is clear and free from doubt.[105] An associated concept is that of *acte éclairé*, which denotes the case where a previous ruling of the ECJ leaves no doubt as to the question of EU law before the national court of final adjudication. In relation to cases where the previous ruling and the present question are materially identical; or where previous decisions of the ECJ have already dealt with the point of law in question, the ECJ has signaled that a preliminary ruling need not be sought.[106]

The CFA apparently declined, consciously or unconsciously, but nonetheless emphatically, to countenance making a judicial reference in the Flag Desecration case and in the *Ng Siu Tung* case on the basis that the answer would have been clear. Could the CFA be said to have applied the concept of *acte clair*? The question that should be asked is: maybe it is clear to us, but how about to them? The controversy in the spring of 2005 over the term of office of a chief executive elected to fill a casual vacancy may have revealed many differences between "the two systems."[107] If the criterion is that of "clear and free from doubt," then the required degree of assurance must necessarily be high. The *CILFIT* case in the ECJ indeed attached importance to the need to "leave no scope for any reasonable doubt."[108]

The practice of the European national courts in relation to the concept of *acte clair* may give solace to the CFA, since, as Douglas Scott[109] and Alter[110] chronicled, national courts do find questions to be *actes clair* and therefore decline to make a reference, when the true position may not be so clear. The most notorious case in this regard was a 1978 decision of the French Conseil d'Etat called the *Cohn-Bendit* case, where the Conseil interpreted on its own a provision of the EEC Treaty contrary to ECJ case law, after using the *acte clair* doctrine to decline to make a reference for a preliminary ruling.[111]

Although the acts of defiance of the CFA's European counterparts generated no reprisals, the plenary power of the NPCSC to interpret all provisions of the Basic Law simply means, and has been demonstrated in practice to indicate, that failure on the part of the CFA to make a judicial reference when the NPCSC believes it should have will be met by a NPCSC interpretation designed to displace the CFA's interpretation (if any) of the relevant provisions of the Basic Law.

Turning to *acte éclairé*, there is a similar history of seeming defiance on the part of the CFA, in relation to the NPCSC Interpretation of June 26,

1999. This interpretation indicates that the legislative intent of all categories in Article 24(2) was reflected in an Opinion of the Preparatory Committee for the HKSAR on the implementation of that provision adopted on August 10, 1996. In subsequent litigation, the CFA declined to act on this statement, after securing from counsel the acceptance that the statement was not a binding NPCSC interpretation of that provision.[112] Viewing the CFA's approach by reference to *acte éclairé*, it appears that it looked at whether there was a "previous ruling," applying a strict and formal conception of that expression, so that analogies and notes for guidance would not qualify. This approach of conceding compliance only in identical circumstances again enabled the CFA to retain room to maneuver within the common law principles of interpretation. In addition, it appears that the NPCSC can displace any CFA interpretation that it disapproves of with an interpretation of its own.

Engagement

The CFA has thus far avoided classifying a Basic Law provision as an excluded provision, which does not of course mean that the CFA will never do so. If the CFA is pressed to the corner, then, apart from being openly and perhaps unreasonably defiant, how can it further its cherished values of judicial independence and the autonomy of Hong Kong's separate system? The court still has some pieces on the board, with a few moves open to it.

The subject of the reference

Although the CFA will listen to the parties, it is the CFA's own deliberation that determines the outcome of the request for reference. From what the CFA has indicated, one would expect the subject of the reference to be a provision rather than a question. And even if a question were submitted, the CFA may phrase it in such a way that the NPCSC would give so vague and general an answer that the CFA would still retain leeway in its application.

Materials to be transmitted to the NPCSC.[113]

Should the CFA forward, as do its European counterparts in a reference for preliminary ruling, the entire record of the case?[114] If the CFA does so, the NPCSC interpretation obtained can be expected to be specific, possibly leaving the CFA to perform an empty act of application. But if it does not, could the court expect the NPCSC and the Committee for the Basic Law[115] to be entirely ignorant of the relevant context and for that reason return a vague and general interpretation? Or should it risk that the Central Authorities would be so misinformed by its information gathering machinery in Hong

Kong about the case that the resulting interpretation, when applied, would lead to an undesired consequence? The prudent course in the dilemma may be for the court to provide the complete information.

The CFA still has one last move to make: it has to decide whether to transmit to the NPCSC its own views on the meaning and effect of the excluded provision. This move may sometimes be regarded as courageous, particularly if the NPCSC's Legislative Affairs Commission has already expressed a view in the media about the "question of interpretation involved generally."[116] Transmission in such delicate circumstances will be an attempt to persuade, rather than to seek endorsement.

Rethinking the Necessity of Judicial Reference

Chief Justice Barak stated a universal truth: "When we [judges] sit in judgment, we are subject to judgment."[117] The CFA's interpretation of the provisions of the Basic Law is being judged by those who have the means to displace that interpretation. The relative importance of securing a judicial reference from the CFA during adjudication may therefore have diminished.

Article 158(3) of the Basic Law is, as Sir Anthony Mason acknowledged, a link between the courts of the HKSAR and the NPCSC on the regulation of the interpretation of the Basic Law. The right of abode saga of 1999 and the constitutional development dispute of 2004 resulted in the opening of a new link and a new initiative respectively.[118] In the meantime, as the link of judicial reference has received no traffic, it can be said that the link does not exist.

The CFA has not yet undertaken a reexamination of the methodology for judicial reference, and it is doubtful whether it will ever complete this task. The CFA will have to wait for the "suitable case," while applying the principles discussed earlier to avoid and delay touching on the judicial reference issue.

The CFA has not, understandably, yet classified a provision of the Basic Law to be an excluded provision. Each classification decision draws a line, exposes a fissure, and concedes a Basic Law provision to the Central Authorities. Rather than handing the authorities in the Mainland and in Hong Kong the "loaded weapon" that once released will become enlistable case law,[119] the CFA has left the matter to the NPCSC, indicating merely its obedience to the letter of NPCSC interpretations, without accepting complicity in the application of their reasoning.

The ground rules have been laid.

Notes

1. Basic Law of the Hong Kong Special Administrative Region of the People's Republic of China (Adopted at the Third Session of the Seventh National People's Congress on April 4, 1990) (1990) 29 ILM 1511.
2. Basic Law, Article 158(2).
3. Basic Law, Article 158(3).
4. *Ng Ka Ling and Others v. Director of Immigration* (1999) 2 HKCFAR 4, CFA. In this case, right-of-abode claimants appealed to have HKSAR immigration legislation tying their entitlement to exercise of their right of abode provided under Art 24(2)(3) of the Basic Law with their obtaining from the responsible Mainland authorities one-way exit permits declared invalid. They sought to protect a "core right," a right on which other rights and freedoms guaranteed under the Basic Law are to be enjoyed; ibid., 34F.
5. Ibid., 29F–G.
6. Ibid., 33B–C (where the CFA considered that a judicial reference for the interpretation of an excluded provision so far as relevant to the interpretation of a nonexcluded provision would withdraw from the court's jurisdiction the interpretation of a provision within the limits of the HKSAR's autonomy, which would be a *substantial derogation from the autonomy of the HKSAR* and "cannot be right").
7. *Ng Ka Ling*, 30E–I.
8. Ibid., 30I–31C (emphasis added). The CFA made a similar holding in respect of the necessity condition; ibid., 31D–E.
9. The CFA did acknowledge in a later part of the judgment that it applied a purposive *interpretation* of Article 158(3) in deciding what test was to be applied in considering whether the classification condition was satisfied; ibid., 32H–J.
10. *Kompetenz-Kompetenz* refers to the jurisdiction to give a binding ruling on the extent of one's own jurisdiction. See P. Y. Lo, "Master of One's Own Court," *Hong Kong Law Journal* 34 (2004): 47.
11. *Ng Ka Ling*, 31F.
12. Ibid., 33F.
13. Denis Chang, "The Reference to the Standing Committee of the National People's Congress under Article 158 of the Basic Law: The Question of Methodology," in *Hong Kong's Constitutional Debate: Conflicts over Interpretation*, ed. J. M. M. Chan, H. L. Fu, and Yash Ghai (Hong Kong: Hong Kong University Press, 2000), 144.
14. See *Ng Ka Ling*, 33C–E.
15. Ibid., 32H.
16. Yash Ghai, *Commentary* [1999] 1 HKLRD 360, 363I–J.
17. Albert H. Y. Chen, "The Court of Final Appeal's Ruling in the 'Illegal Migrant' Children Case: A Critical Commentary on the Application of Article 158 of the Basic Law," in *Hong Kong's Constitutional Debate*, 124–25. For a similar approach, see Weiyun Xiao, *Lun Xianggang Jiebenfa* [*On Hong Kong Basic Law*] (Beijing: Peking University Press, 2003), 857.
18. *Ng Ka Ling*, 35C–D.
19. Ghai, *Commentary*.
20. Chang, "The Reference to the Standing Committee of the National People's Congress," 143, 145, 148, 149.
21. Yash Ghai, "The Imperatives of Autonomy: Contradictions of the Basic Law," in *Hong Kong's Constitutional Debates*, ed. Johannes Chan and Lison Harris (Hong Kong: Hong Kong Law Journal, 2005), 37.

22. Per Lord Steyn in *R (Daly) v. Secretary of State of the Home Department* [2001] 2 AC 532, HL at 548C–D.
23. Roscoe Pound, *The Spirit of the Common Law* (New Brunswick, NJ: Transaction, 1999; repr. 1921 ed.), 171.
24. *Chan Chi-hung v. R* [1996] AC 442, PC, at 452H–53A.
25. See *The Interpretation by the Standing Committee of the National People's Congress of Articles 22(4) and 24(2)(3) of the Basic Law of the Hong Kong Special Administrative Region of the People's Republic of China* (Adopted by the Standing Committee of the Ninth National People's Congress at its Tenth Session on June 26, 1999) in *Hong Kong's Constitutional Debate*, 478–79.
26. Qiao Xiaoyang, *Explanatory Note on "The Interpretation by the Standing Committee of the National People's Congress of Articles 22(4) and 24(2)(3) of the Basic Law of the Hong Kong Special Administrative Region of the People's Republic of China (Draft)"* (Tenth Session of the Standing Committee of the Ninth National People's Congress on June 22, 1999) in *Hong Kong's Constitutional Debate*, 483 (emphasis added). Chang emphasized to this author in response to the conference paper that the NPCSC Interpretation of June 26, 1999, referred to Articles 22(4) and 24(2)(3) *together*, and the NPCSC, having looked at the two provisions in the *context* in which the *issue* of interpretation arose, came to a conclusion that was different from that reached by the CFA by the same exercise. According to Chang, the NPCSC did not go as far as laying down any test of which Basic Law provision is or is not an excluded provision; or indicating that both provisions should have been referred to the NPCSC for interpretation, because it merely said that the CFA did not seek a NPCSC interpretation as required under Article 158(3). As Article 24(2)(3) is not confined to Mainland-born children of Chinese nationality of HKSAR permanent residents and not all such Mainland-born children are physically in Mainland China, it is linked to Article 22(4) only in a limited sense and only in the context of the issue or issues which gave rise to the need to interpret any provision(s) in the first place.
27. *HKSAR v. Ng Kung Siu and Another* (1999) 2 HKCFAR 442, CFA, also known as the Flag Desecration Case.
28. This author was a member of the team of counsel representing the second respondent in the *Ng Kung Siu* case and did receive a copy of the said sheet of paper.
29. The National Flag and National Emblem Ordinance (No. 116 of 1997).
30. "NPC Role in Flag Case Floated," *South China Morning Post*, October 22, 1999, p. 1.
31. Ibid. The chief justice queried whether the contention would prevent the courts of the HKSAR ruling that a local implementing ordinance, which abolished the presumption of innocence, was unconstitutional. Litton PJ asked whether the contention would mean judges were incapable to intervene to invalidate a local implementing ordinance that penalized the waving of a desecrated flag by amputation of the offender's hand.
32. The National Flag and National Emblem Ordinance (No. 116 of 1997), s 7, and the Region Flag and Regional Emblem Ordinance (No. 117 of 1997), s 7.
33. The International Covenant on Civil and Political Rights (Adopted on December 16, 1966), 999 UNTS 171. Article 19 of the Covenant guarantees the freedom of expression in the HKSAR through its incorporation under Article 39 of the Basic Law.
34. As to how the question before the CFA was presented, *see Ng Kung Siu*, 447G–H (per Li CJ) and 462E–G (per Bokhary PJ).
35. *Ng Kung Siu*, 461A–D. Cf. *Percy v. DPP* [2002] Crim LR 835, DC (Eng); and *Hopkinson v. Police* [2004] 3 NZLR 704, NZ HC.
36. *Ng Kung Siu*, 461H.
37. *Lau Kong Yung and Others v. Director of Immigration* (1999) 2 HKCFAR 300, CFA.

38. All other members of the CFA agreed to the chief justice's judgment; Bokhary PJ dissented only on the question of disposition. Ibid., 342D.
39. Per Marshall CJ in *McCulloch v. Maryland* 17 US (4 Wheat) 316 (1819), US SC, though, it is conceded that, the epithet is more apposite to the earlier act, in *Ng Ka Ling*, of declaring the Immigration (Amendment) (No. 3) Ordinance 1997 unconstitutional.
40. The Immigration (Amendment) (No. 3) Ordinance 1997 (No. 124 of 1997).
41. *Lau Kong Yung*, 327B–D.
42. Ibid., 324F–I. Sir Anthony Mason, who participated in both the *Ng Ka Ling* and the *Lau Kong Yung* cases as the nonpermanent judge, made a similar point in his separate opinion at 346G–I.
43. See Yash Ghai, *The NPC Interpretation and Its Consequences*, in *Hong Kong's Constitutional Debate*, 213, observing that if the CFA were "more liberal" in agreeing to requests for judicial reference, there would be less incentive for the chief executive of the HKSAR to request the Central Authorities to invoke the NPCSC's plenary power under Article 158(1). Ghai warned however that that would be at the expense of the perception of judicial independence of the HKSAR courts.
44. *Director of Immigration v. Chong Fung Yuen* (2001) 4 HKCFAR 211, CFA.
45. It was common ground that the necessity condition was satisfied. Therefore, the CFA left for "serious consideration" Chen's argument that the correct approach to considering judicial reference was to assess the necessity condition first; ibid., 229I–30A.
46. Ibid., 230A–C.
47. Ibid., 225I–26E. In the context of the case at hand, the relevant effects on implementation relied on were "immigration control and law and order in the Mainland" and "immigration of persons to Hong Kong."
48. The validity of the assumption, as pointed out earlier in this chapter, is debatable. One would have to continue to make the additional assumption that the consensus built by the CFA in *Ng Ka Ling*, on the *Kompetenz-Kompetenz* of the CFA to decide for itself whether it would make a judicial reference subsisted.
49. *Chong Fung Yuen*, at 229A–H (emphasis added).
50. On the same date, the CFA handed down its judgment in another set of right-of-abode cases, also declining to make a judicial reference and interpreted the provision (which it considered as a matter of character to be a nonexcluded provision) on its own, in the absence of, in the CFA's view, a binding NPCSC interpretation of the relevant portion or expression of the provision: *Tam Nga Yin and Others v Director of Immigration* (2001) 4 HKCFAR 251, CFA. Although Bokhary PJ wrote a dissenting judgment, he agreed with the CFA's holdings on the NPCSC Interpretation of June 26, 1999, and judicial reference.
51. Albert H. Y. Chen, "Another Case of Conflict between the CFA and the NPC Standing Committee?" *Hong Kong Law* Journal 31 (2001):179 at 184.
52. *See* text to note 112.
53. *Ng Siu Tung and Others v. Director of Immigration* 5 HKCFAR 1 (2002), CFA.
54. Ibid., 165 (emphasis added). Bokhary PJ joined them on this point (401).
55. The NPCSC Interpretation of June 26, 1999, does not refer to the temporal effect of Article 22(4).
56. See, for example, Ghai, *Commentary*, and Chen, "The Court of Final Appeal's Ruling."
57. Sir Anthony Mason read the preamble of the NPCSC Interpretation of June 26, 1999, to mean that the NPCSC considered that the CFA should have referred Article 22(4), an excluded provision, for interpretation; see *Lau Kong Yung*. See also the discussion of the effect of the preamble of the NPCSC Interpretation of June 26, 1999, in *Chong Fung Yuen*,

227A–28J as to whether the NPCSC did intimate that Article 24(2)(3) was an excluded provision.

58. The CFA "assumed that art 22(4) is an excluded provision and held that art 24 is a provision within the Region's autonomy": *Chong Fung Yuen*, 219D–E, recounting the CFA's judgment in *Ng Ka Ling*.
59. See, however, P. Y. Lo, *One Living Tree* (Hong Kong: Ming Pao, 2005), 61–74.
60. *See Draft Basic Law of the Hong Kong Special Administrative Region of the People's Republic of China (for Solicitation of Opinions)* (Hong Kong: Consultation Committee for the Basic Law, April 1988), 23 (introduction, para. 52); Yash Ghai, *Hong Kong's New Constitutional Order*, 2nd ed. (Hong Kong: Hong Kong University Press, 1999), 200; Chen, "The Court of Final Appeal's Ruling," 116–17; Shuwen Wang, *Introduction to the Basic Law of the Hong Kong Special Administrative Region* (Beijing: Law Press, China, 2000), 216.
61. Treaty Establishing the European Community/ Treaty of Amsterdam (EC Treaty), Article 234 (formerly the European Economic Community Treaty/ Treaty of Rome (EEC Treaty), Article 177).
62. Henry G. Schermers and Denis F. Waelbroeck, *Judicial Protection in the European Union*, 6th ed. (The Hague: Kluwer Law International, 2001), 218. The authors cite the German and Italian legal systems as examples, and also briefly mention the existence of a "certification" system in the United States; see Jeffrey C. Cohen, "The European Preliminary Reference and US Supreme Court Review of State Court Judgments: A Study in Comparative Judicial Federalism" *American Journal of Comparative Law* 44 (1996): 421, 455–57. Contrast with Mainland China, where the Supreme People's Court in Beijing ensures uniform interpretation and application of the laws through rule making by judicial interpretations and specific rulings by intercourt correspondence (*qingshi-pifu*). See, generally, *Judicial Interpretation (New Edition)* (Beijing: Law Press, China, 2004).
63. *H. P. Bulmer Ltd v. J Bollinger SA* [1974] Ch 401, CA (Eng) at 418F–G.
64. Dorothy Yiu Chu Liu, *Legal System of the HKSAR and its Relationship with the National Legal Structure* (Third Thematic Report submitted to the First Subgroup of the Basic Law Drafting Committee, October 18, 1986). Liu reported to a panel under the Central-Regional Relationship Subgroup of the Basic Law Drafting Committee (BLDC) on the topic of the Legal System of the HKSAR and its Relationship with the National Legal Structure (copy with Hong Kong Collection, The University of Hong Kong Libraries and accessible online via Basic Law Drafting History Online). Liu was a member of the BLDC and a Hong Kong solicitor.
65. Ibid., 31–32.
66. Ibid., 35–36.
67. *Bulmer v. Bollinger.*
68. Ibid., 419C–E.
69. Wang, *Introduction to the Basic Law of the Hong Kong Special Administrative Region*, 216–17.
70. Schermers and Waelbroeck, *Judicial Protection in the European Union*, 237. The authors consider that the ECJ's task "will be made much more difficult if it has to give purely abstract and theoretical answers without being aware of the circumstances in which its reply is needed"; Ibid., 246.
71. Ibid., 239.
72. Such a move would have involved implicit application of what in ECJ jurisprudence is known as the doctrine of *acte clair*.
73. See Sionaidh Douglas-Scott, *Constitutional Law of the European Union* (Harlow: Pearson Education, 2002), 225–26.

74. See Alec Stone Sweet, "Integration and the Europeanization of the Law," in *Law and Administration in Europe: Essays in Honour of Carol Harlow*, ed. Paul Craig and Richard Rawlings (Oxford: Oxford University Press, 2003), 219. See also Karen J. Alter, *Establishing the Supremacy of European Law* (Oxford: Oxford University Press, 2001).
75. Ibid., 219–21.
76. James Crawford, *Rights in One Country: Hong Kong and China* (Hong Kong: Faculty of Law, University of Hong Kong, 2005), 9.
77. Ibid.
78. See *Ng Siu Tung*, [25]–[39].
79. The ECJ indicated in the *Da Costa* case ([1963] CMLR 224) that the preliminary ruling procedure "always allows a national court, if it considers it desirable, to refer questions of interpretation to the Court again," but that there would not be much point in referring a question of interpretation if the ECJ had already given a ruling on a "materially identical" question. National courts thereafter took account of prior ECJ rulings in deciding whether to make a reference. The ECJ recognized this practice in the *CILFIT* case ([1983] 1 CMLR 472) stating that prior rulings "which have already dealt with the point of law in question" may be relied on in adjudication "irrespective of the nature of the proceedings which led to those decisions, even thought the questions at issue are not strictly identical." Some commentators considered that these cases were the beginnings of a "system of precedent" in European law; see Douglas-Scott, *Constitutional Law of the European Union*, 244.
80. The preliminary ruling procedure has been described as an "instrument of co-operation" between the ECJ and the national courts; see *Erich Gasser GmbH v MISAT Srl* [2005] QB 1, ECJ, at 9E–F (per Advocate General Léger) and further 27H–28B (per ECJ).
81. The European Commission's power in this regard is admittedly more theoretical than practical, bearing in mind its stated reluctance to take such action; see Douglas-Scott, *Constitutional Law of the European Union*, 247.
82. Federico Mancini, "The Making of a Constitution for Europe" *Common Market Law Rev* 24 (1989): 595, 606.
83. Ghai, *Imperatives of Autonomy*, 39–40.
84. Cf. Mark V. Tushnet, *Taking the Constitution Away from the Courts* (Princeton, NJ: Princeton University Press, 1999).
85. Charles Fried, *Saying What the Law Is: The Constitution in the Supreme Court* (Cambridge, MA: Harvard University Press, 2004), 14.
86. The NPCSC Interpretation of June 26, 1999, was an interpretation made after final adjudication. The NPCSC Interpretation of April 6, 2004 (on Article 7 of Annex I and Article III of Annex II of the Basic Law of the HKSAR), was an interpretation made without litigation. The NPCSC Interpretation of April 27, 2005, was an interpretation made during litigation, namely *Chan Wai Yip Albert v SJ* (HCAL 36/2005), which was withdrawn afterward.
87. Michael Kirby, *Judicial Activism* (London: Thomson/Sweet & Maxwell, 2004), xv.
88. *Ng Kung Siu.*
89. *See Burton v. United States* 196 US 283 (1905) at 295 (per Peckham J). Cf. Chief Justice Roberts' commencement statement before the congregation of Georgetown University on May 21, 2006, where he opined that "if it is not necessary to decide more to dispose of a case, in my view it is necessary not to decide more," available at http://www.law.georgetown.edu/webcast/eventDetail.cfm?eventID=142.
90. *Ashwander v. Tennessee Valley Authority* 297 US 288 (1936) at 346–47 (per Brandeis J). *See* also *State of Rajasthan and Others v. Union of India* [1978] 1 SCR 1, SC (Ind); *McDaid v. Sheehy* [1991] 1 IR 1, SC (Ire) at 17; *Zantsi v. Council of State, Ciskei and Others* 1995 (4)

SA 615, CC (SA) at 617–18 (per Chaskalson P); *Re Patterson ex p Taylor* (2001) 182 ALR 657, HC (Aust) at 719–20 (per Gummow and Hayne JJ).

91. Ibid.
92. See *Secretary for Security v. Sakthevel Prabakar*(2003) 6 HKCFAR 397, CFA (App Ctte). See also *Yeung Chun Pong and Others v HKSAR* (unreported, March 2, 2006, FAMC 101/2005), CFA (App Ctte).
93. See *Solicitor v. Law Society of Hong Kong & Secretary for Justice (Intervener)* (2003) 6 HKCFAR 570. P. Y. Lo, "Master of One's Own Court," subjects the CFA's approach to critical examination.
94. See *Leung Kwok Hung and Others v. HKSAR* [2005] 3 HKLRD 164, CFA. At [66], the majority judges noted that "the focus of the constitutional challenge is on the contention that the Commissioner's discretion to restrict the right of peaceful assembly for the purpose of 'public order (*ordre public*)' fails to satisfy . . . constitutional requirements for restriction." Having ruled the discretion to be unconstitutional and ordered severance, the majority judges said in [97]: "The offences for which the appellants were convicted did not relate to the statutory provisions conferring on the Commissioner the discretion . . . The offences arose out of the holding of a public procession without complying with the statutory notification requirement. The holding that 'public order (*ordre public*)' in the relevant statutory provisions is unconstitutional and that public order should be severed from it does not affect the convictions. Accordingly, the appeal must be dismissed and the convictions upheld."
95. Kirby, *Judicial Activism*, 90.
96. A trio of final appeals decided in the summer of 2006 may be illustrative. While the CFA declared a provision of the Bankruptcy Ordinance (Cap. 6) as an unconstitutional restriction of the guaranteed right to travel in *Official Receiver & Trustee in Bankruptcy of Chan Wing Hing and Another v. Chan Wing Hing and Another & Secretary for Justice, Intervener* [2006] 3 HKLRD 687, it preferred to express no conclusive views as to whether the HKSAR courts may grant temporary validity to laws judicially declared to be unconstitutional (*Koo Sze Yiu and Another v. Chief Executive of the HKSAR* [2006] 3 HKLRD 455) and whether and to what extent the HKSAR courts have the power to engage in prospective overruling of a previous view on a legal question (*HKSAR v. Hung Chan Wa and Another* [2006] 3 HKLRD 841), holding that the circumstances of the two cases were not such as to make it necessary to determine those two questions of fundamental importance.
97. *Ng Kung Siu*, 460I–J.
98. For further cases, see *Lau Cheong and Another v. HKSAR* (2002) 5 HKCFAR 415, CFA (on mandatory life imprisonment for murder); and *Leung v. Secretary for Justice* [2006] 4 HKLRD 211, CA (on criminalizing buggery with a male under 21).
99. See, for example, Murray Hunt, "Sovereignty's Blight: Why Contemporary Public Law Needs the Concept of 'Due Deference'," in *Public Law in a Multi-Layered Constitution*, ed. Nicholas Bamforth and Peter Leyland (Oxford: Hart, 2003), 337–70; Jeffrey Jowelland Jonathan Cooper, Introduction in *Delivering Rights: How the Human Rights Act is Working ed.* Jeffrey Jowell and Jonathan Cooper (Oxford: Hart, 2003), 3–4; Anthony Lester and David Pannick, eds., *Human Rights: Law and Practice*, 2nd ed. (London: LexisNexis/Butterworths, 2004), 3.19–3.20.
100. The prevailing view is that Article 19(3) preserves the common-law position, which is that acts of state are nonjusticiable and that the courts may determine whether an act is an act of state; see Ghai, *Hong Kong's New Constitutional Order*, 318; and *Halsbury's Laws of*

England, 4th ed., Vol. 18(2), para. 616. See also Wang, *Introduction to the Basic Law of the Hong Kong Special Administrative Region*, 232–33.

101. *Ng Ka Ling*, 27I–J. Cf. Aharon Barak, "The Role of a Supreme Court in a Democracy and the Fight against Terrorism," *Hong Kong Law Journal* 35 (2005): 287 at 302 (where Chief Justice Barak stated that the Supreme Court of Israel opens its doors to hear complaints about the activities of that country's military authorities in the fight against terrorism on the merits and does not summarily reject any complaints using the act of state doctrine or by acknowledging the political nature and thus the non-justiciability of the issue).
102. Per Sears J in *Ng King Luen v. Rita Fan* (1997) 7 HKPLR 281, HC, at 283E.
103. See *Chim Pui Chung v. President of the Legislative Council* (1998–99) 8 HKPLR 767, CFI.
104. For an account of the evolution of the American doctrine of "political questions," see David M. O'Brien, *Storm Center: The Supreme Court in American Politics* (New York: W. W. Norton, 2000), 180–82. However, in the case of HC 910/86 *Ressler v. Minister of Defence* (1988) 42(2) PD 441, the Supreme Court of Israel developed the distinction between "normative justiciability" and "institutional justiciability" and held that *all* actions of the government were normatively justiciable, while a restricted number of categories of cases, such as the internal administration of the Knesset (the Israeli Parliament), were not institutionally justiciable; *see* Itzhak Zamir and Allen Zysblat, *Public Law in Israel* (Oxford: Clarendon Press, 1996), 269–70.
105. Chen, "The Court of Final Appeal's Ruling in the 'Illegal Migrant' Children Case" 118–19.
106. See the *Da Costa* case and the *CILFIT* case.
107. See Lin and Lo, Chapter 7 of this volume.
108. See the *CILFIT* case. The existence of such possibility, according to the ECJ, "must be assessed in the light of the specific characteristics of Community law, the particular difficulties to which its interpretation gives rise and the risk of divergences in judicial decisions within the Community." Schermers and Waelbroeck has counseled against too readily accepting that a rule of EU law is clear on account of differences in legal concept, language and interpretative methodology; the fact that a dispute of interpretation is properly presented before it should make the national court think twice; Schermers and Waelbroeck, *Judicial Protection in the European Union*, 279–80.
109. See Douglas-Scott, *Constitutional Law of the European Union*,246–48.
110. See Alter, *Establishing the Supremacy of European Law*, particularly in respect of the transition of the German and French courts.
111. Douglas-Scott also reported that the German Bundesfinanzhof performed a similar exercise in 1981. As to the British experience, *see Garland v. British Rail Engineering Ltd.* [1983] 2 AC 751, HL, at 771H–72A; and *British Fuels Ltd v. Baxendale* [1999] 2 AC 52, HL.
112. See *Chong Fung Yuen* and *Tam Nga Yin.*
113. *Chong Fung Yuen*, 230C–E.
114. See Cohen, "The European Preliminary Reference," 429.
115. See Basic Law of the HKSAR, Article 158(4).
116. Albert H. Y. Chen, "The NPCSC's Interpretation in Spring 2005," *Hong Kong Law Journal* 35 (2005): 255 at 257, noted that the NPCSC's Legislative Affairs Commission expressed a view on the term of a chief executive of the HKSAR elected to fill a causal vacancy in that office on March 12, 2005; see Xinhua Net at http://news.xinhuanet.com/newscenter/2005-03/12/content_2689790.htm; and "Beijing's Case for Tung's Successor to Serve Two-Year Term," *South China Morning Post*, March 24, 2005.

117. Barak, "The Role of a Supreme Court in a Democracy and the Fight against Terrorism," 290–91 (referring to his judgment in the case on the legality of the security fence in the West Bank).
118. The new link refers to the way by which the chief executive of HKSAR secures, by submitting a report in 1999 and 2005, the Central People's Government's assistance in moving the NPCSC to exercise its plenary power of interpretation of the Basic Law. The initiative refers to the 2004 exercise by the Council of Chairmen of the NPCSC of its prerogative to move for an interpretation of the Basic Law by the NPCSC.
119. *See Korematsu v. United States* 323 US 214 (1944), US SC, at 245–46 (per Jackson J, dissenting).

CHAPTER 9

Formalism and Commitment in Hong Kong's Constitutional Development

*Yu Xingzhong**

Constitutional formalism stresses the formal aspects of constitutionalism, such as constitutional rules, procedures, and conventions and not the substantive aspects of constitutionalism, such as constitutional ideals, values, and principles. The pedigree thesis of legal positivism, a well-known jurisprudential perspective, sees the validity of legal rules purely in terms of the source of power and holds that the ultimate criterion in a legal system resides only in the explicitly articulated power system or rule system within a given jurisdiction.[1]

Hong Kong's constitutional development is founded on two assumptions: constitutional development in Hong Kong means interpretation of the Basic Law and the interpretation of the Basic Law entails the exercise of the ultimate political power by the National People's Congress and the central government (Central Authorities). Since 1997, ad hoc political activism reacting to habitual paternalism has driven Hong Kong's constitutional development. This stimulus-response pattern of development demonstrates a strong tendency toward constitutional formalism based on the pedigree thesis of legal positivism. Although any constitutional law is by its nature a political law and the theory of law as interpretation may serve as a theoretical defense for the current constitutional practices in Hong Kong, constitutional formalism has inherent limitations if it does not give due respect to substantive constitutional commitments.

* I would like to thank Hualing Fu for inviting me to the conference and Albert Chen for very encouraging and instructive comments. My thanks also go to Lison Harris and others who assisted in editing this chapter. The work described in this chapter was substantially supported by a grant from the Research Grants Council of the Hong Kong Special Administrative Region, China (Project No. CUHK4641/05H [2005] [Law]).

Barely observable in current constitutional development in Hong Kong but nevertheless clearly defined in the Basic Law and other authoritative texts related to Hong Kong are the constitutional commitments made by the Central Authorities and shared by the Hong Kong government, of which the most important is the principle of "one country, two systems" (OCTS). These substantive constitutional values and principles, as higher requirements for such development, could compensate for or rectify the formalist inadequacies of constitutional practice. This dimension of Hong Kong's constitutional resources, however, has been obscured by the formalist overtures.

This chapter discusses constitutional formalism and constitutional commitments, the two dimensions of Hong Kong's constitutional development, in an effort to articulate a better practice of constitutionalism in Hong Kong, one which is less antagonistic but more conducive to Hong Kong's emerging constitutional identity. It evaluates and compares the relative significance of the two dimensions and advocates the combination of both approaches, rather than focusing only on either of them in engaging in the current constitutional practice and in envisaging Hong Kong's constitutional future.

The chapter argues that constitutional formalism based on the pedigree thesis limits the possibilities for Hong Kong's constitutional autonomy because the pedigree thesis provides a justification for the Central Authorities to step in at any time when a constitutional controversy emerges in Hong Kong. Constitutional formalism, however, does not preclude substantive constitutional commitments made by the Central Authorities and shared by Hong Kong government, such as OCTS and "high degree of autonomy." A more ideal way for Hong Kong's constitutional development lies in the proper balance of constitutional formalism and substantive constitutional commitments.

The chapter is divided into three parts. The first part reflects on characteristics of Hong Kong's constitutional development since the handover in 1997. The second part addresses the issues of constitutional formalism, pointing out its limitations and negative consequences. The third part explores an alternative way of conceiving of constitutional development, that is, the commitment thesis, for the purpose of enriching Hong Kong's constitutional experience and overcoming the limits of constitutional formalism. The chapter concludes with an optimistic note on the emerging constitutional identity of Hong Kong, which underscores the significance of the common-law constitutional tradition and its integration with the Basic Law.

Hong Kong's Constitutional Development Since 1997

Since 1997, Hong Kong's constitutional development has been marked by a number of constitutional controversies. The right-of-abode cases inaugurated a new constitutional practice and consciousness, which tested the new constitutional order founded on the Basic Law and the existing Hong Kong law. The decisions of the Court of Final Appeal (CFA) on the right-of-abode cases and the National People's Congress (NPC) Standing Committee's interpretation of Articles 22 and 24 of the Basic Law revealed a competition for the ultimate authority in Hong Kong's legal order and cast shadows over the possibility of judicial independence in Hong Kong after 1997.[2] Controversies over Article 23 national security legislation sharpened Hong Kong people's vigilance against any abridgment of their freedoms. Controversies over the Basic Law provisions on the election of the chief executive and the members of the Legislative Council beyond 2007 reflected different attitudes toward universal suffrage and greater democracy. All these controversies contributed, one way or another, to Hong Kong's constitutional development and increased Hong Kong people's constitutional consciousness. At the same time, and more quietly, Hong Kong courts, especially the CFA, have made judicial decisions implementing the provisions of the Basic Law that are less controversial and more concerned with the interests of small individual groups or institutions.[3] The government, too, has taken a proactive attitude toward implementation of the new constitutional order by various means. For instance, it has set up a task force to act as an intermediary between Hong Kong people and the Central Authorities, conveying the opinions of Hong Kong people to the Central Authorities, and explaining the concerns of the Central Authorities to Hong Kong people.[4] Various social sectors, concerned groups, intellectuals, professionals, and the general populace have demonstrated an unprecedented interest and enthusiasm in promoting Hong Kong's constitutional order. In sum, all those developments have ushered in a constitutional movement in which Hong Kong is now constitutionally engaged.

Briefly speaking, this constitutional movement is characterized by the following traits:

1. *Basic Law focus.* The focus of Hong Kong's constitutional development is almost exclusively on the Basic Law, with positive as well as negative implications for Hong Kong's constitutional future. The positive side is that the focus on the Basic Law means acceptance of it by various social strata of Hong Kong people who have diverse political, social, and economic interests, even though the Basic Law was initially imposed on Hong Kong people with the handover, much the same as when Britain

seized Hong Kong and imposed its legal order on Hong Kong one and a half centuries ago.

The negative side is that the focus on the Basic Law alone has created an impression that in Hong Kong constitutional development only means the implementation of the Basic Law, highlighted by the interpretive controversies, while ignoring the fact that Hong Kong's new constitutional order is partly established by the Basic Law and partly exists in the common law constitutional tradition of Hong Kong.

Before 1997, Hong Kong's constitutional framework had two major components: the royal prerogatives such as the Letters Patent and Royal Instructions, and the relevant doctrines, principles and practices of the common law. Modern constitutional law usually plays two roles and is correspondingly composed of two major parts: provisions setting out the power structure of the state and provisions protecting citizens' rights.[5] In Hong Kong's case, the former role was played by the royal prerogatives and the latter role was assumed by the time-honored common-law constitutional tradition in a rather unsystematic manner. Since 1997, the royal prerogatives have been replaced by the Basic Law, but the common law part of the constitutional order has been retained under the Basic Law.[6] Focus on the Basic Law alone does not do justice to Hong Kong's constitutional tradition.

2. *Concentration on the interpretive power.* Theoretically, constitutional development, or more precisely, the implementation of the Basic Law may take three main forms: legislative embodiment, judicial adjudication, and statutory interpretation. While the first two forms have not been neglected, the attention of the officials, lawyers, scholars, activists, and the media in Hong Kong has been largely on the interpretations of contested provisions of the Basic Law as they apply to certain cases. The right-of-abode cases and the Article 45 controversy had to be decided on by interpretation of the Standing Committee of the National People's Congress (NPCSC). Through rendering the interpretations, the NPCSC has effectively established itself as the ultimate authority of Hong Kong's constitutional order. The NPCSC not only interprets but also makes decisions on controversies involving the Basic Law.
3. *Stimulus-response pattern.* The NPCSC's interpretations of the Basic Law provisions are not based on careful and systematic post-legislative study for the purpose of further clarification or explanation, or based on a perceived inadequacy or contradiction, which makes the implementation of the relevant provisions of the Basic Law impossible. Rather they are propelled by disputes arising from different understandings of the provisions based on different political stances and claims. The pattern is of

a stimulus-response effect: controversy emerges in the HKSAR and the Central Authorities respond to it by making a political decision, exercising its power of interpretation.

4. *Ad hoc political activism as an impetus to constitutional development.* The stimuli are not considered or rational requests but are consequences of ad hoc activism representing diverse group interests. The right-of-abode appeals represent the interests of a kind of minority. The Article 45 issues reflect the consciousness of the supporters of democratic change. Ad hoc activism, economic or political, pushes the government along the road of constitutional advancement, but because of the lack of planning, constitutional development lacks an overall map and long-term commitment that would distinguish Hong Kong from other jurisdictions.
5. *Social groups versus government.* The stimulus-response pattern of the constitutional development propelled by ad hoc political activism, characteristic of the constitutional expediency since the handover, has polarized the participants in the constitutional process, with the government on one end and the various political and social groups on the other. Each may be as well intentioned as the other in promoting constitutional and democratic governance, and antagonism exists between them simply because of the interests concerned and the ways their interests are presented. Hong Kong's constitutional development could be smoother if different patterns of behavior were adopted.

Constitutional Formalism and the Pedigree Thesis

An obvious theoretical assumption underlining these constitutional developments in Hong Kong has been the pedigree thesis of legal positivism. The core idea of the pedigree thesis is that there must be a hierarchy of rules in any given legal system, in which there is an ultimate authority who gives validity to the rules of that legal system.[7]

The Pedigree Thesis

The three major versions of the pedigree thesis are John Austin's sovereign imperative, the rule centrism advocated by Hans Kelsen and H. L. A. Hart, and the class domination model of Marxism.

Borrowing heavily from Jeremy Bentham, Austin argues that the principal distinguishing feature of a legal system is the presence of a sovereign who is habitually obeyed by most people in the society but who is not in the habit of obeying any determinate human superior.[8] According to Austin, a rule R is legally valid (i.e., is a law) in a society S if and only if R is commanded by the sovereign in S and is backed up with the threat of a sanction.[9]

Austin's version of the pedigree thesis, however, has been severely criticized by other legal positivists. Hart, for instance, points out that Austin's theory provides, at best, a partial account of legal validity because it focuses on one kind of rule, namely, that which requires citizens "to do or abstain from certain actions, whether they wish to or not."[10] Whereas every legal system must contain so-called primary rules that regulate citizen behavior, Hart believes a system consisting entirely of the kind of restrictions on liberty found in the criminal law is, at best, a rudimentary or primitive legal system.[11]

Hart then put forward the concept of a rule of recognition for justifying the validity of a legal system and its rules, which later attracted extensive discussion.[12] The basic idea is that there is a rule in a given legal system that plays the role of a legitimizing standard for the whole legal system. That rule is called the *rule of recognition*. But unlike Hans Kelsen who explicitly articulated his view of the *Grundnorm*, Hart did not make it clear whether the rule of recognition is a rule, a convention or a social fact.[13] He therefore left room for legal positivists to debate the issue of whether morality is included in the ultimate criterion of law.

The Marxist view, a branch of legal positivism, sees law as hierarchically constructed with the lawmaker as the ultimate authority. Even though law is substantively an expression of the will of the ruling class, its form is necessarily rule based and there are strict hierarchical levels of the rules made by different entities within a legal system. The constitution is seen as the fundamental law of the country, and no legal rules are allowed to contradict the provisions of the constitution.[14]

How the Pedigree Thesis Affects Hong Kong–Mainland Constitutional Interaction

The pedigree thesis, especially the Hartian concept of a rule of recognition, became relevant to Hong Kong in 1999 when debates were waged over the right-of-abode cases decided by Hong Kong's CFA and the subsequent interpretation of Article 24 of the Basic Law by the NPCSC at the request of the Hong Kong government. The NPCSC enacted and is empowered to interpret the Basic Law. Its interpretations have significant implications for the judicial independence in Hong Kong and put the issue of ultimate authority in Hong Kong's legal system in the spotlight. Some scholars resorted to the legal positivist theory of the rule of recognition to justify the superiority of the NPCSC and its interpretation over the CFA decision, arguing that the

Basic Law is only part of a larger constitutional framework of the PRC and the ultimate rule of recognition in Hong Kong law since 1997 must defer to the PRC constitution.[15] Others have, implicitly or explicitly, argued that the Basic Law, as an arrangement to implement the OCTS policy in the Sino-British Joint Declaration and as a mini-constitution for Hong Kong, should play the role of the ultimate rule of recognition in Hong Kong law after 1997.[16] A third view, employing a related concept of Kelsenian terminology of *Grundnorm*, argued that there could be a splitting *Grundnorm*. Instead of one, there could be two *Grundnormen*: one based on the *Grundnorm* in the common law and the other from the socialist origin of China. This view saw the *Grundnormen* settlement as a means to escape the conflicts of ultimate authority due to the change of sovereignty.[17]

Constitutional formalism and the pedigree thesis would allow a series of steps to be taken in the constitutional interaction between Hong Kong and the Mainland that would lead to unfavorable consequences for Hong Kong's constitutional autonomy.

First and most apparent, the pedigree thesis would acknowledge the rule of recognition or *Grundnorm* in Chinese law, arguably embodied in the PRC Constitution, as the ultimate criterion of the validity of Hong Kong law.[18] As the Basic Law was enacted under Article 31 of the PRC Constitution, it has been argued that the rule of recognition in Hong Kong law is not in the Basic Law itself. Rather, it resides in the PRC Constitution, even though the constitution is not in practice the final authority.[19]

Furthermore, the NPCSC, rather than the CFA, would be treated as the sole defender and interpreter of the Basic Law, even though the Basic Law expressly delegates most of the power to interpret the Basic Law to the CFA while keeping NPCSC interpretive power only as to the issues relating to Central Authorities and central-HKSAR relations. The lack of clear definition of that relationship has already proved to be a source of contention. The pedigree thesis would allow only one legal institution as the ultimate defender and interpreter of the Basic Law.

A consequence of such an institutional framework would be the reliance on legislation rather than adjudication to flesh out the provisions of the Basic Law, as is the case in a civil law jurisdiction.[20] The Basic Law contains general provisions relating to the protection of citizens' rights and the regulation of the state structure that require further elaboration, either through legislation or adjudication. The use of legislation to embody the principles and spirit of the Basic Law is another step toward the integration of Hong Kong's system into the larger system of the PRC, whose legal system also resembles the civil-law tradition.

Whether common-law rules should be made into statutes to regularize them has been a matter of debate for centuries.[21] As China has embraced the civil-law tradition, no doubt proposals to systematize the common-law rules in Hong Kong will be made. A move to systematize the common-law rules in Hong Kong would be a radical step toward constitutional integration, rather than interface.

Finally, Chinese theories of interpretation generally assume that rule-makers know best the rules they have made and therefore are the natural interpreters of the rules. Major pieces of legislation promulgated by the NPC or by the State Council or the ministries under the State Council therefore contain a provision explicitly stating that the power to interpret the law is retained by the rule-makers. This fallacy relies on institutional memory—often the original rule-makers do not have an opportunity to interpret the rules they made because of either job transfer, demotion, death, or other reasons. Their successors, who may themselves know little about the legislation, undertake the interpretation. The NPCSC's practice of Basic Law interpretation is a prime example: None of the people who rendered the interpretation was an original drafter of the Basic Law. The provision regarding interpretation is in fact a statement of the power to make a final decision in a dispute over the meaning of provisions of the law, rather than a matter of objective or rational consideration.

Consequences of the Pedigree Thesis in Hong Kong

Constitutional integration would mean unity without separate identities. Hong Kong's legal system and constitutional framework would be incorporated into the Chinese system and lose its own identity. Hong Kong's constitutional development would be determined by China's constitutional development, which has a long way to go before it reaches constitutional maturity, despite the recent rise in constitutional consciousness on the Mainland.[22]

This constitutional incorporation has virtually blocked Hong Kong from developing its political autonomy and is not conducive to the implementation of OCTS. Regional autonomy takes many forms and may even, as Yash Ghai argues, be sustainable in a unitary system, but constitutional incorporation erases or blurs the boundaries between the Central Authorities and the HKSAR. Constitutional autonomy has no meaning for Hong Kong if its constitutional development has to comply with the parameters of the PRC Constitution.

The hierarchy of rules is the direct outcome of the hierarchy of legislative institutions, which is common in civil-law systems. Constitutional formalism and the pedigree thesis therefore work well in civil-law systems, although their advocates include scholars from common law traditions. In common-law systems, the hierarchy of rules is not so easily understood because of its unsystematic nature. Adopting constitutional formalism and the pedigree thesis in Hong Kong's constitutional development would mean giving preference to the civil law over the common law.

Constitutional formalism and the pedigree thesis tend to be rule centered. Rule centrism exalts the importance of rules in a legal system and focuses on issues relating to lawmaking while neglecting other important aspects of a legal system, such as judicial decision making, the enforcement of rules, and the legal consciousness of the populace. Conformity to rule centrism may not entirely comply with substantive constitutional commitments. The substantive commitments made by the Central Authorities to Hong Kong's constitutional arrangements are such that Hong Kong is considered to be different from the Mainland, but the conformity to constitutional formalism erases this difference to the extent that the "one country" of OCTS absorbs the "two systems" element.

Constitutional interpretation in any jurisdiction is inevitably influenced by political factors, even in a well-functioning legal system. The judges' task is to try to minimize or even eliminate those factors so that constitutional controversy can be resolved objectively. The exercise of an interpretive power as a pure political power should be avoided, but the current practice of interpreting the Basic Law is in fact heavily politicized.

Despite their rational bases, constitutional formalism and the pedigree thesis may not be conducive to Hong Kong's constitutional autonomy. For Hong Kong to develop its constitutional autonomy, substantive constitutional commitments must be taken seriously by the Central Authorities as well as Hong Kong government.

Constitutional Commitments and Constitutional Interface

The Basic Law enshrines the constitutional commitments the Central Authorities has made to Hong Kong's autonomy, but they have not yet been seriously enforced. Hong Kong's constitutional future and its constitutional identity may be better served by understanding and pursuing these commitments. As long as there are deep and genuine commitments by the Central Authorities and Hong Kong government to the constitutional ideal of OCTS, Hong Kong's constitutional development can move beyond the confines of constitutional formalism and the pedigree thesis, despite the differences in interpretive approaches and the different understandings of certain provisions of the Basic Law.

In other jurisdictions, constitutional commitments can act as the substantive constitutional parameters, guiding constitutional interpretive practice. For instance, Jed Rubenfeld argues that "American constitutional law has in fact conformed to a determinate interpretive structure" that, until now, has been "largely or even completely unrecognized."[23] While pragmatists, realists, and deconstructivists have given up on a coherent theory of constitutional interpretation, Rubenfeld writes, there is a "framework within which to evaluate episodes of radical reinterpretation," which "emerges from the deepest democratic commitments of constitutional law."[24] By crafting a commitment-based theory of constitutional interpretation, Rubenfeld seeks to rescue the U.S. Constitution from both originalism and the "living document" theories.[25]

According to Rubenfeld, constitutional intention is not important and should be distinguished from constitutional commitments, which do matter. Rubenfeld remarks that "the point of constitutional law is to hold the nation to its self-given, fundamental commitments over time, and discharging this task requires courts to distinguish, as they have, between commitments and intentions."[26] Constitutional commitments are important because they serve as the foundation for interpretive or doctrinal paradigms. Judges acknowledge and apply the core constitutional principles in paradigm cases.[27]

The constitutional commitment thesis requires an enlightened understanding of central-peripheral relations, which would allow the central government to win the respect of the periphery by giving the periphery maximum authority to govern its own affairs and by respecting the periphery's identity and traditions.[28] The periphery shall be loyal to the central government only to the extent that territorial and sovereign integrity is concerned. The Central Authorities need to oversee passively the periphery's development and the introduction of new ideas and institutions within the peripheral region. This understanding does not compete with the theory of sovereignty but rather refines it by way of a new constitutional thinking that exalts peripheral constitutional autonomy. The constitutional interaction between Hong Kong and the Mainland would in this way adopt the interface model, rather than the incorporation model.

The interface model presupposes that Hong Kong has a distinct constitutional identity that accommodates the Basic Law and the constitutional principles, institutions, and practices embedded in the common law.[29] But since 1997, the common law has been overshadowed by the controversies involving the Basic Law. In Chinese history, one of the most damaging practices is the erasure of the deeds of previous dynasties by succeeding ones, which may be a major reason why Chinese culture progressed only slowly. It would be a pity if the common law, which is a vital part of Hong Kong's constitutional identity, were to be similarly neglected or underarticulated.

Only after Hong Kong scholars and politicians form a clear understanding of what comprises Hong Kong's constitutional identity will it be possible for Hong Kong to interface with the Mainland constitutionally. Hong Kong needs a constitutional theory that can recognize the parameters by which Hong Kong's constitutional identity can be measured. Such parameters should be able to articulate the common-law part of Hong Kong's constitutional tradition in line with the provisions and spirit of the Basic Law. Recent constitutional scholarship in Hong Kong has left much to be desired in that regard.

The interface model would allow the coexistence of the two separate systems, rather than one incorporating the other. Unity with separate identities is consistent with the spirit of the OCTS policy. Hong Kong could maintain its rule of law tradition and political and legal identity, in which case Hong Kong would develop on its own, generally free from unwarranted Mainland constraints, and also serve as a reference point for the Mainland's constitutional development. Such an approach would be consistent not only with the OCTS commitment in the Sino-British Joint Declaration and the Basic Law but also with the similar concerns of the PRC Constitution.

The constitutional commitment thesis reflects this new mentality and has the potential to guide the integration of the Basic Law provisions with the common-law constitutional tradition of Hong Kong. The main constitutional commitments in this context include the constitutional ideal and principles, multi-interpretive authorities, and two-level constitutional review institutions.

Commitment to the OCTS ideal celebrates Hong Kong's constitutional identity as well as its future. OCTS is a pragmatic solution to a thorny problem, which became a political and constitutional ideal held by the leaders of the Mainland and Hong Kong governments. In the relationship between the Mainland and Hong Kong, this constitutional ideal works as a guide to, as well as a constraint on, the ultimate criterion for imagining interactive possibilities and institutions. The pedigree thesis of legal positivism must be subject to the constitutional ideals.

Constitutional principles are the values and standards on which constitutional laws and institutions are founded and may be "general" or "special." General constitutional principles are those applicable universally in any given modern constitutional framework and which are therefore adopted by both the PRC Constitution and the Basic Law. These general principles usually include the rule of law, human rights, democracy, separation of powers, and judicial independence.[30] Special constitutional principles are those specifically designed for certain political purposes, applicable only to specific jurisdictions. In Hong Kong's case, special constitutional principles include OCTS, "Hong Kong people ruling Hong Kong," "high degree of autonomy," and "fifty years no change to Hong Kong's way of life." In general, jurisprudence, special principles, and rules take the precedence over general principles and rules.

The sharing of the interpretive power is another major commitment in Hong Kong's constitutional framework. The NPCSC wisely delegated the power to interpret the Basic Law to the CFA, as the NPCSC is not in any position to interpret the provisions of the Basic Law. The NPCSC is not an adjudicatory institution nor a collective legal authority and hence is incapable of determining what and how to interpret unless it is requested to do so by inferior entities. The NPCSC's incapacity has contributed to the lack of enforcement of the PRC Constitution. In the case of the interpretation of the Basic Law, the NPCSC is in an even more unfavorable position because it is not familiar with Hong Kong's reality and its legal system. For efficiency's sake, it is sensible for the NPCSC to delegate its power of interpretation to the CFA. Furthermore, future constitutional development in Hong Kong requires coordination of the Basic Law provisions and the common–law constitutional principles and practice. The NPCSC cannot do this job, but the CFA can.

Nonetheless, the Basic Law reserves for the NPCSC the power to interpret Basic Law provisions regarding affairs concerning the Central Authorities and the relations between the central government and the HKSAR. These affairs may be those concerned with the institutional arrangements between Hong Kong and the central government, although the matter is not clearly specified. They are certainly not affairs involving specific individuals; otherwise, whatever happens between Hong Kong people and the Mainland, individually or collectively, would be subject to NPCSC interpretation. The purpose of reserving that power for the NPCSC was to deal with the issues arising from interinstitutional conflicts between Hong Kong and the central government, rather than covering all citizens.

The power to interpret law is connected to the power of constitutional review. Models for constitutional review can generally be divided into two types: one is a centralized constitutional review by a separate or a specifically established constitutional court or another institution, such as the legislature of the state. Such review extends to legislative acts and administrative acts. The other model is a decentralized constitutional review by ordinary courts, which is most often practiced in common-law systems.[31] Because the power to interpret the Basic Law lies with the NPCSC, which represents the Central Authorities in such matters, the constitutional review process will inevitably be centralized.

China in theory follows the centralized model while Hong Kong's system is decentralized. The type of constitutional review to be adopted in the new constitutional order of Hong Kong has become a matter of contention. The NPCSC theoretically should be the final authority for constitutional review in Hong Kong, but it is more practical for the CFA to act as Hong Kong's final constitutional review entity because that power has traditionally been exercised by the common-law courts in Hong Kong and other common-law jurisdictions. The question, then, is whether the CFA has the power to review legislation promulgated by the NPC that relates to Hong Kong. It would have that power if the special constitutional principles are upheld as the rule of recognition in Hong Kong law, binding both the NPC and the CFA. Practically speaking, the CFA is in a better position than the NPC to assess whether a piece of legislation passed by the NPC or by the Hong Kong legislature complies with the Basic Law. A two-level constitutional review structure, combining both centralized and decentralized review mechanisms, may be the solution.

Constitutional formalism based on the pedigree thesis limits the possibilities of constitutional autonomy in Hong Kong, but constitutional formalism does not preclude substantive constitutional commitments. A proper balance of the two would be the greatest hope for Hong Kong's constitutional future. Hong Kong's current constitutional development leans too much toward formalism while almost neglecting the substantive commitments and must be balanced by more attention to the constitutional commitments.

A commitment to the constitutional ideal of OCTS, the integration of the Basic Law with the common-law constitutional tradition, a combination of universal and special constitutional principles, the practice of interpretation by a multi-interpretive authorities, and a two-level constitutional review mechanism can all contribute to the formation of Hong Kong's constitutional identity. Hong Kong may then create a distinctive constitutional model that suits its unique legal and political characteristics.

Notes

1. Kenneth Einar Himma, "The Epistemic Sense of the Pedigree Thesis," *Pacific Philosophical Quarterly* 80, no. 1 (1999): 46.
2. See Weiyun Xiao, "Why the Court of Final Appeal Was Wrong: Comments of the Mainland Scholars on the Judgment of the Court of Final Appeal," and Bing Ling, "The Proper Law for the Conflict between the Basic Law and Other Legislative Acts of the National

People's Congress," in *Hong Kong's Constitutional Debate*, ed. Johannes M. M. Chan, H. L. Fu, and Yash Ghai (Hong Kong: Hong Kong University Press, 2000). This useful book contains detailed discussions on the CFA decisions and has an appendix of the relevant documents. See also Albert H. Y. Chen, "The Interpretation of the Basic Law—Common Law and Mainland Chinese Perspectives," *Hong Kong Law Journal* 30 (2000): 380–431. See also press release by the *New China News Agency*; *Ng Ka Ling v. Director of Immigration* (1999) 1 HKC 291.

3. See http://www.info.gov.hk/basic_law/fulltext/, Basic Law related judgments.
4. See Legislative Council Panel on Constitutional Affairs on Task Force on Constitutional Development, available at http://www.info.gov.hk/gia/general/200401/14/taskforce-e.pdf.
5. F. A. Hayek, *The Constitution of Liberty* (Chicago: University of Chicago Press, 1960).
6. See the Basic Law of the HKSAR, especially Articles 8 and 18.
7. Himma, "The Epistemic Sense of the Pedigree Thesis," 46.
8. John Austin, *The Province of Jurisprudence Determined* (Cambridge: Cambridge University Press, 1995), 166.
9. Kenneth Einar Himma, "Legal Positivism," entry for *The Internet Encyclopedia of Philosophy*, available at http://www.iep.utm.edu/l/legalpos.htm.
10. H. L. A. Hart, *The Concept of Law* (Oxford: Oxford University Press, 1961), 81.
11. Himma, "Legal Positivism."
12. Hart, *The Concept of Law*, 99; J. Raz, *The Concept of a Legal System*, 2nd ed. (Oxford: Clarendon Press, 1980); L. Fuller, *The Morality of Law*, rev. ed. (New Haven, CT: Yale University Press, 1969); Kent Greenawalt, "The Rule of Recognition and the Constitution," *Michigan Law Review* 85 (1987): 621; Jules Coleman, "Negative and Positive Positivism," *Journal of Legal Studies* 11 (1982): 139.
13. Hans Kelsen, *Pure Theory of Law*, trans. Max Knight (Berkeley: University of California Press, 1967), 214–15.
14. P. Beirne and R. Sharlet, eds., *Pashukanis: Selected Writings on Marxism and Law* (London: Academic Press, 1980).
15. Xiao, "Why the Court of Final Appeal Was Wrong," 53-60.
16. Chan, Fu, and Ghai, *Hong Kong's Constitutional Debate*.
17. Raymond Wacks, "One Country, Two Grundnormen? The Basic Law and the Basic Norm," in *Hong Kong, China and 1997*, ed. Raymond Wacks (Hong Kong: Hong Kong University Press, 1993).
18. See Bing Ling, "The Proper Law," 151–70.
19. PRC constitutions have been enacted by the NPC under the leadership of the Chinese Communist Party (CCP). By convention, the CCP has the power to change the constitution, as has been demonstrated by the four amendments to the constitution introduced since the reform. For a detailed discussion of the CCP's relation to PRC Constitution and the constitutional revisions, see Jihong Mo, *A Constitutional Primer for the Government and the Citizens* (Beijing: Zhongguo Renmin Gongan Daxue Chubanshe, 1999).
20. Hong Kong seems moving toward this direction, as evidenced by the move of the government to make a law to elaborate the Basic Law provisions on crimes against the state. See further Hualing Fu, Carole J. Petersen, and Simon N. M. Young, eds., *National Security and Fundamental Freedoms: Hong Kong's Article 23 Under Scrutiny* (Hong Kong: Hong Kong University Press, 2003).
21. For instance, Jerome Bentham was one who did not think very highly of the common-law tradition, preferring a more systematic presentation of common-law rules. See Gerald J. Postema, *Bentham and the Common Law Tradition* (Oxford: Oxford University Press, 1986).

22. The PRC has had four formal constitutions and an informal constitution called the Common Program of the Chinese People's Political Consultative Conference, briefly in effect during the beginning years of the PRC. The current constitution was made in 1982 and has been revised for four times. The constitution has not been effectively implemented. The frequent changes have reduced it to a mere piece of legislation. Recently, there have been discussions, termed *judicialization* of the constitution, aimed at enforcing the constitution by the judiciary. There have been few cases in the PRC's history where constitutional provisions were cited to back up a judicial decision indirectly.
23. Jed Rubenfeld, *Revolution by Judiciary: The Structure of American Constitutional Law* (Cambridge, MA: Harvard University Press, 2005), 12–13.
24. Ibid.
25. Ibid., 12.
26. Ibid., 15.
27. Kyle L. Kreider, review of *Revolution by Judiciary: The Structure of American Constitutional Law*, by Jed Rubenfeld, *Law and Politics Book Review* 15 (2005): 867–71.
28. For a discussion on the center and periphery relationships in China, see Michael Davis, "The Case for Chinese Federalism," *Journal of Democracy* 10 (1999): 124–37.
29. Albert H. Y. Chen, "The Interpretation of the Basic Law—Common Law and Mainland Chinese Perspectives," *Hong Kong Law Journal* (2000) 30: 380–431.
30. Michael Davis, "Constitutionalism under Chinese Rule: Hong Kong after the Handover," *Denver Journal of International Law and Policy* 27 (1999): 275.
31. Edward Samuel Corwin, *Court over Constitution: A Study of Judicial Review as an Instrument of Popular Government* (Princeton, NJ: Princeton University Press, 1938).

PART III

Legislative Interpretation and the PRC Constitution

CHAPTER 10

Of Iron or Rubber?

People's Deputies of Hong Kong to the National People's Congress

Hualing Fu and D. W. Choy

Introduction

A regional autonomy system is now commonly regarded as an optimal constitutional mechanism to manage and resolve regional, ethnic, or other conflicts within a state. The sustainable operation of an autonomy system depends on the existence of legally-entrenched processes and institutions at the national level that can effectively manage and accommodate regional identity and difference.[1] The opportunities for and ability of an autonomy region to represent itself meaningfully in the national political process are a crucial index of the degree and strength of regional autonomy. Active engagement and effective representation in national politics by autonomous regions not only maintain and strengthen regional autonomy but also generate an integrative force that unites the region with the nation. The existence of procedures and institutions that form a bridge between autonomous regions and the nation is the prerequisite for the successful operation of autonomy, and the participation and representation of the autonomous regions in those bridging institutions create a dynamic process in which regional autonomy and national integration mutually reinforce each other.[2]

The Basic Law of the Hong Kong Special Administrative Region (Basic Law) serves the dual purposes of maintaining Hong Kong's unique political and economic identity, and forming the bridge between Hong Kong and the rest of the People's Republic of China (PRC). The Basic Law both separates and marries the two different political traditions.[3] Although the Basic Law is largely successful in recognizing and preserving the internal differences, the institutional structures and processes that it has created to facilitate dialogue and to generate a consensus between Mainland China and Hong Kong have largely failed. This chapter examines one key bridging institution, the National People's Congress (NPC) as applied in Hong Kong and Hong Kong deputies to the NPC.

Constitutionally, the NPC is the highest organ of state power, representing the interests of all people in all parts of China, including Hong Kong. Hong Kong has both a right and a duty to participate in this political institution. Hong Kong participated in the congressional system during the colonial era, and there is no reason why Hong Kong people should not continue to be represented in the highest organ of state power.

But application of the congressional system to Hong Kong is limited, both constitutionally and politically. The people's congress system does not form part of the political system of Hong Kong, since the "one country, two systems" doctrine is based on the isolation of the Hong Kong system from the socialist system as practiced in the Mainland. Furthermore, Hong Kong deputies are a special political group created and imposed by the NPC on Hong Kong without substantive linkage to Hong Kong's political structure and community at large. Because of these political and legal constraints, the functions of the Hong Kong deputies to the NPC are much more limited than their counterparts in Mainland China.

Hong Kong deputies are therefore criticized in Hong Kong and Beijing alike, by people of different political persuasions. They are said to be political vases, who do little to contribute to Hong Kong and the nation, or are disparaged for making unsolicited comments on controversial issues relating to the operations of the Hong Kong government, thus eroding the high degree of autonomy of Hong Kong.

Relying mainly on semistructured interviews with four Hong Kong deputies to the NPC, two NPC Standing Committee officials as well as secondary sources, this chapter discusses the tension between the legal and political limits placed on Hong Kong deputies and their increasing assertiveness in representing Hong Kong in both national and Hong Kong-related matters. It discusses how the Central Authorities control the membership of the Hong Kong deputies to the NPC through controlling its electoral mechanism, and analyzes the rights and duties of the Hong Kong deputies in Hong Kong and in the Mainland, and the obstacles they encountered in performing their functions.

The most controversial issue concerning the Hong Kong deputies to the NPC since the handover is whether the deputies should participate in (or simply discuss) Hong Kong affairs. This chapter analyses this issue through case studies and illustrates the gradual change of the Central Authorities from prohibiting comments by deputies on Hong Kong affairs to encouraging deputies to support the Hong Kong government. The chapter concludes that while the political influence of the Hong Kong deputies are increasing, their role, as well as the extent of the application of the NPC system in general, within Hong Kong's political structure remains ambiguous. To enable the Hong Kong deputies to better serve their bridging functions between Hong Kong and the Mainland, their functions must be institutionalized and regularized.

The principal argument of this chapter is that Hong Kong deputies are likely to play a more active and instrumental role in facilitating cross-border relations because of the increasing demand on the deputies from three distinct sources. First, Hong Kong people demand more representation of their interests in the Mainland because of the increasing social and economic interaction between Hong Kong and Mainland China; second, because of Hong Kong's further integration into the Mainland economy, the Hong Kong government needs the deputies' political and social capital to assist with coordinating relations between Hong Kong and local governments in the Mainland; and third, the Central Authorities rely on deputies to promote national interests in Hong Kong due to Beijing's increasingly hands-on approach to managing Hong Kong's political affairs. The NPC is potentially an important political institution in China's future political reform. It no longer just rubber stamps the proposals put before it and is playing a distinct role in developing the rule of law and supervising state organs. Can Hong Kong deputies to the NPC maintain the historical trend and forcefully—like iron—represent Hong Kong's interests in China?

Small Circle Elections and the Membership of the Hong Kong Delegation to Beijing

Hong Kong's deputies have been in the NPC since the Fourth NPC (1975–78), but the region did not have an independent NPC delegation until after the handover. Under colonial rule, a NPC election for Hong Kong was not possible and therefore Hong Kong deputies participated in NPC sessions as part of the Guangdong delegation.[4] The deputies were nominated by Beijing and "elected" into office by the Guangdong provincial people's congress. Whoever was nominated was deemed "elected" because there was no connection between the candidates from Hong Kong and the voters in Guangdong.[5] 28 Hong Kong deputies took part in the Guangdong delegation in the Eighth NPC (1992–97).[6]

Hong Kong deputies participated in the NPC as an independent Hong Kong delegation for the first time at the Ninth NPC (1998–2003), which was also the first time that Hong Kong deputies were elected through competitive election. Because of Hong Kong's special status, the region was given seven more seats in the NPC in addition to the twenty-nine seats allocated according to NPC's formula for local representation,[7] totaling 36 seats. Article 15 of the Electoral Law of the People's Republic of China on National People's Congress and Local People's Congresses (Electoral Law) stipulates that the total number of NPC deputies should not exceed 3,000; 2,986 deputies attended the Tenth NPC,[8] so the Hong Kong deputies accounted for 1.2 percent of the total number of deputies in that plenary session.

The NPC designed the electoral system to ensure that its membership would be acceptable. According to a special measure for each plenary of the NPC for Hong Kong, Hong Kong deputies are elected by an NPC Electoral Conference (Electoral Conference) established in Hong Kong. The Electoral Conference is a nonpermanent body constituted solely for conducting the election of Hong Kong deputies to the NPC. The Central Authorities determine the result of the election by controlling the membership of the Electoral Conference and the electoral process.[9]

Only 435 and 1,029 people were eligible to vote in the Ninth and Tenth Hong Kong NPC elections, respectively, giving rise to the term "small circle elections".[10] Members of the Selection Committee for the first HKSAR government, which was also responsible for selecting the first Chief Executive of the HKSAR (CE), along with the Election Committee for the second CE, respectively, constituted 92 percent and 84 percent of the membership of the Electoral Conferences in the two elections. The majority of the voters in the Hong Kong NPC election therefore concurrently had the right to vote in the CE election.

Because of the Central Authorities' ability to control the membership of the Electoral Conference, the Electoral Conferences have been able to elect deputies who are mostly traditional supporters of the Chinese government. Before the handover, deputies came mainly from the so-called patriotic persons in Hong Kong, normally the patriotic labor unions, enterprises, schools, and other grassroots organizations. The Chinese General Chamber of Commerce (CGCC) and the Hong Kong Federation of Trade Unions (HKFTU) were the two main organizations from which deputies were drawn. The post-handover NPC delegations were characterized by more diversity, with many coming from professional backgrounds, particularly business and professionals outside the pan-democratic camp. Hong Kong deputies still remain dominated by the Democratic Alliance for the Betterment of Hong Kong (currently known as the Democratic Alliance for the Betterment and Progress of Hong Kong) (twelve members), the HKFTU, and the CGCC. The Hong Kong delegation is, controversially, led by the officials of the Liaison Office of the Central People's Government in the Hong Kong Special Administrative Region (CLO)[11] and excludes not only democrats but also moderate professionals.[12] Because of the existing electoral system, NPC deputies will continue to be monopolized by a few traditional patriotic organizations.

Initial Expectations and Subsequent Dismays

Deputies expected that the environment for NPC work would improve after the handover so that they could perform more meaningful functions within the political system of the HKSAR and the nation, such as representing people in Hong Kong and supervising the implementation of the Basic Law.[13] When the first 36 post-handover NPC deputies were returned, the deputies exercised their role in the new constitutional order, but the scope and use of their powers in Hong Kong remained vague. At the banquet organized by the NPC Standing Committee, deputies discussed matters such as the establishment of a NPC representative office in Hong Kong, privileges and immunities to be enjoyed by deputies, and even VIP treatment at the airport.[14] They also proposed regular meetings with the CE and optimistically suggested that the HKSAR government might assist the Hong Kong deputies to visit Hong Kong government departments, so that they could supervise the local government as did their Mainland counterparts, and also take the Hong Kong experiences to Beijing.[15]

The broader community in Hong Kong held two prevailing views about the congressional system and the Hong Kong deputies to the NPC. First, as an institution, the delegation was thought to be an important future player, as it would represent Hong Kong in China's highest organ of state power and have access to political power at the highest level in China: the deputies would be "a force to be reckoned within the new political scene" which would "play a crucial role in the new game of 'two systems under one country'."[16] At the same time, people feared that the NPC elections would erode the gap between the two systems.

The second view seriously questioned the deputies' ability to represent Hong Kong. As a "small circle" elected the deputies, it was commonly thought that the deputies would lack a popular mandate in Hong Kong. The election was regarded by many as "a comedy of errors," which, "instead of instilling a sense of pride . . . alienated people from their nation. This is a shame."[17]

These two conflicting themes were apparent in public opinion surveys conducted in 1997. On the importance of NPC deputies to Hong Kong, 66 percent of the persons interviewed were of the opinion that deputies were either "very important" (13.3 percent) or "quite important" (52.7 percent). Only 17.2 percent thought they were "not quite important" (16 percent) and "absolutely not important" (1.2 percent). Reflecting this perception, the majority of the people surveyed thought that Hong Kong deputies to the NPC should be elected by Hong Kong people through universal suffrage (78.7 percent) as soon as possible, preferably within one year (46.3 percent).[18] Clearly, there is significant support for extending the congressional system to Hong Kong.

Nonetheless, Hong Kong residents were overwhelmingly disappointed by the election process. While the NPC Standing Committee hailed the 1997 election as "transparent, equal and fair," public opinion was negative. In a survey conducted on the day of the election (December 8, 1997) and the day after, a large proportion of the public said they did not know the electoral process (33.2 percent), the result of the election (34.7 percent), or the arrangement made by the Electoral Conference (40.2 percent). Among those who knew about the election, the majority were "very dissatisfied" or "quite dissatisfied" with the electoral process (56.5 percent), the election result (50.8 percent), and the arrangements (54.4 percent). The level of dissatisfaction would reach 60 percent if those who did not express an opinion were omitted. Significantly, the majority of the respondents said the election as carried out "did not respect public opinion at all" (23.9 percent) or "not quite" (28.6 percent). Only about 13 percent said it either "very much" did (1.1 percent) or "somewhat" did (11.5 percent) respect public opinion.[19]

The early image of Hong Kong deputies to the NPC was as follows: first, they were politically powerful, posing a genuine threat to the high degree of autonomy in Hong Kong; and second, their lack of a convincing popular mandate meant that they would not be able to represent the interests of Hong Kong people.

Despite the deputies' eagerness to play an influential role in the politics of Hong Kong and the Mainland, to their disappointment, neither their status nor their working environment in Hong Kong improved after the handover. On the contrary, the Hong Kong deputies found that they were subject to more restrictions and criticism. Nearly a year after the return of the first delegation of Hong Kong deputies, the NPC Standing Committee had not yet provided any guidelines as to the status of the deputies and the scope of their functions in Hong Kong, except informal reminders from Chinese officials that Hong Kong deputies should keep a low profile in Hong Kong and not interfere with the high degree of autonomy of the Hong Kong government. During the NPC session in March 1998, a few upset deputies called for a clearer role for the deputies, demanding the ability to exercise their power as members to the "highest organ of state power."

During the implementation of the "one country, two systems" doctrine in the first few years after the handover, expectations were that the new system would work and so the Central Authorities were taking all measures to ensure that the high degree of autonomy promised under the Basic Law would be realized. Critical voices were to be silenced even if they came from the traditional supporters.

After Xu Siming's high-profile criticisms of Radio Television Hong Kong (RTHK), the NPC moved swiftly to restrain Hong Kong deputies. In November 1998, the NPC Standing Committee sent a delegation, headed by Shi Jingcheng, the deputy secretary-general of the NPC Standing Committee, and Hu Kangsheng, deputy director of the Legislative Affairs Commission (LAC), to Hong Kong to announce the Measure Concerning the Execution of Deputies' Duties by the Deputies of Hong Kong to the National People's Congress ("Duties Measure") to the deputies. The Duties Measure prohibited any deputy from undertaking activities related to the Hong Kong government and from interfering with affairs that are within the autonomy of Hong Kong. According to the Duties Measure, the deputies:

1. Cannot conduct any inspection visit in Hong Kong;
2. Cannot convey opinions or complaints of Hong Kong residents regarding the Hong Kong government or other organs in Hong Kong;
3. Cannot enjoy in Hong Kong the immunity from being arrested while the NPC is in session, a right which they enjoy in the Mainland.[20]

Instead, the deputies were asked to focus their work exclusively on national matters, including:

1. Discussing relevant state affairs;
2. Commenting on the Mainland's legislative bills when opinions are sought;
3. Inspecting the work of relevant state organs and units in the Mainland;
4. Conveying the opinions and complaints of Hong Kong residents regarding the government work in the Mainland;
5. Paying inspection visits to Mainland authorities and units;
6. Putting forward suggestions, criticisms, and opinions about any work in the Mainland to the NPC Standing Committee while the NPC is not in session.[21]

The principal function of Hong Kong deputies to the NPC is to participate in the management of national affairs through the activities organized by the NPC Standing Committee. The high degree of autonomy prevailed, making Hong Kong government work off limits for Hong Kong deputies' general supervisory power under the PRC Constitution.

Deputies protested strongly against the Duties Measure on substantive and procedural grounds. Substantively, the Duties Measure would limit the Hong Kong deputies' powers and deprive them of any supervisory authority over the Hong Kong government. A common complaint was that the position of Hong Kong deputies had diminished after the handover, as the Duties Measure emphasized the Hong Kong deputies' political triviality and that deputies were to merely rubber-stamp whatever had been decided in Beijing and Hong Kong.

Many deputies openly expressed their disappointment about the heavy-handed and disrespectful manner with which the NPC Standing Committee handled the matter.[22] Deputies were called to a meeting and the order issued without much explanation. No consultation took place before the meeting, and no discussion took place during the meeting. In addition, the Duties Measure is in the form of administrative guidelines without the force of law, and was created by the working committees of the NPC Standing Committee.[23] The actions of this five-man delegation are difficult to reconcile with the Standing Committee's frequent claims that it respects the Hong Kong deputies.[24]

Functions in Hong Kong

Receiving Complaints against Mainland Authorities

The handling of Mainland-related complaints has inadvertently become the most important task of the Hong Kong deputies to the NPC. Most of the deputies feel that helping Hong Kong people who receive unfair treatment is their most urgent business and something that they have the ability to do.[25] Lacking other more institutionalized channels, aggrieved Hong Kong residents turned to the Hong Kong deputies (especially the more popular deputies) for assistance. For example, Cheng Yiu-tong received more than 600 complaints in the five years before 2003,[26] while Allen Lee handled more than 100 complaints in 2000.[27]

The deputies have received no support for handling complaints from either the NPC Standing Committee or the CLO, so the personal resources of the deputy determine the kind of assistance he can render. Cheng Yiu-tong, for example, received support from the HKFTU, which provided him with the equivalent of half a secretary, but many other deputies work without such institutional support. A complaint may require more than one round of communication and, since the deputy serves as a "middle man" between the complainant and a government department, the task takes a great amount of a deputy's time.

Before the transition, all complaints relating to the Mainland received by Hong Kong deputies were forwarded to the related provincial or city people's congress standing committee for handling, unless the deputies took personal responsibility for them. After the transition, the complaints handling process has been centralized at the General Office of the NPC Standing Committee, though it makes little difference. Allen Lee forwarded more than seventy complaints to the NPC Standing Committee in 2000, but received a reply only in 10 percent of the cases. From 1998 to 2001, Ma Lik secured the release of only four Hong Kong persons who were unlawfully detained in the Mainland.[28] Cheng Yiu-tong has handled a few successful cases, but his success rate remains low. Among the 200-plus cases he handled, less than 1 percent was successfully solved.[29] Some deputies attributed this lack of response to the fact that the national law on the power of NPC deputies has not been extended to Hong Kong so that the mandatory requirement that the allegedly offending institution respond within ninety days does not apply,[30] while others blamed the Mainland authorities for refusing to cooperate with Hong Kong deputies.[31]

Deputies are willing to receive complaints from Hong Kong residents as a "project for people's hearts," to win the support of Hong Kong people by providing practical assistance for them when they encounter difficulties in the Mainland. Although the deputies have both the duty and ability to undertake this task, they also realize that it is a risky project. Whatever they do for the complainants may amount to little, given the low rate of success. One deputy, for example, said his office received frequent abuse from complainants, and a number of his secretaries resigned as a result. Another deputy was reluctant to handle complaints, in part because of the lack of institutional support. Deputies without strong political affiliations do not have the necessary resources to handle grievances. Some deputies also find it difficult to evaluate the validity and merit of complaints they receive. For them, a dispute which occurs in the Mainland should be left to the competent authorities in the Mainland to handle.

The CLO treats the matter more cynically. A CLO official explained that since the deputies are voted into office, they are accountable to the Hong Kong voters. More importantly, if the deputies want to run for office during the next election, they need to report their service to the community and seek the voters' support. According to this official's perspective, deputies should handle fewer complaints from Hong Kong for two reasons. First, both the Hong Kong government and the CLO perform the function of receiving and transferring complaints against Mainland authorities from Hong Kong residents, so the work of the NPC deputies is redundant. Second, Hong Kong deputies should focus on "mainstream" tasks such as supervising state affairs.

Should There Be an Office in Hong Kong?

The issue of whether the Hong Kong delegation should have a permanent office in Hong Kong surfaces regularly, and is one of the few issues over which the deputies and the NPC Standing Committee openly disagree.[32] Hong Kong deputies requested the establishment of a complaints office in Hong Kong when they were still members of the Guangdong delegation.[33] The NPC rejected the possibility of permanent office in Hong Kong mainly out of the fear that the NPC may be perceived as creating another "power center" in Hong Kong.[34] If the office were a representative office of the NPC Standing Committee, it would be official and enjoy a high status. But its existence is not sanctioned by the Basic Law and would present a challenge to both the CLO and the Hong Kong government. Furthermore, the office would operate and interact with the Hong Kong political institutions in the name of the NPC Standing Committee. This would defeat the essential characteristic of the "one country, two systems" policy, which is to limit and contain the influence of the Mainland institutions.

Similar concern was also shared by some Hong Kong deputies who disagreed with the idea of a permanent office.[35] They also argued that since the workload of the Hong Kong deputies is not heavy it would be more convenient and efficient for them to meet the complainants in their own offices. The creation of a central office would therefore be a waste of resources.[36] One deputy predicted that a central office would not be used frequently.[37]

An office would serve both symbolic and practical functions, however. To many deputies, resource support is not their primary concern. They seek a more formalized, systematic and effective mechanism for them to perform their functions in Hong Kong. Without a central office, the deputies cannot develop an independent identity. As deputy Victor Sit said, it was ironic to ask a Mainland body to make logistical arrangements for Hong Kong residents who want to meet their national representatives in Hong Kong.[38] For Sit, Hong Kong matters, including Hong Kong NPC matters, should not be left to the Central Authorities. For the deputies, the lack of a permanent office prevents them from better serving both the Hong Kong government and the people in Hong Kong.

On a more practical level, an independent office would be more accessible for the ordinary people of Hong Kong than the CLO. Asking Xinhua (and later the CLO) to provide services to a representative body is inconvenient, especially when deputies need to be in direct contact with Hong Kong people. The deputies suggested that a central office could be manned by deputies in rotation, making it easier for people to discuss their concerns. An independent office is needed because deputies have been largely unsatisfied with services and support provided by Xinhua and the CLO.

In late 2000, a conference room in the CLO was provided to the deputies and each deputy also has a mailbox in the CLO.[39] Because of the inconvenient location of the CLO, however, deputies generally prefer to meet complainants in their own offices or the offices of their affiliated organizations.[40]

Meetings in Hong Kong

The Hong Kong deputies to the Ninth NPC were initially divided into two groups, and each group was led by two conveners elected by the deputies and among themselves.[41] Because of the difficulties in arranging meetings, deputies would meet as one group. Initially, the deputies were to meet once every month, and later meetings were scheduled once every two months for the convenience of the deputies.

The organization of the meetings appears dismal, with no agenda for the meetings and no minutes taken. Allen Lee revealed that before 2001 no formal meeting had been held. The local deputies were ignored by the NPC Standing Committee and their internal meeting effectively became *cui shui hui* (an empty talk meeting). Hong Kong's congressional system thus existed in name only and was not institutionalized.[42] Indeed, until June 2001 when a conference room was allocated to deputies in the new CLO, they did not even have a fixed venue for meetings.

Not surprisingly, members did not attend the meetings frequently.[43] The CLO official said Hong Kong deputies are not as "disciplined" as their Mainland counterparts, but he acknowledged that deputies were all busy with their work, and seemed to be satisfied with the attendance record. The CLO seems to have tried to accommodate the deputies in their meetings.

Status and Functions in the Mainland

The status of the Hong Kong deputies to the NPC under the political framework of Mainland China is clear. As with the representatives from other regions, they represent Hong Kong people in the NPC, participating in the governance of the state. Given the limited adoption of the NPC system in Hong Kong, however, the deputies may lack an effective channel or network to develop a meaningful understanding of national issues. For example, deputies complained that they were only informed of the candidates for the senior positions of the PRC the day before the election[44] and that they were not informed of the workings of the NPC Standing Committee, including the time of its meeting, its agendas, and the state's legislative plan.[45]

To remedy this problem, the NPC Standing Committee arranged for central government officials to briefly report on that year's work of the central government to the Hong Kong NPC deputies before the NPC meeting.[46] But the matters covered in such reports are restricted to "economic plans and fiscal budget as stated in the government work report."[47] The brevity of the report and its limited briefing may not greatly improve the knowledge or understanding of the Hong Kong deputies.

Communication between the deputies and the NPC Standing Committee is particularly unsatisfactory. The contact point between Hong Kong deputies and the NPC Standing Committee is the Hong Kong member to the Standing Committee, Tsang Hin-chi.[48] Deputies complain that Tsang rarely reported to them about the meetings and the work of the NPC Standing Committee,[49] and doubted his willingness and ability to do so. This missing link is most striking due to the importance of the NPC Standing Committee. Fei Fih, one of the Hong Kong NPC deputies, moved a motion for strengthening the communication between the Hong Kong NPC deputies and the NPC Standing Committee during the Second Session of the Ninth NPC.[50] However, the lack of communication may also be caused by the absence of institutional support and the lack of understanding of national matters on the part of Hong Kong deputies due to either their unwillingness or inability. Many deputies were frequently absent from meetings but were prepared to blame others for their ignorance.[51]

The lack of communication can also be blamed on the political culture in China, which is characterized by a lack of transparency and consultation in the decision-making process.[52] When the bureaucratic style was extended to Hong Kong through the congressional system, the differences between governing styles became conspicuous. But a more important explanation is the lack of respect for the NPC as a political institution. The earlier examples of communication problems cannot be solely attributed to traditional Chinese political behaviors. Bureaucrats treat people differently, depending on their political importance. The lack of an institutional base for the Hong Kong deputies is the result of their powerlessness, not its cause.

Suggestions and Motions

These difficulties notwithstanding, the Hong Kong representatives perform their duties enthusiastically, even more so than their Mainland counterparts.

They actively participate in the annual meetings of the NPC, making suggestions and tabling motions. For example, from the Ninth NPC meeting to the Second Session of the Tenth NPC, the Hong Kong deputies moved five motions and 192 suggestions. Henan moved the highest number of suggestions (1,423). Excluding the Macau delegation, which started to participate in NPC meetings only in 2000, the Hainan delegation moved the fewest number of suggestions (186), followed by the Hong Kong delegation (192), the Taiwan delegation (213), the PLA delegation (238), and the Tibet delegation (241).[53]

In total, the NPC deputies in China from the First Session of the Ninth NPC to the Second Session of the Tenth NPC moved 7,163 motions. The average number of motions moved in each NPC session is 1,023. Zhejiang province moved the highest number of motions (546) during this period, while Macau moved one motion from the Third Session of the Ninth NPC to the Second Session of the Tenth NPC. Macau aside, Qinghai moved the fewest number of motions (3), followed by Tibet (5) and Hong Kong (5), and Taiwan (6). Given Hong Kong's size and the lack of legitimacy and representativeness of its delegation, the performance of Hong Kong's deputies is satisfactory.

The themes of these suggestions and motions by Hong Kong deputies include rectification of corruption, legal reform, social and educational issues, and commercial, economic, and financial development.

Promoting Cross-Border Interaction

The Duties Measure may not be meaningful or effective in restricting the speech of Hong Kong deputies, as Hong Kong deputies are officially allowed to raise cross-border issues. Cross-border issues are by definition partially Hong Kong issues. When attending the meetings, Hong Kong deputies actively put forward motions and suggestions on matters relating to cross-border crimes and mutual legal assistance between Hong Kong and the Mainland, and enhancement of economic cooperation and communication between the region and the center. From the First Session of the Ninth NPC to the Second Session of the Tenth NPC, 49 out of the 197 motions and suggestions moved by the Hong Kong deputies were related to Hong Kong. For Maria Tam (and many other deputies), the primary task for Hong Kong deputies is to improve cross-border relations between Hong Kong and the Mainland, including "anything that links Hong Kong to the local governments or the Central Government in the Mainland."[54]

Deputies might be viewed more favorably by Hong Kong residents if they raise issues which are of practical concern to Hong Kong, and incentives and opportunities now exist for them to do so. The increasing social integration between

Hong Kong and Mainland is resulting in a greater demand for mutual understanding and negotiation and greater demand for cooperation and assistance from the central government. Deputies apparently intentionally maintained a low profile in Hong Kong for the first five years after the handover to respect the "one country, two systems" concept. The increasing interaction between Hong Kong and the rest of China necessitates a more direct channel of communication with the central government and a stronger voice from the deputies. Matters such as the growing numbers of individual visitors to Hong Kong, the daily quota of one-way permits, recognition of professional qualification in the Mainland and the opportunity to engage in a professional practice all need the good will of the governments in the Mainland. Hong Kong deputies are better placed than the Hong Kong government to play an important, sometimes even the leading, role in raising issues with the central government during NPC sessions. Hong Kong NPC members can capitalize on the lack of cooperation between Hong Kong and the Mainland at the official level, to gain a certain legitimacy and even respect from Hong Kong society, especially when the deputies deliver on their promises. For Hong Kong deputies, their strength is not their contribution to national affairs and interests, but to Hong Kong's unique interests.[55]

Site Visits

When the NPC is not in session, the Mainland deputies enjoy the authority to supervise the work of the localities they represent through site visits. The restriction is that they are not allowed to inspect any other provinces.

In Hong Kong, the "one country, two systems" principle has turned the inspection mechanism on its head. The Hong Kong deputies are prohibited from conducting any inspection tour in Hong Kong and were instead organized to inspect provinces in the Mainland.[56] Before the transition, deputies were invited to tour a Chinese province once a year, often before the annual session, and the deputies could prepare for the annual meeting while on the inspection tour.[57] Since the Ninth Session of the NPC, the NPC Standing Committee has organized two tours for Hong Kong deputies every year. For example, some deputies had been invited to pay inspection visits and conduct surveys in Guizhou, Xinjiang, Nansha, and Liaoning.[58] All the expenses are covered by the NPC Standing Committee.

The tours undoubtedly assist Hong Kong deputies to understand the social and economic conditions in the Mainland[59] but can hardly play any meaningful or distinctive supervisory function. The visits were meticulously arranged by Mainland authorities, effectively becoming "a tour for honored guests" without any element of supervision.[60] But inspection tours may become meaningful when conducted in conjunction with other more specific functions and together with Mainland NPC members.

Discussing Hong Kong Affairs

The most significant challenge facing Hong Kong deputies is the prohibition on any discussion on political issues relating to Hong Kong in Hong Kong, Beijing or elsewhere. Before the transition, Chinese government actively encouraged the deputies to challenge the colonial government and to speak out and act as the master of the country. Deputies spoke and acted on behalf of Beijing when circumstances did not allow Beijing to speak or act directly. But immediately after the transition Beijing started to silence the Hong Kong deputies.

The First Assault on Radio Television Hong Kong (RTHK)

The Duties Measure was triggered by the first assault on RTHK, the official radio station and broadcasting company of the Hong Kong government, during the NPC session in 1998. In March 1998, at a meeting in Beijing, a delegate of the Chinese People's Political Consultative Conference (CPPCC), Xu Simin, criticized RTHK for not being objective and urged the then CE of HKSAR Tung Chee-hwa to tighten control over RTHK.[61] Although Tung and his top officials subsequently defended RTHK,[62] and the head of the CPPCC also indirectly disapproved of Xu's comments,[63] Xu's comments aroused great concern for press freedom in Hong Kong.

Xu's criticisms and the reactions in Hong Kong prompted some unusually high level responses. In his speech at the First Session of the Ninth Hong Kong NPC in March 1998, Jiang Zemin, the then President of the PRC, stated, "According to the principle of 'one country, two systems,' as a special administrative region of our country, Hong Kong does not implement the people's congress system, NPC deputies returned in Hong Kong only represent the Hong Kong compatriots to participate in administering the state affairs, but not to *interfere* in the affairs of Hong Kong" (emphasis added).[64]

Immediately after Jiang's speech, the NPC Standing Committee's news bureau chief, Zhou Chengkui, announced that it was "inappropriate for the Hong Kong NPC deputies to comment on Hong Kong affairs when the NPC is not in session."[65] Undoubtedly, the gag rule in the Duties Measure was imposed as an immediate reaction to the increasing criticisms of the Hong Kong government by NPC deputies and CPPCC members.

Hong Kong deputies were divided on this issue. Some deputies, including Allen Lee and Ng Hong-mun, insisted that deputies were entitled to speak about Hong Kong affairs as long as the speech did not violate any law. Indeed, they saw it a duty of a deputy to speak up: "No one can stop me, not even the Standing Committee," said Lee.[66] Others seemed more willing to exclude pure Hong Kong affairs and to limit their deliberations to national affairs and affairs relating to cross-border relations. As Maria Tam said, "if one wants to talk about Hong Kong affairs, go and run for Legislative Councilor."[67] Deputies are mostly critical of the gag rule and vowed to challenge Hong Kong government policies in their personal capacity, rather than in their official capacity. But the lack of any institution for the Hong Kong deputies makes distinguishing a deputy's personal capacity from his or her official capacity difficult.

Despite repeated verbal reminders by senior Chinese officials and the explicit provisions in the Duties Measure to prevent "intervention" in the autonomy of Hong Kong, many deputies have spoken on Hong Kong affairs, arguing that, as Hong Kong residents as well as Hong Kong deputies representing Hong Kong people, making comments on Hong Kong affairs should be as a matter of right, and does not amount to "interference."[68]

Second Assault on RTHK

The deputies were effectively silenced, and when the RTHK was attacked for broadcasting Lee Teng-hui's "Two States Theory," the reaction of Hong Kong deputies was unsurprisingly low key. While being interviewed by a German Broadcasting company, on July 9, 1999, the then president of Taiwan Lee Teng-hui claimed that ever since Taiwan amended its Constitution in 1991, Taiwan had already established its relationship with China as one between two nation states, or at least a special state-to-state relationship.[69] China strongly condemned the "Two States Theory" and some Hong Kong deputies and CPPCC delegates criticized Lee in the Hong Kong media.[70] On July 17, RTHK invited Cheng An-kuo, the managing director of the Chung Hwa Travel Service and Taiwan's de facto envoy in Hong Kong, to present his view on Lee's "Two States Theory" in the radio program *Letter to Hong Kong*.[71] Expressing his support for the "Two States Theory," Cheng described the relationship between Taiwan and China as resembling the relationship between West Germany and East German before their reunification.[72]

Cheng's comments on RTHK caused another round of assaults on RTHK. Wang Rudeng, assistant to the Director of Xinhua News Agency (who subsequently became a Hong Kong deputy to the Tenth NPC in 2002), chastised Cheng for "promoting" a two-Chinas policy in Hong Kong.[73] The comment of then Information Coordinator for the CE's office, Stephen Lam Shui-lung, was especially interesting: he said that "as the head of a travel agency in Hong Kong, it is more appropriate for [Cheng] to focus on economics, tourism and associated matters. It is not appropriate for him to get involved in political issues."[74]

Except for a few critical comments by individual deputies, [75] the response of the Hong Kong NPC delegation was slow and not "sensitive" enough.[76] They held only one meeting to discuss Lee's theory and Cheng's comments a full month after Lee Teng-hui had made his speech.[77] During the meeting, many deputies also denounced RTHK for allowing Cheng An-kuo's comments to air in Hong Kong. Tsang Hin-chi commented that "As the broadcasting station of the Hong Kong government," he said, "RTHK should exercise self-control and should not arbitrarily facilitate some people to publicize secessionist speech."[78] Tsang said that he would take the matter to the impending NPC Standing Committee meeting in Beijing for discussion.[79] Other deputies diplomatically claimed that what Cheng had done was "inappropriate" and called on the Travel Agency to be aware of its special status in Hong Kong and to exercise "self-discipline and be watchful over his own deeds and words as a guest of the Hong Kong government."[80]

NPC Standing Committee Interpretations of the Basic Law

The 1999 Interpretation of the Basic Law by the NPC Standing Committee changed the position of the Central Authorities regarding Hong Kong NPC deputies' status and function in relation to Hong Kong. The deputies did not play any role in formulating the first Interpretation, and they were called to attend a meeting in Shenzhen to receive the Interpretation without any discussion. But the subsequent strong reactions may have caused the central government to rethink its role in Hong Kong governance and adjust its relations with the Hong Kong deputies and other traditional supporters. According to the deputies,[81] the 1999 Interpretation was the first time in the post-handover era that the Central Authorities realized that their traditional supporters, particularly the Hong Kong deputies to the NPC, play an important role in central-local relations.

Interference is difficult to define and is subject to different interpretations in different circumstances. By 2002, the Central Authorities had changed their attitude. In May 2002, Li Peng, the then NPC Standing Committee chairman, said to the Hong Kong deputies, "You are Hong Kong people. If you don't have a view on Hong Kong affairs or are not concerned about it, what's the point of being NPC deputies? You can speak out."[82] When Wu Bangguo became the chairman of the NPC Standing Committee in 2003, the Duties Measure was effectively discarded, though only de facto. Instructions from the NPC have changed expressly: deputies are entitled to discuss Hong Kong affairs while attending NPC meetings in Beijing, and they may also discuss Hong Kong affairs while in Hong Kong in their personal or other capacities.[83]

The Central Authorities have reconsidered the restraints they placed on the deputies. Hong Kong's economic status and political landscape changed substantially during the ten years after the transition. The trust placed by the Central Authorities in the Hong Kong government and the Hong Kong people is waning and shifting. For the Central Authorities, it is becoming clear that the Hong Kong question was not resolved with the handover, and a high degree of autonomy does not mean that the central government can take a "hands-off" approach. Certain positive interventions in social, economic and even political matters may be necessary to "stabilize" Hong Kong and reconfirm Beijing's influence.

One can see the subtle changes in what the NPC Standing Committee has required of Hong Kong deputies. If the demand on Hong Kong deputies in the Ninth NPC was largely negative in the sense that deputies were restrained from acting on, or speaking about, Hong Kong affairs, the demand from the Tenth NPC was that they actively support CE Tung and the policies of the Hong Kong government. Gradually, the Central Authorities are recognizing that NPC deputies are an important political force in cross-border political and legal relations. Beijing may not be able to win the hearts of Hong Kong's middle class in the near future, and is turning to traditional supporters to implement Beijing's policies.

The change is gradual but highly visible. For example, while the deputies were merely notified of the first NPC Standing Committee Interpretation, they were given full explanations of the second and the third Interpretations, and deputies were able to engage in extensive discussion with the NPC Standing Committee, although the result of the discussion was never meant to alter the Interpretations.

"Sheng Huaren's Instructions"

In August 2003, Sheng Huaren, Deputy Chairmen of the NPC Standing Committee and the NPC Standing Committee's Secretary-General, paid a special visit to the Hong Kong deputies who were on an inspection tour to Inner Mongolia and gave them four instructions:

1. Deputies should treasure and protect the stability and prosperity of Hong Kong.

2. Deputies should support the work of Hong Kong government under Tung's leadership.
3. Deputies should support the Article 23 national security legislation.
4. Deputies should focus their attention on promoting Hong Kong's economic development.[84]

Sheng's instructions were a disguised criticism of the deputies. After the unprecedented antigovernment demonstration in Hong Kong on July 1, 2003, the territory's government plunged into a deep legitimacy crisis.[85] The government's relentless push for national security legislation back-fired. The demonstration of anger and frustration on such a massive scale shocked both the Hong Kong and the Central governments. More shocking and perhaps more disappointing was the open challenge to the Tung administration by some Hong Kong deputies to the NPC, who called for the national security legislation to be delayed and Tung's resignation.[86] The deputies had elected Tung into office, so their calls for his resignation effectively amounted to a voters' recall.

The key part of Sheng's instructions was the reference to Hong Kong's stability: "Hong Kong NPC deputies enjoy very high political status in Hong Kong and are very influential. Therefore when expressing opinions in public forums, [deputies] should take Hong Kong's stability, Hong Kong's overall interest and public interest as the priority. In the eyes of Hong Kong people, what is said by deputies represent the patriotic forces. When the speech is correct, it can guide [the people] positively; but when the speech is incorrect, it will have negative impact."[87] Sheng imposed two more specific requirements on the deputies: first, deputies should not say or do anything detrimental to the stability of Hong Kong and Hong Kong's overall interest; and second, deputies should actively support the Hong Kong government in its renewed promotion of Article 23 legislation and ensure the safe passage of the legislation. Deputies were further required "to let known his or her own positions and to be firmly against anything that is inconsistent with the Constitution and the Basic Law."[88] Sheng's speech was part of a larger effort on the part of the central government to help the Hong Kong government to re-group after the failure to push through the Article 23 legislation. The efforts eventually failed and Tung resigned from the CE post as a result. The response of some of the deputies to Sheng's instructions illustrated the level of defiance and rebellion among the traditional supporters of the Hong Kong government.

Upon returning to Hong Kong, Allen Lee publicized the details of the Sheng instructions on his radio program[89] and Ma Lik wrote about the meeting in detail.[90] Both used the occasion to make the point that the central government has allowed Hong Kong deputies to play a more active role in Hong

Kong. While the role was limited to *supporting* the Hong Kong government and mandated deputies to challenge dissent relating to the national security legislation, Sheng's veiled criticism has been read as officially releasing the deputies from their previous constraints of speaking on Hong Kong affairs.

Ma Lik also remained defiant in his article published in the *Hong Kong Economic Times*. In response to Sheng's request that he support Tung's government, Ma said that as the deputies were Tung's voters, they would support him. But Ma continued, saying "if the CE failed to govern according to law or made errors in governing, and as a result the interests of Hong Kong and the nation were violated, Hong Kong deputies should be entitled to make criticisms to protect the interests of Hong Kong people, Hong Kong and the nation."[91]

Ma was equally firm in rejecting the suggestion that deputies should pledge their unconditional support for the Article 23 legislation and insisted that the Bill should be withdrawn to prevent further polarization of Hong Kong society. Ma called upon deputies to expand their influence in Hong Kong and especially to make comments and provide suggestions on matters of great public interest. Only through more active engagement *within* Hong Kong society can the deputies shed their rubber stamp image and gain acceptance from Hong Kong people.[92]

Conclusion

Ten years after the handover, the status and functions of Hong Kong deputies are vastly different to those predicted. Soon after the handover the Central Authorities reminded the Hong Kong deputies that they should not "interfere" in Hong Kong affairs, to ensure the implementation of the "one country, two systems" principle. Whenever deputies openly criticized Hong Kong affairs, the Central Authorities would quickly reissue the "non-intervention" policy. These deputies were not politically strong and not an important political force within Hong Kong or in China. The issuing of the heavy-handed Duties Measure was a significant restraint on the activities of the Hong Kong deputies.

But the role that Hong Kong deputies may play is changing. In the first five years after the handover, deputies maintained low profiles due to a lack of experience, lack of opportunities, and caution about paying the highest degree of respect for Hong Kong's autonomy. Since 1999, however, one can see a clear development towards political activism on the part of the deputies. The failures of the Tung administration allowed deputies the opportunity to address important Hong Kong matters and increased their communications with the Central Authorities. The increase in cross-border social and economic interactions has also created incentives for the deputies to bridge the divide between the two places for the benefit of Hong Kong. The deputies are gaining political legitimacy and are achieving a certain popular mandate in dealing with the less political issues of cross-border legal relations, in particular helping Hong Kong people of different political persuasions who have troubles in the Mainland.

The deputies are no longer content with their symbolic role, merely acting as Hong Kong's nominal representatives in the NPC. They have active role models: many of the deputies have been members of both the NPC and Legislative Council, which has acted assertively to ensure the accountability of the Hong Kong government. The two positions may be difficult to distinguish, as some have predicted, and the role a deputy has in Hong Kong will affect his or her behavior in the NPC activities. One cannot quarantine one's pattern of political behavior.

The mentality of the deputies has also undergone a gradual but visible change. They take pride in their supreme constitutional status, but are aware of the gap between the formal authorities, the lack of any institutionalized powers, and the disrespect they have received from the Hong Kong government. Deputies are speaking out and reaching out; they have also become more defiant of any attempts to silence them. But the ultimate test for deputies is whether they can change the impression that they are merely speaking for the Central Authorities, and not for the people of Hong Kong.

The Hong Kong government has also started to pay more respect to the Hong Kong NPC deputies since Donald Tsang became the CE of Hong Kong. Tsang's consultation with the Hong Kong NPC deputies in respect of the contents of his first Policy Address before official public dissemination and his invitation to eleven incumbent Hong Kong NPC deputies to sit in the Commission on Strategic Development[93] clearly demonstrate his recognition of the importance of the Hong Kong NPC deputies.[94] In addition, before attending the NPC session in March 2006, CE Tsang invited the Hong Kong NPC deputies and CPPCC members to hold a gathering to exchange views. According to the report, the issues discussed during the gathering included Hong Kong's development and economy. Tsang reportedly promised that he would appoint more Hong Kong NPC deputies to the advisory committees of the Hong Kong government.[95] Most significantly, Hong Kong members of the CPPCC's Guangdong chapters set up a club in Hong Kong.[96] This unprecedented event may be a cause both for celebration, because of its potential bridging function, and fear, because of its potential for interference.

At the national level, the NPC has been asserting its own authority in performing its legislative and supervisory functions. No longer a rubber-stamping organization, the NPC is gaining increasing legitimacy and power. At the regional level in particular, deputies are inventing different accountability mechanisms to place government departments and the judiciary under more effective control. The Hong Kong deputies are aware of the recent developments and are eager to contribute to the process. But to claim legitimacy in Hong Kong, deputies sooner or later would have to stand firm—like iron—side by side with other Hong Kongers, to resist encroachment on Hong Kong's high degree of autonomy by the Central Authorities.

NPC deputies in Hong Kong straddle the two systems, but neither the Central Authorities nor the Hong Kong government is certain which constitutional functions the deputies are expected to serve. The NPC system as applied in Hong Kong is unsatisfactory to all the parties concerned, including the Standing Committee of the NPC, the CLO, the Hong Kong government, the pan-democrats, and the deputies themselves. The Hong Kong NPC system is perceived by many as having been created hastily at the time of transition, without careful and serious consideration. Clearly the existing model is not a long-term solution and was not meant to be one. The model as practiced in Hong Kong was designed and redesigned in an ad hoc manner in response to the changing political landscape in Hong Kong. It needs a long-term and systemic overhaul to make it more representative, more effective, and better integrated into Hong Kong's political structure. Despite the political and legal limitations within which they work, Hong Kong deputies are already a political force that cannot be simply written off.

Notes

1. *See* Hurst Hannum, *Autonomy, Sovereignty, and Self-Determination: The Accommodation of Conflicting Rights* (Philadelphia: University of Pennsylvania Press, 1990); and Yoram Dinstein, ed., *Models of Autonomy* (New Brunswick, NJ: Transaction Books, 1981).
2. Ibid.
3. For a detailed discussion about the political relationship between Mainland China and Hong Kong under the Basic Law, *see* Yash Ghai, *Hong Kong's New Constitutional Order: The Resumption of Chinese Sovereignty and the Basic Law*, 2nd ed. (Hong Kong: University of Hong Kong Press, 1999).
4. Ng Hong-mun, *Renda Xuanju Beiwanglu: Jiujie Renda Huigu yu Shijie Xuanju* (*Memorandum of the Election of the National People's Congress: A Review of the Ninth NPC and the Election of the Tenth NPC*) (Hong Kong: Cosmos Books, 2002), 26.
5. "'Brother Tong' Wants to Be the Glue between the Two Places—Interview with Hong Kong NPC Deputy Cheng Yiu-tong," *Bauhinia Magazine Online*, available at http://www.zijing.com.cn/BIG5/channel3/200301/03/428.html (accessed August 9, 2005).
6. Ng, *Renda Xuanju Beiwanglu*, 5.

7. Chs. 2–5, Electoral Law.
8. For the details about the number of deputies in each delegation, *see Zhongguo Renda Wang*, the website of the National People's Congress, available at http://www.npc.gov.cn; hereinafter NPC website.
9. Article 1, Measure for the Election of Deputies of the Hong Kong Special Administrative Region of the People's Republic of China to the Tenth National People's Congress.
10. Cao Zhi, "Explanation Concerning the Name List of Members of the Electoral Conference of the Hong Kong Special Administrative Region of the People's Republic of China to the Ninth National People's Congress (Draft)," (October 29, 1997) (on file with authors); "'Significant Responsibility of the Electoral Conference' of the Hong Kong NPC," *Ta Kung Pao*, August 30, 2002. For the composition of the Ninth Electoral Conference and the political affiliation of the members of the Electoral Conference, *see* Suzanne Pepper, "Hong Kong Joins the National People's Congress: A First Test for One Country with Two Political Systems," *Journal of Contemporary China* 8 (21) (1999): 319, 322, and 331.
11. Since the Fourth NPC in 1975, the norm has been that heads or deputy heads of the former Hong Kong branch of the Xinhua News Agency and the current CLO are Hong Kong deputies to the NPC. Li Guoqiang and Zhong Lijuan, eds., *Gangqu Quanguo Renda Daibiao Fengcai Lu* (*A Record of the Charm of the Hong Kong Deputies to the National People's Congress*) (Hong Kong: Hong Kong Culture Association Limited, 2003), 14.
12. Some traditional leftist candidates also admitted that strategic voting by the pro-China elements was at work. "Four Senior Deputies Resigned, Two New Candidates being Defeated, the Younger Are Replacing the Seniors, It Is Good to Have New Members," *Wen Wei Po*, December 4, 2002, p. A4; "Allen Lee Implicitly Criticized Casting Votes in Enterprises to Oust the Opponents," *Hong Kong Economic Times*, December 4, 2002, p. A4. For the details about the alleged strategic voting scheme of the pro-China camp in the Ninth HK NPC Election, *see* Pepper, "Hong Kong Joins the National People's Congress," 331.
13. Linda Choy, "NPC Role 'to Check Basic Law'," *South China Morning Post*, May 19, 1997, p. 6. Wong Man-kong had moved a similar motion to the Tenth NPC in 2004, calling for setting up a Basic Law Supervision Committee. However, such a motion was dropped because of failure to seek a minimum of thirty deputies' support. "Only Three Hong Kong NPC Deputies Supported, Another Withdrew Signature, Wong Man-kong's Motion May Fail," *Singtao Daily*, March 10, 2004, p. A10. David Chu was one of the deputies who had expressly stated his belief that Hong Kong deputies could be "an important new force . . . as catalytic agents" for China's reform and "serve as a bridge between Hong Kong and China by among other things, moving beyond the narrow confines of their own pro-China circle to win the trust of ordinary Hong Kong people through active involvement in local cocerns." David Chu, "The Five Future Tasks of the Hong Kong SAR's Delegates to the NPC," *Ta Kung Pao*, August 20, 1997, translated and cited in Pepper, "Hong Kong Joins the National People's Congress," 325.
14. Chris Yeung, "Deputies Must Prove Role," *South China Morning Post*, December 11, 1997, p. 19.
15. Ng, *Renda Xuanju Beiwanglu*, 55.
16. Yeung, "Deputies Must Prove Role".
17. Christine Loh, "Election Reduced to Comedy of Errors," *South China Morning Post*, December 15, 1997. For criticisms from the Frontiers and Democratic Party, *see* "HK's Pro-democracy Camp Rallies against Selection of Chinese MPs," *Agence France Presse*, December 7, 1997; and Sharon Cheung and Clarence Tsui, "Cease Hostility, Democrats Told," *South China Morning Post*, January 2, 1997, p. 4.

18. Social Sciences Research Centre of the University of Hong Kong (SSRC), "Opinion Survey on the Election of the Hong Kong Deputies to the NPC," *POP Express*, November 1997. (On file with authors.)
19. SSRC, "Opinion Survey on the Election of the Hong Kong Deputies to the NPC," *POP Express*, December 1997. (On file with authors.)
20. "NPC Deputies Do Not Involve in the Work of the SAR and Do Not Enjoy Any Privilege in Hong Kong, NPC Directives Released after Repeated Calls," *Ming Pao*, November 10, 1998; "Hong Kong NPC Deputies Execute Deputies' Duties, No Intervention in HKSAR Work," *Hong Kong Commercial Daily*, November 20, 1998.
21. The details of the guidelines were published in "Hong Kong NPC Delegation's Functions Finalized," *Hong Kong Commercial Daily*, December 1, 1998. *See also* "NPC Deputies Do Not Involve in the Work of the SAR."
22. These deputies were Cheng Yiu-tong, Tso Wung-wai, Wong Kong-hon, and Ng Hong-mun. *See* "Hong Kong NPC Delegation's Functions Finalized."
23. Ibid. *See* also, "Hong Kong NPC Deputies Claim That the Guidelines Are Clear, Legal Justification Sufficient and in Accordance with the Circumstances of the SAR," *Ta Kung Pao*, November 20, 1998.
24. For example, *see* "Hong Kong NPC Deputies Claim That the Guidelines Are Clear."
25. For a detailed discussion of the assistance provided for the Hong Kong residents who were being unlawfully detained in the Mainland, *see* Hualing Fu and Pinky Choy, "Unlawful Detention in the Mainland and the Concerns of Hong Kong," *Hong Kong Law Journal* 30 (2000): 290.
26. "'Brother Tong' Wants to Be the Glue."
27. "Allen Lee Urged to Institutionalized the NPC Election," *Oriental Daily*, March 14, 2001.
28. Ma Lik, "Reflections on NPC Work," *The Sun*, March 11, 2002, p. D8.
29. "Convenient to Gather Forces, Citizens Have Channel to Seek Help, Hong Kong NPC Deputies Propose to Set up Office of Duty Deputy," *The Sun*, March 2, 2003.
30. "Allen Lee Urged to Institutionalized the NPC Election."
31. "Convenient to Gather Forces."
32. For the most recent call, *see* Michael Wei, "Local NPC Deputies Plead for the Space to Do Their Jobs," *South China Morning Post*, September 9, 2005; and Editorial, "Work of NPC Deputies Hindered by Lack of Home," *South China Morning Post*, September 9, 2005.
33. Ng Hong-mun, *Renda Binfen Lu* (*The Colourful Record of the National People's Congress*) (Hong Kong: Mingpao Press, 1997), 157. After the formation of an independent Hong Kong delegation, such a proposal has also been one of the issues frequently discussed by the Hong Kong NPC deputies.
34. Zhou Zhimin, "A Good 'Measure' That Reflects 'One Country, Two Systems'," *Wen Wei Po*, November 22, 1998.
35. "Hong Kong NPC Deputies Propose to Set up Office," *Hong Kong Commercial Daily*, March 11, 2003; Wei, "Local NPC Deputies Plead."
36. "Quite Big Internal Discrepancy among the Deputies of the Hong Kong Delegation, the NPC and the CPPCC Have Not Declared Their Stands, NPC and CPPCC Office in Hong Kong is Hardly Established for the Moment," *Hong Kong Commercial Daily*, March 17, 2003.
37. There have been suggestions that deputies could set up their personal representative office in their personal capacity. But for apparent financial reasons, no deputy has taken this step.

38. "NPC Deputies Do Not Want to Rely on to Xinhua on Everything," *Ming Pao*, November 21, 1998, p. A10.
39. "Quite Big Internal Discrepancy among the Deputies."; Kong Lai-fan, "Local NPC Deputies to Get Complaints Office," *South China Morning Post*, March 10, 2000, p. 4; Gary Cheung, "Cross-Border Issues Given Priority by a New Breed of Local Deputies," *South China Morning Post*, December 5, 2002, p. 3.
40. "Hong Kong NPC Deputies under the Organizational System of Hong Kong," *Ming Pao*, March 6, 2003, p. D9.
41. The conveners were Ng Hong-mun, Maria Tam, Yuen Mo, and Ng Ching-fai.
42. *See* "Allen Lee Urged to Institutionalized the NPC Election."
43. "Asian Affairs Interview with Maria Tam: Hong Kong Deputy at the NPC," *Asian Affairs* (Autumn 1999), available at http://www.asian-affairs.com (accessed on October 30, 2005). (On file with authors.)
44. "Confirmed the Work of the Standing Committee over the Last Five Years, but Communication Is Still Insufficient, HK NPC Deputies Hope to Fully Participate in the Legislative Work," *Ta Kung Pao*, March 11, 2003, p. A7.
45. "Tsang Hin-chi Is Expected to Have His Term of Office as Member of the NPC Standing Committee Renewed," *Oriental Daily*, March 11, 2003, p. A27.
46. Ng, *Renda Xuanju Beiwanglu*, 185.
47. Ibid.
48. Given Jiang Enzhu was a member of the Standing Committee of the NPC, together with Tsang Hin-chi, Hong Kong had two NPC deputies sitting in the Standing Committee of the NPC during the Ninth Hong Kong NPC. However, after Jiang ceased to be a Hong Kong NPC deputy in the Tenth Hong Kong NPC, Hong Kong only had one representative in the Standing Committee. Tsang succeeded in renewing his term of office and became the only Hong Kong deputy in the NPC Standing Committee.
49. Tsang admitted that he failed to perform his role as conduit between Hong Kong NPC deputies and the NPC Standing Committee satisfactorily in the Ninth NPC, but he explained that this was largely due to his poor health. "Insufficient Communication between NPC Standing Committee and Hong Kong NPC Deputies, Tsang Hin-chi: Will Try My Best," *Ming Pao*, March 11, 2003; "Promise to Report the Work to the Hong Kong Members More Often, Tsang Hin-chi Succeeded in Renewing His Term of Office as NPC Standing Committee Member with Fewer Votes," *Singtao Daily*, March 16, 2003; "Ng Hong-mun: Insufficient Consultation before Voting and States That Hong Kong NPC Standing Committee Member Lacks Communications with the NPC Deputies," *Wen Wei Po*, March 11, 2003.
50. NPC website.
51. Interview with NPC deputies.
52. Ibid.
53. For the details about the NPC statistics and the motions and suggestions moved by the NPC deputies, *see* NPC website.
54. "Asian Affairs Interview with Maria Tam."
55. Editorial, "Hong Kong NPC Deputies Should Make Good Use of Their Unique Status," *Ming Pao*, March 4, 2002, p. A2. For a different view, *see* Zhong Zhi, "Hong Kong NPC Deputies Acted Improperly," *Hong Kong Economic Times*, March 5, 2002, p. C9. The author pointed out that Hong Kong deputies are ignorant because they raised the safety concerns of tour buses in the Mainland while other delegations raise more political issues such as further political reform.

56. "NPC Deputies Do Not Involve in the Work of the SAR"; and "Hong Kong NPC Deputies Execute Deputies' Duties."
57. Li Weiting, "Seriously Performing the Functions as Hong Kong NPC Deputies," *Wen Wei Po*, November 30, 1998.
58. Ng, *Renda Xuanju Beiwanglu*; Li and Zhong, *Gangqu Quanguo Renda Daibiao Fengcai Lu, 299*–326.
59. "'Democrats' Are Not Welcome to Run for NPC Deputies," *Bauhinia Magazine Online*, available at http://www.zijing.com.cn/BIG5/channel3/200207/18/251.html (accessed August 9, 2005).
60. Ng, *Renda Binfen Lu*, 157.
61. Chris Yeung and Jimmy Cheung, "RTHK Guidelines 'Boost Standards,' Rules Based on International Broadcast Principles Aimed at Halting Accusations of Bias," *South China Morning Post*, September 15, 1998. *See* also, Chris Yeung and No Kwai-yan, "RTHK Independence and a Matter for HK People," *South China Morning Post*, March 7, 1998.
62. Ibid.
63. Linda Choy, "Xu's Attack on RTHK Dismissed, Local Delegates Told CPPCC Has No Role in SAR," *South China Morning Post*, March 8, 1998.
64. For the full-text of Jiang's speech, *see* Ng, *Renda Xuanju Beiwanglu*, 99–102.
65. "Hong Kong NPC Deputies Barred from Commenting on Hong Kong Affairs When the NPC Is Not in Session," *Ming Pao*, March 11, 1999, p. A16.
66. Ibid.
67. Ibid.
68. "Concerning about SAR Affairs and Expressing Opinions Are Perfectly Justified, Ma Lik Hopes to Establish the Constitutional Status of the Hong Kong NPC Deputies," *Ta Kung Pao*, January 20, 2003.
69. "Lee Teng-hui Claimed the Cross-Strait Relationship as 'State-to-State'," *Singtao Daily*, July 10, 1999, p. A4.
70. "Various Sectors Condemned Lee Teng-hui's Secessionist Fallacy, Accusing Him of Creating Obstacles for the Cross-Strait Relationship and Violating the People's Wish of Unification," *Ta Kung Pao*, July 13, 1999, p. A12.
71. Kong Lai-fan, "RTHK Blasted by Xinhua Chief for Taiwan Broadcast," *South China Morning Post*, August 7, 1999, p. 2.
72. Ibid.
73. Ibid.
74. "Hong Kong Advised Not to Publicize Taiwan Leader's Theory," *Hong Kong Standard*, August 20, 1999, p. A1. Lam's statement was criticized on two grounds. First, treating Cheng simply as a head of a travel agency was both unrealistic and misleading, as it was clear that Cheng was in fact a de facto representative of Taiwan in Hong Kong. Second, his argument that Cheng, as a head of a travel agency, should focus on economics and tourism but not politics, was criticized by many as occupational discrimination and undermining the right to freedom of expression in Hong Kong. "Stephen Lam's Speech being Attacked, Legislators Request the Government to Clarify the Line of Freedom of Expression," *Ming Pao*, August 20, 1999, p. A6.
75. "Hong Kong NPC Deputies Will Discuss the Two States Theory Next Week, Cheng Ankuo's Speech Will Be Subjected to Attack Again," *Ming Pao*, August 6, 1999, p. A7.
76. "HK NPC Deputies Will Discuss the 'Two States Theory' Today, Cheng Yiu-tong: It Is Suspected to be 'Outdated'," *Ming Pao*, August 9, 1999, p. A8.
77. Ibid.

78. "HK Deputy to the NPC Standing Committee Decides to Complain to the Central Government about RTHK and Cheng An-kuo," *Central News Agency*, August 11, 1999.
79. Ibid.
80. "Cheng An-kuo Was Criticized That He Should Be Watchful over His Own Speech, Hong Kong NPC Deputies Unanimously Condemned the 'Two States Theory'," *Singtao Daily*, August 10, 1999, p. A15.
81. Interview with NPC deputies.
82. Angela Li, "NPC Deputy Wants More Action," *South China Morning Post*, March 17, 2002, p. 4.
83. Interview with NPC deputies.
84. Ma Lik, "New Positioning of the Hong Kong NPC Deputies," *Hong Kong Economic Daily*, August 18, 2003, p. A33.
85. The immediate cause of demonstration was the discontent with the HKSAR government's approach in handling the enactment of the legislation to implement Article 23 of the Basic Law, though participants of the demonstration actually had multiple purposes such as requesting the HKSAR government to establish an independent body to investigate the SARS Incident, requesting certain senior government officials to resign, expressing discontent with the general performance of the HKSAR government and requesting the government to introduce measures to help people with negative assets. It was reported that as many as 500,000 people participated in the demonstration, and among them include people coming from the middle class, and medical and legal professionals. For the reports about the demonstration, *see*, for example, Carole J. Petersen, "Hong Kong's Spring of Discontent: The Rise and Fall of the National Security Bill in 2003," in *National Security and Fundamental Freedoms: Hong Kong's Article 23 Under Scrutiny*, ed. Hualing Fu, Carole J. Petersen, and Simon N. M. Young (Hong Kong: Hong Kong University Press, 2005), ch. 1.
86. "Pro-China Figure Said a Crisis of Governance Is Facing Tung, Allen Lee: No Use for Government to Give 'Candies' Anymore," *Ming Pao*, July 2, 2003, p. A7.
87. Ma, "New Positioning of the Hong Kong NPC Deputies."
88. Ibid.
89. "Content of Sheng Huaren's Instructions Exposed," *The Sun*, August 19, 2003, p. A6.
90. Ma, "New Positioning of the Hong Kong NPC Deputies."
91. Ibid.
92. Ibid.
93. The Commission on Strategic Development now oversees Hong Kong's constitutional development.
94. Jimmy Cheung, "Greater Role Urged for City's NPC Deputies," *South China Morning Post*, September 10, 2005; "Appointment to the Commission on Strategic Development," Government Information Centre Press Release, November 15, 2005, available at http://www.info.gov.hk/gia/general/200511/15/P200511150128.htm (accessed November 16, 2005); "Brief Introduction of Members of the Commission on Strategic Development," Government Information Centre Press Release, November 15, 2005, available at http://gia.info.gov.hk/general/200511/15/P200511150128_0128_8385.doc (accessed November 16, 2005).
95. "Tsang Vows to Improve Ties with NPC Deputies," *South China Morning Post*, February 25, 2006.
96. "More Balanced View Needed on Advisers," *South China Morning Post*, June 2, 2006.

CHAPTER 11

Legislative Interpretation by China's National People's Congress Standing Committee

A Power with Roots in the Stalinist Conception of Law

*Sophia Woodman**

The idea that the roots of the power of the National People's Congress Standing Committee (NPCSC) under Article 67(4) of the Constitution to interpret the law lie in the civil-law system has featured in a number of articles on the subject.[1] In statements defending the first interpretation of the Hong Kong Basic Law by the NPCSC in 1999, the Hong Kong government asserted that various European legal systems have or had an analogous power.[2]

I believe this claim is misleading. While the idea of legislative interpretation may originate in the separation of powers instituted in France in the immediate postrevolutionary period, the NPCSC's particular variant comes from the legal order established under Stalin to serve "victorious socialism" and the fusion of powers in the Soviet state. This chapter will focus on the genealogy of the NPCSC's interpretation power to elucidate some aspects of its nature.

The Chinese Communist Party (CCP) has never undergone de-Stalinization—Stalin's picture still appears in the Chinese version of the pantheon of Marxist heroes. In fact, de-Stalinization in the Soviet Union was one of the causes of the Sino-Soviet split in the early 1960s.

* I am grateful to Robert Morris and Lison Harris for their helpful comments on this chapter. I would also like to thank Yash Ghai for inspiration and guidance and Antoine Garapon for help in understanding the French *référé-législatif*.

Of course the Chinese state and its legal system are not mere clones of their Soviet precursors. As a number of authors have pointed out, pragmatism may have been more important than ideology in shaping the Chinese legal order in the reform era.[3] The influence of Soviet thinking on some of the key elements of the Chinese legal system should not be discounted, however; in the key period of the early 1950s when the PRC's first constitution was drafted, Soviet influence was at its height, and the legal thinking received was that of the Stalin era.[4] The main reason the CCP moved to begin drafting a constitution in 1952 was that Stalin had three times pressed the party to do so, some writers assert.[5] The current Chinese Constitution, promulgated in 1982 and revised four times since then, is modeled on the 1954 Constitution, harking back to what is still seen as the formative moment for socialist law in China.

Interpretation of Law, Not Constitution

Discussions of the interpretation question have generally failed to distinguish between the exercise of the constitutional power to interpret *laws* (Article 67[4]) and the power to interpret the constitution and supervise its enforcement (Article 67[1]). These powers are listed separately in the enumeration of the NPCSC's powers in the 1982 Constitution. The power of constitutional interpretation did not appear in the 1954 Constitution, which, like the 1936 Stalin Constitution,[6] which was its model, only listed the power to interpret law (Article 31[3]).[7]

The NPCSC has not exercised its power under Article 67(1). As Cai writes, "In our country, as yet there is no specific procedure for the NPCSC to exercise its power to interpret the Constitution, so this type of interpretation has not been practised."[8] This situation reflects the lack of effective mechanisms for enforcing the Chinese Constitution, despite increasing pressure from Chinese jurists to establish some means for addressing unconstitutional acts and conflicts of laws.

But the NPCSC has used its power to interpret laws, even as early as the 1950s.[9] In 1955, the NPCSC issued a "Resolution Regarding Questions of Interpretation of Law," which stipulated that the NPCSC would use this power in situations when clear definitions or additional stipulations were required and also allowed the Supreme People's Court (SPC) to make interpretations on the application of law in adjudication. The 1981 "Resolution on Strengthening the Work of Interpretation of Law" was a response to requests for interpretations of the new laws being issued by the NPC and provided for interpretation powers to be exercised by a number of additional bodies: the Supreme People's Procuratorate and the State Council and its departments, and in the case of local regulations, local people's congress standing committees and provincial government departments. In theory, interpretation by different institutions is also different in nature: "Interpretation of the law by the [NPCSC] is often defined as legislative interpretation, while interpretation of the law by other organs is defined as interpretation of particular applications of the law."[10] NPCSC interpretation is not directed at specific cases, and for this reason has been labeled "abstract interpretation" by some scholars.[11]

Prior to the enactment of the Legislation Law in 2002, however, no procedure had been laid down for NPCSC legislative interpretation.[12] The provisions in Chapter 2, Section 4 of the law supersede the 1981 NPCSC resolution and only allow for interpretation in two situations: when the specific meaning of a provision of a law requires clarification (Article 42[1]) and when new circumstances have arisen since the passage of a law and clarification is needed on the grounds for application of the law (Article 42[2]). The Legislation Law thus eliminated a function of interpretation that, according to some scholars, based on the 1981 resolution, had been within the powers of the NPCSC: amendment of a law through interpretation.[13] According to Lin, "It is fair to say that the grounds for seeking interpretation from the NPCSC are very limited" under the Legislation Law.[14] The law also specifies the bodies that may request interpretations, limiting standing to the State Council, the Central Military Commission, the SPC, the Supreme People's Procuratorate, special committees of the NPCSC, and the standing committees of provincial/autonomous regional/directly governed municipal people's congresses (Article 43).

Legislative interpretations by the NPCSC have been rare, and remain so, although the use of this power has increased somewhat in recent years. In the 1950s and 1960s, the NPCSC issued eleven interpretations of law in accordance with the 1955 Resolution. "More than 10" interpretations were issued between 1979 and 2002, but they were only identified as such after 1996, when the NPCSC issued its interpretation of the Nationality Law in relation to Hong Kong.[15] In addition to the three interpretations of the Basic Law, between 2000 and 2005, the NPCSC issued nine interpretations of the Criminal Law. Thus a total of fourteen legislative instruments titled "interpretations" were passed by the NPCSC between 1996 and 2005.[16]

Legislative interpretations by the NPCSC have the same status as its other legislative enactments.[17] But due to the fact that the NPCSC has "relinquishe[d] the power of interpretation" by failing to exercise it, organs implementing the law, in particular the SPC, have regularly been issuing interpretations that go beyond the scope of their authority.[18] While the interpretations of administrative agencies are only supposed to be for the purpose of implementing the law, in fact they regularly exceed these limits, sometimes even effectively creating new legal requirements in the process.[19] In addition, the "working organs" of the NPCSC, particularly the Legislative Affairs Commission, also regularly issue effective interpretations of law in response to questions from administrative agencies, local people's congresses, and governments on the meaning of the law.[20]

Not a Power Used in Civil-Law Systems

The power to interpret laws is not a question of their compliance with constitutional principles. It is the elucidation of what the codified law, in itself, means in application to a particular situation or new development. It reflects a singularly Soviet view of law and its role in society. According to Cai, the allocation of the Article 67(4) power to the NPCSC (rather than allowing courts to exercise such power) is determined by the principle of "democratic centralism" underlying the PRC's people's congress system.[21]

The history of the emergence of constitutional review in Europe has little to tell us about the use of the interpretation power. Legislatures in civil-law countries *never* made issuing interpretations of laws a common practice. Immediately after the French Revolution, French judges were ordered to refer any question regarding the interpretation of law to the legislature (under a procedure known as the *référé-législatif*). This obligation to refer was a product of the revolutionaries' extreme distrust of *ancien régime* judges, who had abused their powers to make regulations that supported the interests of the nobility. Under the new order, judges were obliged to refer to the legislature any question about the meaning of the law emerging from a case they were dealing with. But this system was quickly found to be unworkable and repealed by 1800.[22] In other countries, even where the power did exist, it was used only very rarely, if at all. As Stone Sweet writes, "Parliaments did not in fact exercise continuous control over application of statutes." [23]

Thus in the continental legal systems, interpretation may be essentially divided into two categories: interpretation of law that is entrusted to the judiciary (including, in the French system, the *Cours de Cassation*, which rules on questions of law), and interpretation of the constitution (or the principles of law) that generally remained the prerogative of the legislature until the twentieth century. Now European legal systems have generally established constitutional courts to perform the latter type of interpretation, as part of a realization that the legislature must also be bound by constitutional principles.

A central principle of most civil-law systems is the aim of establishing a comprehensive code of laws that can apply to any situation that a judge may have to deal with. Of course this is a fiction, but it contrasts with the "socialist law" ideal of codification supplemented with interpretation to ensure that law never strays from serving the ends to which the socialist state is dedicated (as determined, of course, by the ruling party). In the latter system, indeterminacy may be intentionally built into the law, to allow the authorities more flexibility to respond to emerging circumstances.

Certainly, the form of the legal order shaped under Stalin owed much to Western legal systems of both civil and common law types. Prerevolutionary Russia had borrowed from Western Europe to develop legal codes, and the adoption of constitutions to govern the new Soviet state reflected the Bolsheviks' admiration for progressive western ideas.[24] The architects of the revival of law under Stalin acknowledged their borrowing from the forms of "bourgeois" legal systems.[25] But the commonality of form should not obscure the different purposes to which law was put.

Origins of the Interpretation Power in the Stalin Constitution

The NPCSC's Article 67(4) power to interpret the law can be linked directly to the Stalin Constitution of 1936 and to its conception of the role of law in a socialist state. The power had not appeared in previous Soviet constitutions.

Under the Stalin Constitution, the power to interpret "the laws of the USSR currently in force"[26] was given to the Presidium of the Supreme Soviet (henceforth, Presidium), a body analogous to the NPCSC. As in the PRC, no other body was given the power of interpretation in the Constitution,[27] including the full Supreme Soviet.[28] A similar power of legislative interpretation appears in most of the post–World War II Eastern Bloc constitutions,[29] although it was dropped from some in post-Stalin revisions. By contrast, the power to interpret the constitution was not specifically allocated to any body in the Soviet system until the constitutional revisions of 1977 under Leonid Brezhnev.

Legislative interpretations by the Presidium were to be issued in the form of edicts,[30] and in a draft of the 1936 Constitution, the Presidium's issuing of edicts is essentially seen as a manifestation of the interpretation power.[31] No stipulations are made regarding the method to be used in making interpretations; the Presidium of the Supreme Soviet was free to determine this without any restrictions.[32] As in the Chinese system, the Presidium issued only a few edicts "in the narrow sense of authoritative rulings clarifying the meaning of legislative acts," in some instances involving prominent criminal cases.[33] The power to issue edicts was used extensively by the Presidium to make new law, even though lawmaking power in the constitution appeared to be granted solely to the Supreme Soviet. In the post-Stalin period, "the great bulk" of legislation was enacted in this form.[34] One commentator calls the power to issue edicts the most important power of the Presidium. Many such edicts were then transformed into statutes at the following session of the full Supreme Soviet.[35]

The conception of statutes[36] and the relationship of edicts to them articulated by the architect of Stalin's legal reforms, Andrei Vyshinskii, show how this system is supposed to work. Statutes were to be sets of general rules drawn from experience and based on "the interests of the toilers."[37] They were not expected to cover all eventualities and thus interpretation through edicts would be an essential aspect of ensuring their "correct" application.[38] Vyshinksii's theory was that: "Details of the development of social relationships cannot possibly be anticipated by legislation nor can it, even in general form, furnish rules for all concrete cases. It enunciates general principles, leaving the details of the statements of principle to be developed in the form of [edicts]. . . . [Edicts] ensure that the statute shall be applied in conformity with the changing conditions of life. By means of [edicts] a statute is extended to all the cases embraced by its meaning and content."[39]

Despite this broad scope, edicts had to be connected to a statute and, according to Vyshinskii, "must neither contradict it nor deviate from it."[40] They were to show the original meaning of the statute, in light of the current situation facing the Soviet state and its leaders' assessment of the needs of the cause of socialism. He explains, "Interpretation of a statute is elucidation of its purposes and content, and of the conditions of its most correct application (in conformity with questions of socialist building), and also of its separate propositions (or of the whole statute) as applied to the concrete facts of life. . . . Interpretation neither creates a new rule nor goes outside the compass and bounds of the statute under interpretation. It merely reveals the meaning and content of the statute, the obligations imposed thereby, starting from concrete circumstances, from the unity of socialist purposes and from socialist law presently in force."[41] According to later Soviet writers, in "extensive interpretation" the Presidium could only extend the operation of a statute "to facts which the legislator foresaw or could foresee but which he did not include in the text of the statute."[42]

The "guarantee" of the correctness of an interpretation is the nature of its author. "According to the Stalin Constitution, the legislator himself establishes who is to interpret the laws. In the USSR that right is given to the Presidium of the Supreme Soviet of the USSR . . . an organ accountable to the Supreme Soviet. Thus the utmost identity (authenticity) of statutory interpretation with the statutes themselves, as expressing the will of the entire Soviet people, is guaranteed. Thereby social legality is strengthened and stabilized, and the character of statutory interpretation in the USSR, its subordination to the statute, is foreordained."[43] Because it is the Presidium that issues the interpretation, it unquestionably *must* embody the meaning of the law. This position is a reflection of the fact that the interpretation power and its use in the Soviet system is a manifestation of the *fusion* of powers in the Supreme Soviet and its Presidium under the Stalin Constitution.

In the Soviet system—and in Marxist theory—the "bourgeois" separation of powers is rejected as not only a sham but also as a limitation on the coercive power of the socialist state.[44] Also, the unity of purpose behind the Soviet organs of governance meant that it was assumed that unanimity of views would prevail, rather than conflict between different institutions of government.[45] Fusion of powers meant that any limitation on the power of the legislature was considered unacceptable, thus precluding any kind of judicial review.[46]

Role of Law in "Socialist Society"

In his speech introducing the draft of the Constitution of 1936, Stalin said it was premised on three major accomplishments of the Soviet state. These were the establishment of socialism, the end of class struggle (relationships between classes in Soviet society were now "friendly"), and, based on the former two, dictatorship was to be transformed into "state guidance of society," which required "stability of laws."[47] As part of the "rehabilitation" of the state in the Soviet Union, entailing a rejection of Marxist orthodoxy on the "withering away" of the state under socialism, law was to play a crucial role, as a principal mechanism for the regulation of society.[48] The violence that had established the Soviet state, however, would continue to have its uses: "Law would not replace 'administrative repression' but take its place alongside it: law and force would jointly constitute the social regulation mechanism of Soviet society."[49]

Barry points out the tension in such a view of law:

> How, then, can one characterize such a system—part arbitrary and part ordinary? Ernst Fraenkel, writing of Nazi Germany, characterizes such a system as a "dual state." In some aspects, it can be a "prerogative state" which is governed arbitrarily with no effective limits on the jurisdiction of state organs. In other aspects, it can be a "normative state" in which government is limited by legal norms which delineate the boundaries of permissible government action. The areas of jurisdiction covered by the "prerogative state" and the "normative

> state" are not fixed. Rather they are constantly expanding and contracting as the situation demands.[50]

Unger contrasts the Stalinist view of law to that embodied in the Rechtsstaat idea, to which some writers had compared it. "The nearest that Soviet law comes to Western tradition is to the law of the Prussian *Polizeistaat*, i.e. the law of a state which seeks to provide orderly and predictable government and, to that end, imposes an elaborate system of rules upon officials and citizens alike; but also one which postulates an identity of interests between the state and its citizens, which grants the citizen no inherent rights against the state, which leaves the arbitrary conduct of officials unsanctioned whenever such conduct conforms to 'reasons of state' and, above all, one which places no restraints whatever upon the state's supreme rulers."[51]

Another problem the Stalinist approach to law aimed to address was the growing complexity of Soviet society, which required some division of labor and more sophisticated mechanisms of state control. If the state was not to wither away, it needed to have rules to constrain its subjects. Thus the Stalin Constitution combined "distinct limitation of jurisdiction with complete supremacy of legislative authority as embodying the will of the entire Soviet people."[52] Power is still absolute, but parceled out among different bodies exercising the popular sovereignty,[53] a reflection of the need for specialization as economic development created a more complex environment.[54] "While a measure of functional division has increasingly been introduced, the official doctrine remains that the exercise of state power is ultimately one and indivisible."[55]

Conclusion

The power of legislative interpretation—as practiced in the Soviet Union and in China today—is a reflection of the Stalinist conception of the role of law in socialist society. Although it has an ideological basis, it is also pragmatic, aimed at ensuring that law is applied correctly, in the interests of socialism as perceived by the rulers of the state. While it would be a mistake to put too much emphasis on the formal similarities of the Soviet and Chinese legal systems, given the obvious differences between the two states in so many spheres, comparing China's legal development to that of Soviet law is nonetheless useful.[56]

As in the Soviet system, the vagueness and generality of Chinese law drafting is in part intentional:

> At the level of basic law and statutes, legislation is customarily written in an ambiguous fashion in the form of principle-like pronouncements, intended, as it is, to provide only a thumbnail sketch of the parameters of regulation. This is because the PRC has adopted a rationale that lends itself to the creation of laws that are inherently flexible so that they may be adjusted according to the vagaries of human behavior. Such laws allow for wide variation in application as they are customarily expressed as general principles (*you yuanze xing*) which are inherently flexible (*you linghuo xing*) in application.[57]

Of course, there are also other reasons for ambiguity. Factors often mentioned as contributing to vagueness of laws are inexperience, the enormous diversity of the country (which means that those responsible for lawmaking see broad and general laws as providing localities with sufficient flexibility),[58] the desire to preserve administrative discretion,[59] and the pragmatic orientation of China's reform era leaders. Like their Soviet counterparts, Chinese legal theorists advocating a socialist view of law as "superstructure" think that law should be flexible enough to respond to changes in the economic "base."[60] Such flexibility is considered beneficial, in contrast to common ideas about law in Western legal systems.[61]

If the question of the completion of a term of a Hong Kong chief executive who resigned was discussed by the Basic Law drafters, why was a provision for such an eventuality not included in the law? One answer might be that consensus could not be reached, another that this provision was *intentionally* left vague to allow for a response to such an event depending on the particular circumstances. What information is available about the drafting history gives some support to the latter idea: apparently more specific language was replaced with a more indeterminate formulation.[62]

Commentators on the NPCSC's use of its interpretation power have noted the small number of NPCSC legislative acts labeled "interpretations." They have thus often viewed this as a power that has not been exercised, except in relation to Hong Kong, and more recently, on provisions of the criminal law. But based on the Soviet comparison and the internal logic of the Chinese legal system, it may make more sense, following Jiang, to categorize the NPCSC's interpretation power as part of its general power to make decisions.[63] This power is a substantive power through which the NPC "expresses its will and settles a problem." Decisions are often the device of choice when achieving a consensus on an issue might be difficult or when it is an emergent matter,[64] as has been the case (at least in the view of the governments in Beijing and Hong Kong) in the NPCSC interpretations related to Hong Kong.

Such a view situates interpretation as a mechanism for ensuring that legal outcomes adhere to "substantive rationality" so that they meet the objectives of those in power. Allowing lawmakers and implementers the discretion to guarantee the right result remains an important feature of the Chinese system, one that also reflects China's historical perspective on law.[65] For example, there are many indications that for the PRC courts, substantive justice is more important than procedural correctness.[66] The interpretation power also has to be seen in the context of the extensive use of interpretation by administrative agencies within the Chinese system which allows for the exercise of discretion on a wide range of subject matters. Looking at the issue even more broadly, it reflects the lack of clear distinction in the Chinese system between law and policy.

Hong Kong has its own legal system, and its courts are one of the only truly independent institutions of government in the SAR. But as a part of the PRC, ultimately, the SAR is subject to the highest organ of state power, the NPC and its Standing Committee. Absent some radical rethinking of the direction of the Chinese state and the role its institutions play (in particular the role of the CCP), it seems likely that, reflecting the Stalinist roots of this power, the NPCSC will continue to use interpretation to resolve political controversies in Hong Kong to ensure the "correct" implementation of the Basic Law. Interpretation is an escape clause, allowing the entry of the principle of democratic centralism and party rule into the Hong Kong polity. As in the Soviet system, ultimately the party and the institutions it controls reserve the power to decide on questions they consider the most important, and the law means what they say. It seems likely that this was the original intent of those who decided on the final content of the Basic Law and included the interpretation power as the expression of the central state's "prerogative power"[67] over Hong Kong.

Notes

1. For example, Lin Laifan et al. state that: "The concept [of legislative interpretation] . . . originates from a long and well-established tradition of the civil law system." See Lin, Laifan, Gu, Minkang and Zhu, Guobin, "An Analysis of the Legislative Interpretation System in the PRC," *Hong Kong Lawyer*, available at http://www.hk-lawyer.com/1999-8/Aug99-56.htm.
2. Special Administrative Region Secretary for Justice Elsie Leung response to questions in Legco in verbatim transcript of the Special House Committee meeting on May 18, 1999 (transcript is in Chinese, but this section is in English), available at http://www.legco.gov.hk/yr98-99/chinese/hc/minutes/hc180599.pdf.
3. Xingzhong Yu, "Legal Pragmatism in the PRC," *Journal of Chinese Law* (1989) 3: 29–51.
4. Ibid., 36–37.

5. Cai, Dingjian, *The Essence of the Constitution* (*Xianfa jingjie*) (Beijing: Law Press, 2004), 24–26. See also, Hua-yu Li, "The Political Stalinization of China: The Establishment of One-Party Constitutionalism, 1948–1954," *Journal of Cold War Studies* 3 (2001): 28–47.
6. Jan F. Triska, *Constitutions of the Communist Party States* (Stanford, CA: Hoover Institution, 1968).
7. Only in the Soviet Constitution of 1977 under Leonid Brezhnev was a provision added allowing the presidium to "supervise the observance of the Constitution of the USSR" (Article 121[4]). The 1977 Constitution is available in William B. Simons, *The Constitutions of the Communist World* (Alphen aan den Rijn, the Netherlands/Germantown, MD: Sijthoff and Noordhoff, 1980).
8. See Cai, *The Essence of the Constitution*, 299. The establishment of some kind of constitutional committee under the NPC has been under discussion since 1981, when the incorporation of such a body into the constitution then under discussion was proposed. Feng Lin, *Constitutional Law in China* (Hong Kong: Sweet and Maxwell Asia, 2000), 296–97.
9. In fact, the power of interpretation existed even before the PRC had its first constitution: Under the Organic Law on the Central People's Government of 1949, the government had the power to make laws and to interpret them. Wang, Xiangzhen, "Judicial Interpretation Should Be Seen as among the Sources of Socialist Law" ("*Sifa jieshi yingshu shehui zhuyi fa de yuanyuan*"), *Explorations in Jurisprudence* (*Faxue tansuo*) 1 (1995): 22.
10. Cai, Dingjian, "Functions of the People's Congress in the Process of Implementation of Law," in *Implementation of Law in the People's Republic of China*, ed. Jianfu Chen, Yuwen Li and Jan Michiel Otto (The Hague: Kluwer Law International, 2002), 36–37.
11. Wang, Zhenmin, *China's System of Constitutional Review* (*Zhongguo weixian shencha zhidu*) (Beijing: Chinese University of Politics and Law Press, 2004), 286, citing Xu Chongde.
12. See Lin, *Constitutional Law in China*, 110.
13. Ibid., 107 n201.
14. Ibid., 109.
15. See Cai, *The Essence of the Constitution*, 39. In 1998, the NPCSC issued a similar interpretation applying to Macau.
16. According to the list generated from a search on the comprehensive legal database operated by Beijing University, available at www.chinalawinfo.com, accessed May 29, 2006.
17. Deng, Shibao, "The NPCSC's Interpretation of Law: Theory and Practice" ("*Quanguo renda changweihui falü jieshi de lilun jiqi shijian*"), paper presented at the conference Interpretations and Beyond, November 2005, p. 1.
18. See Cai, *The Essence of the Constitution*, 38–40.
19. See, e.g., Peter H. Corne, "Creation and Application of Law in the PRC," *American Journal of Comparative Law* 50 (2002): 398–409.
20. Before the enactment of the Legislation Law, these were not even made public, but now they are available on the NPC website in the section "questions and answers on law" (*falü wenda*), available at http://www.npc.gov.cn/zgrdw/home/index.jsp.
21. Cai, *The Essence of the Constitution*, 301.
22. John P. Dawson, *The Oracles of the Law* (Ann Arbor: University of Michigan Law School, 1968), 379.
23. Alec Stone Sweet, *Governing with Judges: Constitutional Politics in Europe* (Oxford: Oxford University Press, 2000), 129.
24. Donald D. Barry and Carol Barner-Barry, *Contemporary Soviet Politics* (Englewood Cliffs, NJ: Prentice-Hall, 1978), 76.

25. Vyshinskii repeatedly cites "bourgeois" practice and then details how the same powers or devices are used for different ends in the Soviet system. Andrei Y. Vyshinkii, *The Law of the Soviet State*, trans. Hugh W. Babb and John N. Hazard (Westport, CT: Greenwood Press, 1979).
26. Article 49(b). "The Presidium of the Supreme Soviet of the USSR shall . . . (b) interpret the laws of the USSR currently in force, and issue edicts."
27. In practice, however, the USSR Council of Ministers (analogous to the State Council) issued interpretations that were considered legally binding (in the form of decrees, see note 30), and the USSR Supreme Court issued judicial interpretations that were binding on judicial agencies. The power to interpret republican law was also granted to republican presidia in their respective constitutions. F. J. M. Feldbrugge, Ger P. van den Berg and William B. Simons, eds. *Encyclopedia of Soviet Law* (Dordrecht: Martinus Nijhoff, 1985), 396–97.
28. Ibid., 605–6.
29. Bulgaria, Czechoslovakia, East Germany, Poland, and Romania.
30. Distinctions between various types of law were not always very clear in the Soviet system, and another problem emerges when different sources translate the same terms in different ways. Barry and Barner-Barry, *Contemporary Soviet Politics*, 148, and a number of other writers on Soviet law use the term *edicts* for substatutory rules issued by the Presidium and *decrees* for those issued by the Council of Ministers (the Soviet counterpart to the State Council), but the translation of Vyshinskii's *The Law of the Soviet State* uses the term "decrees" for "edicts" in this sense. So as not to confuse the reader, I have thus altered the text of the translation of Vyshinskii to be consistent.
31. Aryeh L. Unger, *Constitutional Development in the USSR—A Guide to the Soviet Constitutions* (London: Methuen, 1981), 102.
32. See Vyshinskii, *The Law of the Soviet State*, 340.
33. See, e.g., Unger, *Constitutional Development in the USSR*, 102, 131–32. At least one case involved the retroactive application of the death penalty.
34. Ibid., 103. In a 1947 amendment, the power to issue edicts was separated from the interpretation power, thus granting the Presidium untrammeled power to create legislation in this way.
35. See Barry and Barner-Barry, *Contemporary Soviet Politics*, 90. Transforming edicts into statutes became a major part of the annual sessions of the Supreme Soviet.
36. This term in the Soviet system includes both codes (mainly enacted at republican level on the basis of principles laid down by the center) and specific statutes. See Barry and Barner-Barry, *Contemporary Soviet Politics*, 148–49.
37. Vyshinskii, *The Law of the Soviet State*, 337.
38. Ibid., 338–89.
39. Ibid., 341.
40. Ibid.
41. Ibid., 339. Parentheses are in the original.
42. See Feldbrugge, *Encyclopedia of Soviet Law*, 46–47. This is contrasted with another device in Soviet law for covering all eventualities: analogy. Under the analogy principle, the application of a statute could be extended to situations not foreseen by the legislator.
43. Vyshinskii, *The Law of the Soviet State*, 339. Parentheses are in the original.
44. See Unger, *Constitutional Development in the USSR*, 273.
45. Barry and Barner-Barry, *Contemporary Soviet Politics*, 76.
46. See Unger, *Constitutional Development in the USSR*, 122.
47. Quoted in ibid., 81–82.

48. Ibid., 277–78.
49. Ibid., 280. The "administrative repression" quote is from Vyshinskii.
50. See Barry and Barner-Barry, *Contemporary Soviet Politics*, 134.
51. See Unger, *Constitutional Development in the USSR*, 291–92.
52. See Vyshinkii, *The Law of the Soviet State*, 321–22.
53. Ibid., 318.
54. Ibid., 319.
55. See Unger, *Constitutional Development in the USSR*, 273.
56. Although this is beyond the scope of this chapter, in my view, comparison with the Soviet example would be a useful corrective to some of the more rosy assessments made of recent developments in the Chinese legal system.
57. Corne, "Creation and Application of Law in the PRC," 374.
58. Randall Peerenboom, "Ruling the Country in Accordance with Law: Reflections on the Rule and Role of Law in Contemporary China," *Cultural Dynamics* 11 (1999): 315–51, 335–56.
59. See Corne, "Creation and Application of Law in the PRC," 376.
60. Ibid., 374.
61. Ibid., 375.
62. See, for example, the account provided in speech by the Secretary for Justice Elsie Leung, at the Special Meeting of the House Committee of the Legislative Council on Tuesday, March 15, 2005, which indicates that words that would have made the meaning clearer were deleted from later drafts of the Basic Law. *See* also Chapters 1 (Young) and 7 (Lin and Lo) in this volume.
63. Jinsong Jiang, *The National People's Congress of China* (Beijing: Foreign Languages Press, 2002), 211–18. The NPC and the NPCSC issued 155 decisions between 1979 and 1997.
64. Ibid., 213.
65. Karen G. Turner, "Introduction," in *The Limits of the Rule of Law in China*, ed. Karen G. Turner, James V. Feinerman, and R. Kent Guy (Seattle and London: University of Washington Press, 2000), 12.
66. See Corne, "Creation and Application of Law in the PRC," 377, on practice in administrative lawsuits; another example is the refusal of courts to exclude illegally obtained evidence in criminal cases, although they technically might be able to do so.
67. In the sense used by Barry and Barner-Barry, *Contemporary Soviet Politics*, rather than relating to any powers of the British crown.

CHAPTER 12

China's Constitutionalism

Lison Harris

> In building socialist political democracy, China has always adhered to the basic principle that the Marxist theory of democracy be combined with the reality of China, borrowed from the useful achievements of the political civilization of mankind, including Western democracy, and assimilated the democratic elements of China's traditional culture and institutional civilization. Therefore, China's socialist political democracy shows distinctive Chinese characteristics.[1]

China's extensive legal reforms are often assessed according to its progress toward a liberal democracy, although it has made clear that its intentions lie elsewhere. In the same way, the role of the Constitution of the People's Republic of China is assessed according to Western theories of constitutionalism, sometimes resulting in the conclusion that China has no true legal system. The constitution is nonetheless a vital element of the reform process, as the Chinese Communist Party's broad power of leadership or government over state institutions is set out in its preamble. The constitution is both the symbol of and the legal justification for the power of the Chinese Communist Party (CCP) over government policies in China and is a vital component of the CCP's strategy for survival—the "life and death" of the party.[2] Although the CCP exerts broad ideological control over state policy making and decision making, the growth of the market economy has allowed, or forced, the party to withdraw from the day-to-day affairs of state and to concentrate on consolidating its ideological influence. The constitution defines and legitimizes this ideological framework.

Democracy has transformed from a system derided throughout the ages into a regime that is generally accepted in Western political thought "as the sole legitimate form of government."[3] In the West, democracy's superiority was assumed and unchallenged,[4] and in the late 1980s, the West proclaimed the "unabashed victory of economic and political liberalism" and "the total exhaustion of viable systematic alternatives to Western liberalism." This triumph marked the "end of history," the "end point of mankind's ideological evolution and the universalization of Western liberal democracy as the final form of human government."[5] All roads lead to democracy.

By contrast, Carothers argues that the "transition paradigm," based on the assumption that "any country moving *away* from dictatorial rule can be considered a country in transition *toward* democracy,"[6] has lost its usefulness and that its core assumptions are flawed. The move in the late twentieth century from dictatorial rule to "more liberal and often more democratic governance"[7] in many regions of the world prompted the development of "an analytic model of democratic transition," which became "the universal paradigm for understanding democratization." As a result, political change tends to be erroneously analyzed in relation to an assumed sequence of democratization, and movements that do not conform to that path are disregarded.[8]

For the Chinese government, which is constantly urged to promote domestic democratic reforms, these assumptions, along with the assumed benefits of a democratic regime, must appear incomprehensible in the face of the lack of democratic progress that has in fact been made in postauthoritarian regimes. Many, according to Carothers, are in a "political grey zone," and suffer from "serious democratic deficits" and poor performance by state institutions.[9] These regimes are nonetheless described in terms of qualified democracy, but by "describing countries in the grey zone as types of democracies, analysts are in effect trying to apply the transition paradigm to the very countries whose political evolution is calling that paradigm into question."[10] Carothers calls on analysts to think of these political patterns "as alternative directions, not way stations to liberal democracies."[11] China would want to avoid being stuck in the middle-ground "hybrid" phase, where it would lack the authoritarian power to contain violence and also lack the institutional capacity of an effective democracy.[12]

China has clearly established the principles of its alternative to liberal democracy. Commentators are skeptical of the significance of the Chinese Government's White Paper on democracy. *The New York Times*, for example, dismissed the White Paper as "self-congratulatory,"[13] while others find it predictable, unconvincing, and even laughable. The White Paper is, however, an unprecedented summary of China's perspective on democracy and its practice: "political democracy with Chinese characteristics,"[14] and it represents an attempt to respond to the international and domestic pressure for reform.

Although the White Paper "makes clear that the Communist Party has no plans to relinquish power and deems its grip on power essential to China's development,"[15] it also concedes that democratic reform is essential to the CCP's grip on power. The White Paper therefore reiterates the fundamental principles of Chinese democracy, which is not based on an assertion of individual rights against a government but rather on social harmony and the harnessing of the energy of the masses for the state project.

The Chinese leadership expresses in the White Paper a willingness to establish democracy but only on its own terms. The paper thoroughly rejects the notion of "mechanically copying the Western bourgeois political system"[16] but rather than dwelling on the shortcomings of liberal democracy, it identifies those elements of democracy that may be incorporated into the Chinese political system. In this way, China has taken on elements of the technology of democracy, while rejecting Western ideological elements.

The constitution is fundamental to this development of a distinct legal and political system. It reads, "Guided by the objective of ruling the country by law and building a socialist country under the rule of law, more efforts are being made to build socialist democracy so that it is institutionalized, standardized and in line with prescribed procedures. A socialist law regime with Chinese characteristics and with the Constitution at its core has been preliminarily formed."[17]

Bolstering the status of the constitution is one means of ensuring that the CCP ideology is deeply enough entrenched to resist the forces of liberal democracy. The role that the PRC Constitution plays in China's legal and political system is therefore distinguishable from that of a liberal constitution.

Liberal democratic theories of constitutionalism suggest that a government's powers should be limited by law, in many cases in the form of a written constitution and that a government's authority depends on its observing those limitations. A constitution may also serve to "articulate and preserve a society's fundamental moral principles."[18] The U.S. Constitution, for example, was based on what Loveland describes as a "pervasive distrust of human nature,"[19] making it necessary to create a system that aspired to protect minorities from the whims of the majority. In response to the perceived risks of majoritarian rule, the framers of the U.S. Constitution established a representative government, based on a federation of states with devolved powers, the separation of powers, and a set of "fundamental" rights that were superior to legislation.[20] The U.S. Constitution therefore limits and defines the relationship between government and individual citizens, separating public powers from private affairs.

Chinese constitutionalism, however, originally depended on the perception of the relationship between government and the people, that the people *are* the government: "Here, in our country, the true masters of the state are the overwhelming majority of the people."[21] The first version of the current Chinese Constitution was drafted in 1954, by the Central Committee of the Communist Party of China. It was both a celebration of a victory, and a statement of purpose: it was the "epitome of the historical experience of more than a hundred years of heroic struggles by the Chinese people,"[22] was designed to entrench the country's "gradual transition towards socialist society" and to celebrate the overthrow of "the dark rule of imperialism and feudalism."[23]

The constitution was intended to ensure that the will of the majority, or the "masses," was implemented in government. This will was considered to be unitary, rather than pluralistic, and so the exercise of state power was "completely unified in our National People's Congress"[24] rather than divided between the judiciary, legislative, and executive as in the U.S. model. The interests of the majority and the interests of the state were envisaged as intertwined.[25] Liu proclaimed, therefore, that "from a bourgeois viewpoint, it is impossible to understand the political system of our country," and dismissed foreign criticism of the constitutional foundations of the new political system as a failure "to see the tremendous change that has occurred in Chinese history."[26]

The most recent version of the constitution, promulgated in 1982 and subsequently amended several times to reflect the country's move toward a socialist market economy, "defines the basic system and basic tasks of the state," and is "the fundamental law of the state and has supreme legal force." [27] The image of the constitution as a map of the road to socialism is reiterated. The preamble lists the tasks that the Chinese people are to undertake, "under the leadership of the Communist Party of China." It also reconfirms the ideological importance of Marxism-Leninism, Mao Zedong Thought, Deng Xiaoping Theory, and since the most recent amendments of 2004, the important thought of 'Three Represents'."[28] The aim of the constitution is to provide the means of creating "a socialist country that is prosperous, powerful, democratic and culturally advanced."

The 2004 amendments also included the recognition of private property rights, the development of a modern socialist market economy by building socialism with Chinese characteristics, and the development of the rule of law and respect for human rights. The current version of the constitution, therefore, recognizes that there are constitutional limits on state power, at least in theory.

The text of the PRC Constitution does not mention the CCP, other than in the Preamble. Chinese Communist theory distinguishes between a party in power, and a party that provides "comprehensive leadership."[29] The former is voted into power by the electorate. The leadership of the Communist Party, however, is based on the party's demonstration of "its historic capability of leading the country into independence, prosperity and democracy."[30] The power of the Communist Party is not, as in the Westminster system, the power of the state. Rather, the Communist Party has "a power of leadership for all of society."[31] The party "directs all state institutions from above. It is over the state."[32] It maintains power through educating party members and the public about Marxist doctrine, by demonstrating the quality of its leadership, by guarding against internal corruption and wrongdoings, and by exercising "instruments of discipline and, in extreme circumstances, even force."[33]

The party's Document on Governance Capability issued by the CCP following its plenum in 2004 concedes, however, that the CCP needs to "enhance governance capability to consolidate its ruling status and meet domestic and global challenges." [34] The governance document makes it fairly clear that government will be subject to constitutional constraints, and that the people will be mobilized and organized "to manage state and social affairs, economic and cultural undertakings according to law." To do so, the party must "lead in the formulation and the enforcement of the Constitution and law." Party members are to "adhere to acting within the scope of the Constitution and laws, and play an exemplary role in safeguarding the authority of the Constitution and laws."[35] The CCP has clearly indicated that the constitution is a component of its very survival.

The withdrawal of the party from constitutional activities, lawmaking in particular, appears to confirm this stance. Dowdle, for example, examines the constitutional development of the NPC, concluding that the "NPC's institutional emergence owes much to a corresponding decrease in the CCP's own willingness to intervene in or otherwise oversee a wide range of constitutional activities," as the Party transferred constitutional operations to the appropriate constitutional institutions.[36] In 1991, the CCP "for the first time set out explicit normative limits on its own authority to oversee legislative drafting. This move generally limited the CCP's legislative input to one of broad policy direction."[37] There is now little evidence of CCP intervention in NPC activities,[38] according to Dowdle's research.

The CCP does, however, retain significant influence over the NPC's constitutional activities, by the same means, according to Dowdle, "by which majority parties control national parliaments in many developed constitutional systems." These include "setting policy goals for legislative development, shaping the legislative agenda, and determining who gets what office within the legislature."[39] Nonetheless, even party membership of the NPC delegates is not in itself enough to ensure that the CCP's interests are the paramount considerations of the NPC, as NPC leaders have challenged the CCP orthodoxy in the past.[40]

Dowdle also suggests that constitutional norms have become binding on the political institutions in China: "The true force of constitutional principle comes precisely from the fact that most political actors and institutions do not want to breach constitutional mandates, not from the fact that they 'can't.'"[41]

The NPC plays a vital role in accommodating the increasingly pluralistic nature of Chinese politics and society, being "the most accessible forum through which these various interests can attempt to affect central-level policy making."[42] He claims that the CCP has disavowed this developing pluralism, by continuing to "espouse the ideological primacy of democratic centralism and 'unified thought'."[43] Dowdle sees a "principled consistency" in the workings of the NPC, which is "a defining feature of constitutionalism," [44] and suggests that "constitutional considerations can affect political operations in China" even though, as in most political systems, they are not the sole factors driving political behavior.[45]

Other commentators might not agree with Dowdle's interpretation of the CCP's retreat from the processes of state. Li Buyun, for example, argues that constitutional norms in China have not yet developed so that it has become a habit for the ruling party to act according to the law and that, to elevate the authority of the constitution, the NPC requires further reform.[46]

Stanley Lubman is even more dismissive of the notion of a body of law that permeates Chinese society: "because of the lack of a unifying concept of law, and even more so because of the fragmentation of authority that marks China today" he does not refer to a "Chinese legal *system*, only to Chinese legal institutions."[47] He does not see the constitution as having significant unifying force for China's legal system or for its social and political arrangements. He states that the "grip of CCP authoritarianism"[48] is established by the 1982 constitution, which "expresses the supremacy of the CCP authority." Legislation is therefore treated as "an expression of CCP policies," subject to alteration by CCP directives.[49]

Lubman suggests that the implementation of the rule of law, or constitutionalism, would mean that "the relations between state and Party must change and that the CCP must surrender at least some of its authority to law."[50] Nonetheless, he concedes that policy is increasingly implemented through legislation rather than formulated and applied directly by the CCP.[51]

Randall Peerenboom does not clearly state whether he sees the party's withdrawal from the everyday workings of the state as a sign of the weakening influence of party ideology, or as an indication of a consolidation of the party's authority within a constitutional framework. He writes "even when the Party seeks to assert control, it increasingly lacks the capacity to achieve its goals" due to the burgeoning independence of local governments.[52] Yet, "local governments still operate within a political framework defined largely by the Party," and Peerenboom suggests that the retreat of the party makes it stronger, by allowing it to govern more efficiently and effectively.[53]

Peerenboom states that the party's legitimacy is now based primarily on economic performance, due to a shift from ideology to economics.[54] It could be argued, however, that as control over day-to-day economic matters has been placed squarely with the state apparatus, the party has reaffirmed its authority over the ultimate ideological document and instrument of institutional control, the constitution. The economic policies that the party espouses are still tightly bound to ideology: after all, the stated aim of the party is to establish a *socialist* market economy, so it cannot separate the ideological factors of its policies from the purely economic, any more that a purely capitalist system can. Nonetheless, there has certainly been a shift toward using the language of economics and constitutionalism to bolster the legitimacy of the policies within China, and also no doubt to make them more palatable to external observers, who are able to accept the wielding of constitutional power more readily than ideological power.

Lin Feng agrees that economic achievement is important to the party's legitimacy, but does not see the implementation of the constitution as conflicting with the party's authority, seeing it as a tool for economic development. Compliance with any specific provision depends on "how well it serves the objective the government intends to achieve."[55]

Lubman, however, suggests that nothing, even constitutional power, has replaced the party's ideological power: "China is presently undergoing a crisis of belief in an ideology that has become irrelevant and in a Party whose legitimacy is in doubt. These symptoms of decay limit the effectiveness of the new legal rules and institutions."[56]

Chen is more measured in his approach: "a tension exists between the authority of the law and that of the Communist Party . . . The supremacy of the Party means that the Constitution and the law may not be supreme . . . The Party continues to be the sole interpreter and guardian of the interests of the people and the nation."[57] Chen suggests that there is nonetheless significant support for the relevance of the PRC Constitution: it provides "the vocabulary, terminology and language with the operation of government is described in the official media." Rather optimistically, he suggests that the form of the constitution is based on "Western liberal democratic constitutionalism" so "genuine constitutionalism might germinate in the future." Finally, he notes that some of the institutions established by the constitution have developed great authority and legitimacy, and may have real influence on Chinese political and legal processes.[58]

Peerenboom speculated that "which role the constitution will play in the future depends in part on which version of rule of law prevails"[59] in China. He suggests that "even if Statist Socialism prevails, the Constitution is likely to have a more important role as a baseline for measuring the legitimacy of state actions. To maintain credibility, the ruling regime will have to take the Constitution more seriously. As a result, the ruling regime will appeal to the Constitution more often to justify its acts."[60]

The party's withdrawal from constitutional activities, then, may be seen as a calculated move to enhance its legitimacy. If, as it appears, the party intends to consolidate its governance by enhancing and then drawing on the authority of the constitution, it is vital that it maintains control of both the formulation and the application of the constitution. By channeling its governance power into a constitutional power, the party would appear to risk relinquishing authority, as Lubman suggests. But, as Dowdle points out, the CCP was not forced to remove itself from the NPC constitutional decision-making process.[61] He suggests that the constitution "places limits on the CCP's authority to manipulate constitutional operations, and the CCP's withdraw [sic] from NPC decision-making processes is consistent with these limits."[62]

Paradoxically, then, it may be to the long-term advantage of the CCP to embrace constitutionalism. By confining the pluralistic behavior of the NPC and other institutions within the confines of the constitution, the CCP minimizes direct challenges to its own authority. In this way, debate and dissent can be tolerated and even encouraged. Dowdle suggests that the NPC provides an appealing arena for strong leaders who "may be chaffing against the Party orthodoxy."[63] By allowing the NPC to act as forum for debate and even dissent, as described by Dowdle, the party can contain challenges within constitutional parameters. Criticism of party policies can be couched in relatively neutral constitutional terms, in ways that do not explicitly challenge the authority of the party. In addition, the party can avoid accountability for mistakes and short-term diversions.

The party does not have the power to legislate directly, and must therefore ensure that its policies are legislated for, and that the law is applied in the appropriate manner. The constitution is a valuable tool to achieve this aim, as it establishes the institutions and processes of lawmaking, as well as the ideological framework for the formulation and application of laws.

Although the constitution is the supreme, superior law in China, it is seen as a directive or guideline for legislating, rather than binding in its own right.[64] The Legislation Law applies constitutional principles to lawmaking by requiring that legislative activities abide by the basic principles of the constitution, particularly the four basic principles set out in the constitution's

Preamble.[65] The Legislation Law stipulates that the constitution "has the highest legal authority. All law, administrative regulations, local regulations, autonomous regulations, and separate regulations shall not contravene the Constitution."[66] The Legislation Law applies to "the enactment, amendment and abolition of laws, administrative regulations, local regulations, autonomous regulations, and separate regulations" as well as departmental rules of the State Council, and those of local governments.[67]

The power to make national laws is vested in the National People's Congress and its Standing Committee, with the NPC alone empowered to enact "criminal laws, civil laws, the fundamental laws on the national authorities and other basic laws." The Standing Committee may make all other laws, and, if the NPC is not in session, may amend or supplement laws enacted by the NPC, so long as the substance of the laws remains intact.[68]

Certain areas of law must be legislated for by the NPC and the NPCSC.[69] All other matters may be dealt with by the State Council (and therefore by all its attendant central and local departments and ministries) through administrative regulation "to meet the practical needs of the society." Excluded from this last delegation are "matters regarding crime and punishment, the mandatory measures and punishment regarding deprivation of the political rights of citizens and restriction of personal liberty, and the judicial system." [70]

Provincial and other local people's congresses and their standing committees may, "according to the specific situations and needs of their administrative regions, enact local regulations which shall not contravene the Constitution, laws and administrative regulations." These are to be vetted by the standing committees of the provincial people's congress for compatibility with the constitution and other laws and regulations.[71]

If an organ of state, other government bodies, or a citizen is of the opinion that administrative regulations, local regulations, and so on, contravene the constitution or laws, they may make a written suggestion to the NPCSC for review. A working organ of the NPCSC will forward the matter to a special committee if it finds it "necessary" to do so. If the special committee finds that there is a contravention, it "may give a written opinion to the enacting authority, who has two months to decide whether to make any amendment and report.[72] The NPCSC meets bimonthly, however, and mainly focuses on legislation. The NPC and its Standing Committee therefore seldom have the time to conduct constitutional overviews and investigations of constitutional violations.[73]

In practice, because this dual process of vetting and review is not an effective process, many local laws contravene constitutional and legal principles.[74] As Wang Zhenmin, a prominent mainland academic, pointed out, the conflict of legislation is clearly a reflection of the tussles over the distribution of power between different government departments and local administration.[75]

Commentators agree, therefore, that in order to bolster the authority of the constitution, the process for reviewing legislation must be regularized. To Li Buyun, for example, the most serious defect is the lack of constitutional review, as violations do occur, so if no effective review process is in place the constitution itself is cast into doubt. [76] Chen concurs, saying that the influence of the constitution on lawmaking, particularly at the local level, is undermined by "the lack of any court or specialised tribunal for constitutional adjudication," which tends to "lower the relevance of the Constitution as a device to contain, structure or direct the operation of political forces."[77]

An independent constitutional supervisory organ with the sole task of ensuring that all local and central legislation is consistent with the constitution might seem to be a solution to the problem of the unconstitutionality of laws.

One option that has been suggested is the establishment of an independent constitutional court with the power to review legislation. Judicial review of legislation by an independent judiciary is considered in many countries to be an integral part of constitutionalism, being a key check on government power. The debate about the role of judicial review and the means of implementing it is by no means resolved in developed constitutional systems, however.

Judicial review in democratic constitutionalism is "a means for guaranteeing government's obedience to the Constitution."[78] Judges, or a special constitutional court, make "the necessarily vague terms of constitutional provisions more concrete and gives them practical application."[79] The rationale behind judicial review in developed constitutional regimes is based on a rigid and "relatively immutable" constitution that is considered to be superior law. Because of the constitution's superior status, the judiciary can apply it as "a tool for enforcing the Constitution against ordinary legislation."[80]

Civil law countries have generally adopted a centralized system of judicial review, as the absence of the doctrine of *stare decisis* makes a decentralized system, where all courts have the power to review legislation, impractical.[81] European civil law systems tend to emphasize the political nature of the decisions being made by the courts, so prefer to give the review powers to specialized courts. The ordinary courts lacked the "structure, procedures, and mentality required for effective constitutional adjudication," and were considered "psychologically incapable of the value-oriented, quasi-political functions involved in judicial review."[82]

China faces several issues when it considers the establishment of a constitutional court that is independent of the NPC and its Standing Committee.

As Professor Cai notes, this proposal is "rather idealistic" as it is "outside the current constitutional system, and therefore has a slim chance of realization." [83] For example, because of the rejection of the doctrine of the separation of powers, the Chinese courts must recognize the superior authority of other organs of state powers. Under the present constitutional arrangements, therefore, an independent judicial body would not have the power to issue decisions that were binding on the Standing Committee.

Also, no institution that is given the power to review legislation would have the power to review party documents. The CCP Constitution explicitly states that the party must act within the confines of the law and the constitution, a statement, which "demonstrates CCP acknowledgment of the fact that the Party could potentially be the subject of constitutional supervision." Nonetheless, as the party exercises control over the NPC, and its authority extends "beyond the realm of the state system," the NPC is "simply unable to conduct constitutional supervisions over the CCP."[84] Without constitutional amendment, any supervisory organ could only recommend that CCP decrees that violate the constitution be amended by the party.

Another reason why judicial review may not be appropriate for China is that constitutional judges tend to look to international examples of constitutionalism, to the extent that in "modern constitutionalism there is a clear trend towards a transnational, indeed a universal acceptance of certain values."[85] The internationalization of the constitution may be something that the Chinese leadership wishes to avoid, as the very notion of Western-style judicial review is intertwined with multiparty democratization, the separation of powers, the rule of law, and the decentralization of authority, [86] along with liberal rights–based arguments.

Perhaps more importantly, China's Constitution has been significantly and substantively amended over the years, and could hardly be called "immutable." The rationale for judicial review, which is to protect legislation from majoritarian whims based on a written document that sets out fundamental values, is not applicable in the Chinese context, as the CCP is still refining the values that the constitution is intended to embody, and is not prepared to allow the judiciary to participate in that refinement.

For these reasons, presumably, in May 2004 the Chinese leadership ruled out the possibility of establishing a constitutional court with the powers of judicial review.[87] Two months later, the NPC Standing Committee set up a new agency within its Legislative Affairs Commission with the job of reviewing "whether legislation or a government or court decision accords with the stipulations of the Constitution."[88]

Little information is available about this new agency. Apparently, it has a staff of about ten, who will "step up the examination of administrative regulations, regional law, and judicial interpretations." It will also "be responsible for the collection of information on constitutional violations from the public, including individuals' suggestions and comments on violations of the Constitution."[89] Its form, function, and powers were not made clear in the announcement, but it appears to be an administrative body with no power to issue rulings that are binding on legislators and decision makers. There is no indication that it will have the power to alter legislation made by the NPCSC or other state organs.

The rejection of a constitutional court is entirely consistent with the Chinese leadership's plans "to enhance the governance capability of the Communist Party of China" through the constitution.[90] But is the CCP being forced into embracing constitutionalism in order to retain a modicum of power into the future, or has it taken advantage of the changing attitudes toward constitutionalism to strengthen its position?

The CCP's "retreat" from constitutional activities has been paralleled by the advance of constitutional norms, perhaps illustrating the transformation of ideology into constitutionalism. A clear division of roles now exists between the State and the party: the State has jurisdiction over day-to-day government, while the party retains control over ideological matters, which include constitutional policies. The Constitution may be seen as the legal document that defines and legitimizes China's ideological framework.

It is too soon to tell whether the party's shift in focus means that it will lose the ability to control further reforms, but there is no reason to believe that the party will fall from power.[91] The CCP appears to have embraced the trappings of constitutionalism, while at the same time ensuring that the constitution reflects CCP ideology. The constitutionalism that is developing as a result is not a liberal one based on individual rights, but may well be one that promotes and supports a system of rights based on communitarian values.[92] The party, by establishing the value system that enfolds the constitution, and then aligning itself with the constitution, will thereby enhance its own legitimacy.

Notes

1. Chinese Government White Paper, *Building of Political Democracy in China*, October 2005, ch. 2.
2. CPC Central Committee Decision on the Enhancement of the Party's Governance Capability, adopted at the Fourth Plenum of the Sixteenth CPC Central Committee, held in Beijing from September 16 to September 19, 2004 (hereinafter the "Governance

Document"). "Party's governance capability highlighted," September 20, 2004, http://www.china-embassy.org.

3. Patrick J. Deneen, *Democratic Faith* (Princeton, NJ: Princeton University Press, 2005), 1.
4. Ibid., 1.
5. Francis Fukuyama, "The End of History?" *The National Interest*, Summer 1989, 3. Fukuyama finds a "steady convergence of political and economic institutions around the models of liberal democracy and capitalism and the continued implementation of liberal principles, particularly the principle of equality of opportunity, within liberal democracies." See also Fukuyama, "The Future of Equality," *The National Interest*, Winter 1994/1995. Fukuyama has since moderated and nuanced his views, but they were no doubt a reflection of the times.
6. Thomas Carothers, "The End of the Transition Paradigm," *Journal of Democracy* 13, no. 1 (2002): 6; emphasis in original.
7. Ibid., 5.
8. Ibid., 7.
9. Ibid., 9.
10. Ibid., 10.
11. Ibid., 14.
12. Richard Youngs, *International Democracy and the West* (Oxford: Oxford University Press, 2004), 14. See also Pitman Potter's work on institutional capacity in China.
13. Jim Yardley, "Report Calls Communist Party Rule Essential to Democracy in China," *New York Times*, October 20, 2005, A5.
14. White Paper, *Building of Political Democracy in China*, preface.
15. Yardley, "Report Calls Communist Party Rule Essential to Democracy in China."
16. White Paper, *Building of Political Democracy in China*, chap. 1.
17. Ibid.
18. Ian Loveland, *Constitutional Law, Administrative Law, and Human Rights*, 3rd ed. (London: LexisNexis, 2003), 2.
19. Ibid., 7.
20. Discussed in greater detail in ibid., 8–18.
21. Shao-chi Liu, *Report on the Draft Constitution of the People's Republic of China [and] Constitution of the People's Republic of China* (Peking: Foreign Language Press, 1962), 20.
22. Ibid., 4.
23. Ibid., 5.
24. Ibid., 32.
25. Ibid., 38.
26. Ibid.
27. PRC Constitution, Preamble.
28. The "Three Represents" refers to the notion that the Chinese Communist Party represents the developmental needs of China's advanced social productivity, the direction of China's cultural advancement, and the fundamental interests of the broadest range of the Chinese people.
29. Jinsong Jiang, *The National People's Congress of China* (Beijing: Foreign Language Press, 2003), 72.
30. Ibid., Jiang, 72. Similarly, the White Paper states: "It was the CPC that led the Chinese people to find the correct road to build China into a prosperous, democratic and civilized modern country. It is precisely because of this historical reason that the CPC's leading status is clearly described in the Constitution of the People's Republic of China."
31. Ibid., 73.

32. Ibid., 73.
33. Ibid., 73–74.
34. This is "vital to China's socialist cause, the Chinese nation and the CPC itself." See Governance Document.
35. It does not, however, give any indication of how this adherence will be monitored or supervised, other than to urge the "implementation of the existing rules and regulations, including those on inner-Party supervision."
36. Michael W. Dowdle, "The Constitutional Development and Operations of the National People's Congress," *Columbia Journal of Asian Law* 11, no. 1 (1997): 13, citing Murray Scott Tanner, "Organizations and Politics in China's Post-Mao Law-Making System," in *Domestic Law Reforms in Post-Mao China*, ed. Potter Pitman, Studies on Contemporary China (Armonk, NY: M. E. Sharpe, 1994), 61–62, 72–74.
37. Ibid., 14.
38. Ibid.
39. Ibid., 15–16.
40. Ibid., 17.
41. Ibid., 17, citing Ronald Dworkin, *Taking Rights Seriously* (Cambridge, MA: Harvard University Press, 1977).
42. Dowdle, "The Constitutional Development and Operations of the National People's Congress," 18, 19.
43. Ibid., 20.
44. Ibid., 24.
45. Ibid., 24–25.
46. Li Buyun, Centre for Comparative and Public Law Public Lecture on the Reform in the NPC and Constitutional Development in China, November 24, 2004.
47. Stanley B. Lubman, *Bird in Cage: Legal Reform in China after Mao* (Stanford, CA: Stanford University Press, 1999), 3.
48. Ibid., 3.
49. Ibid., 139.
50. Ibid., 5.
51. Ibid., 139.
52. Randall Peerenboom, *China's Long March toward Rule of Law* (Cambridge: Cambridge University Press, 2002), 207.
53. Ibid., 189, 211.
54. See, for example, ibid., 209 (and elsewhere).
55. Feng Lin, *Constitutional Law in China* (Hong Kong: Sweet & Maxwell Asia, 2000), para. 1.24.
56. Lubman, *Bird in Cage*, 3.
57. Albert Chen, *An Introduction to the Legal System of the People's Republic of China*, 3rd ed. (Hong Kong: LexisNexis, 2004), 40.
58. Ibid., 41.
59. Randall Peerenboom, "Post-Mao Reforms: Competing Conceptions of Rule of Law," in *China's Long March toward Rule of Law*, 89.
60. Ibid., 89.
61. Dowdle, "The Constitutional Development and Operations of the National People's Congress," 12.
62. Ibid., 22.
63. Ibid., 13.
64. Chen, *An Introduction to the Legal System of the People's Republic of China*, 47.

65. Legislation Law, Article 3.
66. Legislation Law, Article 78.
67. Legislation Law, Article 2.
68. Legislation Law, Article 7.
69. Legislation Law, Article 8.
70. Legislation Law, Article 9.
71. Legislation Law, Article 63.
72. Legislation Law, Article 91.
73. See Cai Dingjian, "Constitutional Supervision and Interpretation in the People's Republic of China," *Journal of Chinese Law* 9 (1995): 219.
74. For a critical analysis of this process, see Cai Dingjian, "The Mechanism for Resolving the Conflict of Laws in China: Ratifying, Recording, and Interpreting Law," in *Hong Kong's Constitutional Debates*, ed. Johannes Chan and Lison Harris (Hong Kong: Hong Kong University Press, 2005), 45–52.
75. "New NPC Body to Address Law Conflicts," *China Daily*, June 21, 2004, available at http://www.chinadaily.com.cn, quoting Wang Zhenmin.
76. Li Buyun, CCPL Public Lecture.
77. Chen, *An Introduction to the Legal System of the People's Republic of China*, 40.
78. Mauro Cappelletti, *The Judicial Process in Comparative Perspective* (Oxford: Clarendon Press, 1989), 118.
79. Ibid., 118.
80. Ibid., 132.
81. Ibid., 138–42.
82. Ibid., 142–43.
83. Dingjian, "Constitutional Supervision and Interpretation," 229–31.
84. Ibid., 228.
85. Cappelletti, "The Judicial Process," 119.
86. See Tom Ginsburg, *Judicial Review in New Democracies: Constitutional Courts in Asian Cases* (Cambridge: Cambridge University Press, 2003), chap. 1.
87. "Beijing Rules Out Constitutional Court to Protect Human Rights and Private Property," *Asianews.it*, May 22, 2004.
88. "New NPC Body to Address Law Conflicts."
89. Ibid.
90. Governance Document.
91. Peerenboom, *China's Long March toward Rule of Law*, 571.
92. For a summary of the Chinese government's theories of human rights, see its White Papers on human rights progress in China, at http://www.china.org.cn/e-white/index.htm.

Contributors

D. W. Choy is research fellow, Department of Law, University of Hong Kong.

Michael C. Davis is professor of law at Chinese University of Hong Kong.

Michael W. Dowdle is formerly associate professor of public law at the Chinese University of Hong Kong Department of Government and Public Administration.

Hualing Fu is associate professor, Faculty of Law, University of Hong Kong.

Yash Ghai is honorary professor, University of Hong Kong.

Lison Harris (BA (Hons), LLB) was assistant research officer in the Centre for Comparative and Public Law, University of Hong Kong, in 2003–6. She is currently the legal and constitutional adviser in New Zealand's Department of Prime Minister and Cabinet.

Lin Feng is associate professor of law, School of Law, City University of Hong Kong; Barrister-at-law, and also a member of the Council of the Hong Kong Bar Association (2006–7).

P. Y. Lo is LLB (London); Barrister-at-law (England and Wales, Hong Kong), member of the Bar Council; chairman of the Special Committee on Constitutional Affairs and Human Rights, Hong Kong Bar Association (2006–7); PhD candidate, Faculty of Law, University of Hong Kong.

Robert J. Morris is juris doctor (1980); PhD (2007). He teaches in the Department of Law, University of Hong Kong, further information may be seen online at www.robertjmorris.net.

Carole Petersen is visiting professor, William S. Richardson School of Law, University of Hawaii at Manoa. She was formerly associate professor, Faculty of Law, University of Hong Kong.

Sophia Woodman is a PhD candidate in the Department of Sociology, University of British Columbia, Canada. She was formerly research fellow in the Centre for Comparative and Public Law, Faculty of Law, University of Hong Kong.

Simon N. M. Young is associate professor and director, Centre for Comparative and Public Law, Faculty of Law, University of Hong Kong. He is a member of the bar in Hong Kong and Canada (Ontario).

Yu Xingzhong is B.A. (Lanzhou), L.L.M. (Harvard), S.J.D. (Harvard), associate professor, School of Law, the Chinese University of Hong Kong.

Index